ETERNAL
SHADOWS OR SHADOW MAKERS

FR. STEVE PETERSON OSJ

WestBow
PRESS
A DIVISION OF THOMAS NELSON

Edited by
Fr. John Warburton OSJ, Provincial of the California
Province for the Oblates of St. Joseph.

Reviewed by
Fr. Phillip Masseti OSJ and Fr. Mariusz Beczek OSJ

2nd edition, 2011
3rd edition 2012

All Scripture passages used in this book were taken from The New American Bible.
St. Jerome Press.

Front cover design by Mitch Peterson
mepproductions07@gmail.com

WestBow Press books may be ordered through booksellers or by contacting:

WestBow Press
A Division of Thomas Nelson
1663 Liberty Drive
Bloomington, IN 47403
www.westbowpress.com
1-(866) 928-1240

ISBN: 978-1-4497-5980-3 (sc)
ISBN: 978-1-4497-5981-0 (hc)
ISBN: 978-1-4497-5979-7 (e)

Library of Congress Control Number: 2012912855

Printed in the United States of America

WestBow Press rev. date: 09/09/2013

CONTENTS

PREFACE

When you are in the presence of God, you no longer have any doubts about the reality of heaven. No words can sufficiently describe the infinite complexity of such a reality, yet at the same time, everything about God and surrounding God is so simple and clear; it is self-evident and can be understood by the simplest heart.

We do not have to wait for death to experience heaven and eternal life. All we need to do is become like little children whose hearts are open and ready to explore the unknown. Innocent children speak with their hearts coming from God's country because they can see God.

Peter Kreeft, a well-read author of several philosophical and theological books, describes in one of his books, called *Heaven: The Heart's Deepest Longing*, that we must explore what he called

> An *undiscovered country*, meaning the human heart. Many of us mistake the heart as being a place of feelings only. Instead, the depth of the heart has 'reasons' because it can see the divine secrets of love inside other true human lovers. Such an x-ray type of vision reveals a 'divine secret': the hidden God of the universe to all who can see.[1]

In order to rediscover this hidden, undiscovered country, we need to return to our innocence. We need to unclutter our mortal hearts so we can see God again and His image in each other, thus enabling us to be open and ready to explore the unknown depths of heaven within our immortal and eternal hearts.

---

[1]   Kreeft, Peter. *Heaven: The Heart's Deepest Longing*, Ignatius Press: San Francisco, 36-37.

INTRODUCTION

We Are Eternal, Spiritual Beings

After many years of putting things off, I must put a few words down on paper before I meet my Creator. I say Creator because my being did not evolve from some monkey or ape, and neither did I wish myself into being. It had a divine origin. A loving, divine person made me for a divine purpose—eternal life with my divine Creator.

> After 120 years of life on earth, Moses informed the children of Israel, lucidly and energetically, how to enter the Promised Land. Then God told Moses to climb up and "die on Mount Nebo." However, God also told Moses that he would "join your fathers" (Dt 32:50). In other words, Moses knew he was going to die, but that death was not going to be his final destination. Maybe he knew that something about himself would go on living.

In a statement from the Pastoral Constitution on the Church in the Modern World, the Second Vatican Council talks about the mystery of death and that man's ultimate vocation is eternal.

> In the face of death the enigma of human existence reaches its climax. Man is not only the victim of pain and the progressive deterioration of his body; he is also, and more deeply, tormented by the fear of final extinction. But the instinctive judgment of his heart is right when he shrinks from, and rejects, the idea of a total collapse and definitive end of his own person. He carries within him the seed of eternity, which cannot be reduced to matter alone, and so he rebels against death. All efforts of technology, however useful they may be, cannot calm his anxieties; the

biological extension of his life span cannot satisfy the desire inescapably present in his heart for a life beyond this life.[2]

The church teaches that humankind has always desired to be free from death and decay and is destined to know and share life with God forever.

Perhaps there is something about knowing God that equals eternity. Adam and Eve saw God, but they never really *knew* God. In fact, there is nothing in the book of Genesis that says they spent much time with God. There is no mention of either one of them walking and talking at any length to God except for the day they were expelled from the garden of Eden. Again, in my imagination, it seems like until the time of Noah and the flood, no one really spent much time with God except one little obscure man named Enoch. The account of this one character, however, holds a significant clue to man's ultimate quest and eternal destiny. It alludes to the entire reason for our being on earth. Enoch lived only 365 years on earth. That was a very short lifespan compared to his forefathers and son, who lived an average of nine hundred and some odd years before they died. Until Noah, Scripture uses the phrase "then he died" at the end of every man's life except for Enoch. Hmm, how curious.

What does the inspired Word say at the end of Enoch's life? "After Enoch had walked with God, he disappeared because God took him up" (Ge 5:24). You mean to tell me he didn't die! Why not? The answer to this mysterious question is simple: "he walked with God." Anyone who walks with another person normally does some talking. What happens when you talk to someone? You get to know a little about that person. How long did Enoch walk with God? For 365 years. I would say if you were to walk and talk with someone for that many years, you would get to know that person inside and out.

Not only that, but the person Enoch chose to walk and share himself with was not his son but God. In other words, Enoch discovered there was more value in discussing things with God than with his own son. This is not to say he didn't care about knowing his son; no, this is saying something more about sowing seeds of love and reaping a life that never ends in death. If Enoch had loved his son Methuselah only, he would have ended up doing what his forefathers did: "then [they] he died." Instead, he did as Saint Paul

---

2   Vatican II, Pastoral Constitution on the Church in the Modern World, *Guadiun et Spes* 18.

wrote in his letter to the Galatians when he said, "A man will reap only what he sows. If he sows in the field of the flesh, he will reap a harvest of corruption; but if his seed-ground is the spirit, he will reap everlasting life" (Gal 6:7-8). In his walks and talks with God, Enoch learned that there was more to life than eating, drinking, sleeping, corroding, and dying. Enoch's son could not provide him seed-ground, meaning "words" that promised him eternal life. I dedicate this book to my eternal brother Enoch who sowed the seeds of love in the heart of God while they journeyed together on this planet's surface.

Enoch was not the only biblical character God took from the earth, sparing him from death. A man named Elijah was also taken up into heaven in a chariot of fire before the eyes of another young man named Elisha (2 Ki 2:11). Before he left the earth, however, Elijah asked the young man "What shall I do for you before I am taken away from you?" (2:9). Elisha requested "twice his spirit" (2:9). Elijah was the only true prophet living in the land at the time who knew God. He knew God intimately and lived only to please God. Elijah pleased God, as Enoch did, so God decided to take his beloved prophet Elijah away from corruption and death also.

All of us have experiences with the spirit of men and the spirit of God begging to talk to us. Before Elijah went to heaven, the young man Elisha asked for twice the amount of Elijah's spirit. Thus, Elisha experienced something of Elijah's spirit, but did Elisha experience God's Spirit? Later on, we read that Elisha died. Why? Could it be because he asked for a man's spirit instead of God's Spirit? Maybe the message from this passage is that we need to experience God's Spirit, not someone else's. Before Christ, this took extraordinary work and effort. Only after the coming of Christ can we see clearly how to work for the Spirit of God by modeling ourselves after the Son of God named Jesus. Thanks to Jesus, it's a lot easier to discern a sure-fire and safe path home to God.

I also dedicate this book to all the human characters in sacred Scripture who were determined to take on the difficult task to go beyond the grave, to souls who decided to walk and talk, share and love, hold and touch the hand and heart of God.

PART I

THE QUEST

Where Are You Going to Be for an Eternity?

Eternal life is not something you just die and wake up into. Nobody walks into heaven like opening a door and shutting it once inside the room. Most saints go through a long process of purification that slowly takes place from within a person's heart. Ever since human beings came on the earthly scene, no man or woman has articulated a truer pathway to eternal life than Jesus of Nazareth. Jesus is the only figure in human history that reveals the eternal heart of God. And since the life and death of Jesus, there have risen untold accounts of saintly, purposeful, holy, and perfected people into the world. Christian saints are still on the rise. Before Christ, saintly people were few and far between. The life and teachings of Jesus Christ have given countless souls the opportunity to bring about a fundamental change of character and spirit. No other spirituality known to mankind has moved souls closer to perfection than Christianity. By perfection, I mean the union of the human and the divine. Heaven consists of *divinized* human beings, meaning sharers of the divine nature, while still remaining contingent creatures.

Wanting to enter into the kingdom of heaven has intrigued both believers and nonbelievers since the beginning of time. There are many spiritualities in existence today, but none of them speak of a man coming back to life after being dead for three days inside a tomb. The resurrected body of Jesus Christ was seen and touched by some of His disciples. His ascension into heaven was also seen by hundreds of other eyewitnesses just outside of Jerusalem. It has long been determined that so many people could not have been lying about such accounts. Catholic Church officials have taken careful measures throughout the centuries to safeguard the original accounts of the early Christians.

One of the most important things to remember about the sacrificial life and death of Christ is that Jesus caused mankind to make a tremendous leap of faith into the spiritual unknown. For the most part, mankind was bogged down into following stringent religious rules, rituals, and other superstitions. There have been many impressive cults developed throughout history that required sacrifices of all types. Some of these cults demanded the blood of human beings. Regardless of all the sacrificial fanfare, none of their cult leaders came back to life after their own deaths. The great pyramid-like tombs the world over have never yielded the bodies of their dead. These mummified kings and queens never made a reappearance in the flesh to anyone else in the land they ruled. Are there any records of a pharaoh, a king, a queen, or some great spiritual founder describing their resurrected bodies walking and talking to anybody after they died?

The Great Pyramid: a Monument to Eternal Shareholders

Having spent many years of my life working in masonry construction, I consider the Great Pyramid situated on the Giza Plateau in Egypt to be one of the most perfect monuments of design and engineering in the world. I am convinced the Great Pyramid was built to last forever, or at least until the end of the world. The amazing structure was either built by God Himself or by men possessing God's wisdom and power that enabled them to construct it.

The pyramid was built as a symbol of perfection. Its design holds within it the developmental process of man's gradual ascent into shared divinity. The Catechism of the Catholic Church quotes several saints talking about humankind's quest to share in God's divinity. St. Peter wrote in his second letter to the Church that "the Word became flesh to make us 'partakers of the divine nature.'" St. Irenaeus said, "For this is why the Word became man, and the Son of God became the Son of man: so that man, by entering into communion with the Word and thus receiving divine sonship, might become a son of God." St. Athanasius said, "For the Son of God became man so that we might become God." St. Thomas Aquinas said, "The only-begotten Son of God, wanting to make us sharers in his divinity, assumed our nature, so that he, made man, might make men gods."[3] Human beings have the capability to continue and endure life on earth until the end of time, but they will only go beyond time and space into eternity if they have responded to God's perfecting grace. The Great Pyramid can be seen as a model monument designed to reveal, in time or in stages, man's slow process of perfection—the process toward becoming a potential shareholder in God's divine nature.

The Great Pyramid was carefully designed to last a lifetime and more. It was cautiously placed in the center of the earth's land mass. It was also diligently aligned with all kinds of celestial objects (sun, moon, planets, and stars). The extraordinary attention given to its dimensions (size, degrees, angles, levels, weights, etc.) in proportion to the surrounding universe bears witness to its creator and onlookers that it was designed to endure well into

---

[3]   *Catechism of the Catholic Church*, Libreria Editrice Vaticana, 460.

the future. Scientists over the recent centuries have estimated that there are over two and a half million carefully cut and laid stones in the Great Pyramid. Each one of these stones weighs from two to seventy tons. Each stone was cut with such precision that the mortar space between every block surface is no thicker than the thickness of a man's thumbnail.[4] Every stone is united together to form one, integrated stone monument.

Each individual is like the Great Pyramid. Like the Great Pyramid, each human being was designed to last a lifetime and beyond. The careful and loving placement of a soul in the center of the original fertilized egg will grow into a mass of cells bonded to each other to form one integrated human body from conception until death.

When a person arrives at a stage in his or her life that perceives the existence of God and that God is the *end all* of his or her life, he or she will carefully weigh, measure, and form every decision with precision to secure the constant construction of a holy and healthy body and soul. An average good person is built on thousands or maybe millions of decisions during his or her lifespan. The soul that has integrated itself in union with God will grow and go beyond its natural boundaries to become an integrated divinized creature. The unborn souls and the souls of infants and children who die before the age of reason or decision making see God and are divinized according to God's merciful plan for them.

We Reap Eternal Consequences of What We Alone Sow

Most people, aware of their eternity, will *not* commit themselves to saying or doing stupid things. I remember one of my religious instructors telling the class to "beware what evil you say or do, for the day will come when the one you offended will stand before you weeping and bleeding." The more one grows in the knowledge that there is life beyond the grave, the more one understands the value of every thought and action. One of Isaac Newton's laws of physics says, "For every action there is an equal and opposite reaction." This can be applied to the spiritual as well as the natural world. The more the understanding of eternity intensifies, the more a person's consequences intensify.

---

4   Tompkins, Peter. *Secrets of the Great Pyramid.* Harper & Row: New York (1971) 1, 36, 105.

A person who is aware of his or her immortal self—a self that can never be destroyed—knows that every word, action, and even thought creates consequences. The words, actions, and thoughts of today will cause consequences tomorrow. They either cause good consequences to follow producing good fruits like the fruits of the Holy Spirit, or they cause bad consequences that end in doom, like the fruitless fig tree Jesus cursed one day and found withered and dead the next (Mk 11:14-21).

Every relationship has its eternal consequences. Take the relationship between teachers and students for example. Teachers, the children you had in your class will always remember you. Yes, you planted seeds of information and knowledge of the arts in your students' minds, but more importantly, you planted seeds of your beliefs and your spirit in the hearts of those students as well. Whatever you planted in their hearts will continue to grow. Even if you never see them again in this life, you will see them in the next life. They will either love or hate your indoctrination; they will either draw nearer to you or distance themselves from you. They will either hug you or beat you.

Their souls have received something from their experience with their teacher. You will reap what you have sown in the hearts of the children entrusted to you. If you expressed the love of God to them, then love will grow in their hearts for you, but if you spread hatred and rejection of God to them, then hatred and rejection will destroy their relationship with you. The only way love is destroyed is if you allow it to happen by denying the author of love—God. It is also true that the grace and mercy of God can break a vicious cycle of cause and effect.

A man or a woman who does not try to understand the divine call of his or her lonely state in life is destined for tragic consequences. From the very beginning of man's existence on earth, God saw that everything He created was completely good, except one last thing seemed to be missing: Adam's mate. The first man God created was found to be lonely (Ge 2:18). God had created male and female pairs out of every creature except the man. It was not until Adam had named all these creatures that he recognized his loneliness. The deep sorrow felt within the man's heart of not having someone like himself cried out to God. God heard his heartfelt call and responded by creating a woman for his lonely man-creature. In time, woman would help complete man. Ignacio Larranaga, a modern contemplative, says,

"Human beings are not completed beings, but rather beings 'in process,' by the use of their freedom."[5]

> A stone or a tree is a completely realized being within the boundaries or limits of its essence. I mean to say that it cannot give more than it gives, it cannot be more perfect than it is. The same for a cat or a dog, they are bounded beings, finished, "perfect" within their possibilities. We are not. We, essentially, are "able-to-be." We are the only beings in creation who can feel unfulfilled, unsatisfied, frustrated. And because of this, among created beings, we are the only ones who have the ability to overcome the barriers of our limitations . . . we are also the only ones capable of introspection, transcendence, and freedom. [6]

God then removed a rib, a bone that surrounded the heart of the man, to build up a woman. Notice that God did not remove a leg bone or a hand bone to make the woman. It was a rib bone that surrounds the heart, the very center of man's person, his being, and his soul. In the Torah, the Jews believe that it is in the heart where the soul resides. Evert and Butler say in the *Theology of the Body for Teens,*

> It's in the heart where God's design of love is hidden. It is also in the heart where the kind of complete love we are all looking for, even if we don't know it, is hidden in God's original design of our bodies and souls.[7]

Let us take marriage as an example of eternal consequence. It holds a key that opens the door to the secret of God's perfect and hidden design for not only love but also for integral existence. In other words, marriage contains a divine plan hidden within the union of man and woman destined to lead a person to eternal union with God, the author of complete love. The late Blessed Pope John Paul II concluded:

---

[5]   Larranaga, Ignacio, *Sensing Your Hidden Presence*, Doubleday: New York, 158. (Guadium et Spes, 17).

[6]   Ibid., 158.

[7]   Evert, J.C. Butler B. *Theology of the Body for Teens.* Ascension Press: Pennsylvania (2006) 5.

> Therefore, in his original situation man is alone and at the same time he becomes male and female—unity of the two. In his solitude he is revealed to himself as a person, in order to reveal, at the same time, the communion of persons in the unity of the two . . . In the unity of the couple he becomes male and female, discovering the nuptial meaning of his body as a personal subject.[8]

In other words, any other union outside of this divine plan, since the beginning of time, is destined to fail, leaving unbearable, lonely consequences in its wake.

Yes, the teaching of the Catholic Church states that God has actually hidden in our design as "male and female" (Ge 1:27) a key to the secret of love. And the answer to man's loneliness and search for meaning and purpose in life is to be found in the union of these two opposite designs of a man's body and a woman's body in generous love—God's design for love.

> The two sexes, male and female, are designed to become one according to our Creator's loving plan for human beings. Men and women are designed to share their bodies in generous relationships. Any relationship for selfish reasons and purposes done outside of this perfect design for our bodies is doomed to fail... If everyone loved the other as he or she wished to be loved, we would have virtually no pain, no problems in relationships. Imagine, for example, if marriages never ended in divorce. Think about the pain that both parents and children would be spared. Confusion between the two sexes reigns, and it is leading to some seriously broken hearts. People today seem more confused about the meaning of love and the purpose of sex than ever before."[9]

This is why the Catholic Church teaches that active homosexual relationships are "disordered"[10] because they confuse even more the perfect design God has for conjugal love and sex. Sexually active homosexuals

---

[8]   Pope John Paul II, *Theology of the Body*, Wednesday audiences (January 13, 1982).

[9]   Evert; Butler, 5.

[10]   *Catechism of the Catholic Church*, 2357-2359.

deprive their partners from achieving a complete love and therefore, knowledge that leads to eternal life. Homosexuals are called to chastity to approach Christian perfection.

> We see more "lust stories" than "love stories" in our modern culture. Self-giving has been turned on its head. Love is seen as something you get rather than give. "Why is this important? Because "love" involves being generous—like God—while "lust" is sexual desire that is selfish—apart from the love of God. Not to be confused with sexual attraction (which is good), lust is almost purely self-seeking.[11]

This is so important to understand because if any man or woman communicates nothing but selfish desire to the other, that man or woman will end up in a state of utter isolation, desolation, alienation, and yes, once again just like poor old Adam, incomplete and all alone in the world. The consequence of lust is to end up all alone with no one to love or be loved. The eternal consequence of this kind of loneliness is to be in hell.

The consequential growing tragedy of lovesick, dying human hearts is reaching epidemic proportions. There is a dark cloud creeping in and covering the horizons of the human heart the world over. People don't know how to love. Our materialistic, consumerist, and *self*-interested culture has created a society of cold-hearted independents. Most people possess a misconceived, carnal knowledge of love. Love means nothing more than pleasure fulfillment and superficial talk. There is no depth, no intimate soul searching in relationships. The consequences of these empty relationships end up going to the dogs.

Do you wonder why so many people live alone, sharing their houses, food, and even their beds with pets and other animals? We read stories of people being attacked by dangerous pets. Why? Answer: we are afraid of forming personal relationships with other human beings. People do not know how to reach out to humans, so they grab on to some dog, cat, monkey, boa constrictor, or lion. They spend their money and their lives in relationships with irrational creatures. Meanwhile, the hospitals, prisons, and rest homes are crammed with lonely souls and lovesick hearts. We need

---

[11]   Evert, 6.

to stop this heart disease before it is too late. It is too late when we die. I have heard of no one coming back from the grave to get another chance to love.

People who live alone without God run the risk of getting stuck in the mud of a culture of death and its eternal consequences. Jesus spoke of these ugly consequences in several of His teachings and parables. "There will be wailing and gnashing of teeth" (Mt 24:51). "It would be better for that man if he had never been born" (Mk 14:21). "It would be better to have a millstone tied around your neck and thrown into the sea" (Lk 17:2). "Be afraid of the one who after killing has the power to cast into Gehenna" (Lk 12:5).

What do we do to avoid such horrible, lonely consequences? First of all, "We need to reach back and take the Lord God's hand first before you extend the other hand to anything or anyone else."[12] We can experience a transfiguring courage and love within us every time we bring God into any situation. Second, we need to stop doing stupid things like committing sins, crimes, and offenses toward God, the self, and others that result in painful alienation and isolation. God, however, can transform loneliness into wholeness.

Ronald Rolheiser says in his book *The Restless Heart*, "Loneliness is God's way of drawing us toward the end for which He made us, namely, union with God and with our fellow human beings."[13] Being lonely spurs us on the trails of life to see what is beyond the horizon. With restless hearts

> We yearn for full, all-consuming love and ecstatic union with God or with others. Reality, however, does not always deal in dreams and yearnings. Consequently, we go through life experiencing not just love, but frustration, restlessness, tension, and loneliness, as well. In life, all of us are somewhat frustrated in our deep desire to share our being and our richness with others. We live knowing that others do not fully know and understand us and that others can never fully know and understand us, that they are "out there" and we are "in here." St. Paul calls this living as "through a glass, darkly," a riddle, a veil, a mist of unreality that separates us from God and others, and from what is authentically real (I Cor. 13:12-13).

---

[12]   St Francis de Sales, 2nd Sunday Lent yr. B Homily Notes, March, 1604.

[13]   Rolheiser, Ronald. *The Restless Heart*. Image Books Doubleday: NY (2004) 140.

Our hearts were not built to live as through a "glass, darkly," but to be in consummate union with God and others. And so, as we try to sort our way through the mist of unreality, the riddle of life, our hearts are lonely and, thus, speak to us of not just love, but also of pain. At times, the pain is not so poignant and we feel close to God and others. At other times, the pain becomes unbearable and we are given a foretaste of hell, realizing that loneliness is the ultimate threat, the final terror that can relativize all else. Mostly, though, the pain is tolerable, but nagging: a dissatisfaction with the quality of our life and our relationships to people, a frustration without an object, a yearning without a particular reference, a nostalgia for past moments and friends, a restlessness that prevents us from relaxing and from being present to the moment, a feeling of alienation, a paranoia, a sense of missing out on something, an inexplicable emptiness.

Too often, though, we run from these feelings of loneliness, thinking that there is something wrong with us. We guard our loneliness from others, keeping it private, like an object of shame. Yet other hearts speak the same language as ours. Loneliness is not a rare and curious phenomenon. It is at the center of every person's ordinary life experience. To be human is to be lonely.

To be human, however, is also to respond. The human person has always responded to this pain. The response has varied greatly. Sometimes loneliness has led us to new heights of creativity, and sometimes it has led us to drugs, alcohol, and emotional paralysis; sometimes it has led us to the true encounter of love and authentic sexuality, sometimes it has led us into dehumanizing relationships and destructive sexuality; sometimes it has moved us to a greater depth of openness toward God and others, to fuller life, and sometimes it has led us to jump off bridges, to end life; sometimes it has given us a glimpse of hell; sometimes it has made the human spirit, sometimes it has broken it; always it has affected it. For loneliness is one of the deepest, most universal, and most profound experiences that we have. [14]

---

[14]   Rolheiser, 3-8.

A person prone to fall into evil temptation is the consequence of an untrained, undisciplined mind that is not in union with God. The mind that has not found rest and assurance in God is capable of going insane. Insanity is total loss of self-control. An insane person is the mortal self at large; it is someone who has become reduced to a disintegrated being. When someone lives in such a cracked-up state, he or she easily will fall prey to evil spirits that proceed to invade the imagination to divide and blow a person around like dust in the wind.

For example, I have met several parents who have little faith in God. They suffer from haunting thoughts and images of strangers putting lustful hands on their little children. These poor people are under the influence of dark powers and principalities pulling them apart and blowing their minds in all directions. An integrated person, on the other hand, has the strength to fight off evil spirits. Evil spirits use the imagination to drive a wedge between the mind, the body, and the soul. However, no evil imagination is capable of driving an integrated person from his or her secure union with God.

A person with a God-consciousness has power of integrity. Like light, God's grace pushes away darkness while preserving the person intact, mind, body, and soul. God does not allow dark thoughts from evil powers to completely overcome and disintegrate a person. Such disintegration takes place when someone vehemently rejects God. History is loaded with people driven to insanity because they refused to discipline and train their hearts, minds, and souls on God. Some of these people caused horrific damage to themselves, their families, friends, communities, and even their whole country. Try to imagine the eternal consequences some souls must face in the hereafter for the offenses they are held either directly or indirectly responsible for, especially if they left trails of blood, misery, and death to others caused by their hateful ideas and actions.

Some of the most costly consequences of evil influences recorded in recent history were wrought by one man driven to insanity named Adolf Hitler. This man was personally responsible for the direct and indirect deaths of some forty million people worldwide. There is an inscription erected at the end of one of the death houses in Auschwitz that reads, "Where are you now?" The monument shows a photograph of several German guards sitting in a circle, smiling and drinking from their beer steins. In the middle of the circle stands a German shepherd dog, and in the background, you see the death camp in full killing operation. The photo makes you ponder the question, where are those German guards today? You wonder if they are sitting around drinking beer with glee in the midst of angels and saints. It is a frightening thought to imagine if my thoughts are the same kind of wishful thinking that forty million victim souls are wishing towards these men in the photo. Try to imagine the wishes that millions of tortured and murdered souls harbor toward the soul of Adolf Hitler.

Every thought, every word, and every action holds within it the seed of eternal consequences. Will the soul of Adolf Hitler spend an eternity explaining to 40 million souls why he committed such atrocities? Will every one of those souls forgive him and wish good thoughts toward his soul? How many of them will curse him and demand justice? Will they hug him or beat him? Or worse? St. Louis de Montfort once said, "Hell is an endless blaming game. Every soul in hell blames another for being there. Their hatred seethes like burning embers waiting for fresh wood (more souls) to burn."[15] We either go on loving or hating each other. We pick up and continue right where we left off from our last encounter with someone. We either go on scheming new ways to torture our enemies or create new ways to love our fellow souls at every encounter.

Anyone who thinks he or she is getting away with hidden evil acts done in the dark is fooling only himself or herself because God sees and hears all things. The light of truth, which is the light of God, will always expose the fool. If you always do what you always did, you will always get what you always got. In other words, if a person always does stupid and foolish things in life, that same person is always going to get in trouble and have to be punished for his or her offenses because Satan is with that person, not God. "God promises to remain forever with those who do what is just and right."[16] There is no indication in Scripture or any Church teaching that says God will always remain with the fool.

Nightmares and Hawks

Evil spirits invaded my home, my room, and my personal space very early in life. Like most children, I lived in silent fear of the night. It is difficult for a child to express spiritual realities, especially if the child's parents do not take seriously what is causing the child's fear. Not all children see strange, spirit

---

[15]   St. Louis de Montfort, *The Secret of the Rosary*, 1954.

[16]   *Divine Office* III, 201.

visitors come into their rooms in the middle of the night. My three younger brothers never revealed anything of the sort to me.

As a child, I did not understand what these nightmarish things were trying to do to me. All I knew was that they were extremely dangerous and they wanted to frighten the life out of me. These evil spirits, powers, or entities, however you want to call them, were the catalyst that eventually got my spiritual ball rolling toward an eternal quest. My little mind could not withstand these awful nighttime visitors, and it was thrown into confusion. Like most children, I shoved these visions way down inside because the memory of their appearances scared me half to death. It took years and many nightmares later before I understood their hellish nature and why these dark spirits went after me with a vengeance.

It was not until after my father's tragic and sudden death when I was eighteen years old that I truly embarked on a deep search for the spiritual meaning of life. My parents put my three younger brothers and me in a Catholic parochial school. My Catholic school days planted the seeds of a belief in God and His Son Jesus Christ deep in my heart. As a child, I would spend many hours in the classroom daydreaming about heaven. I do not remember what I saw back then, but my days were filled with spiritual mind wandering. I always wanted to be good so that when I died, I would go directly to heaven because I did not want to burn in hell forever. Many modern atheists feel that this is a foolish fear. Today I can tell them this: I would be dead and this story would never have been written if it were not for my childhood respect and fear of hell. Knowing your enemies helps a person live longer. Anyway, the seasons of Christmas and Easter were exciting times full of joyful expectations and loving adoration of the Christ of God.

Those wonder-filled moments in heavenly, childlike bliss slowly faded away as the teenage years ground them down to a halt. By the time I entered high school, my mind had already slipped into the many worldly distractions and interests. My preoccupation with grades and money filled my days with school and work. My soul was deprived of grace as it fell into a spiritual slumber. I fell in among friends who were not very religious and who enjoyed certain indulgences. My soul rode through some rough times and spiritual badlands. My faith in God dwindled down to almost nothing. Bad company and influences caused the direction of my life to take a turn for the worse. If it were not for the hawk, my life and soul would have fallen deeper into darkness.

One day, a neighbor from down the street came walking by my house carrying a large bird on his wrist. I went out to greet him and to see what he was doing with the bird.

"I'm walking my hawk," he said.

"A hawk!" I exclaimed.

"Yeah, it's a female sparrow hawk. I'm training it to hunt."

I was impressed by its looks and how much he knew about the nature of this bird. As I gazed on the hawk's features, I felt a growing desire to have one too. We talked for a while, and he saw how interested I was in learning more about what he called falconry, so he invited me over to his house. In time, we became friends, and I would go over to his house to watch him train the hawk. Every weekend, I would spend time hanging out with him and the hawk. He showed me how to make a snare trap. I convinced my mother to drive us to areas around central California where there were an abundance of hawks. We would spend all day driving down sparsely populated roads searching for falcons and hawks sitting in trees, on telephone poles, or on fence posts. It took several trips and many attempts to finally catch my first hawk. It was an exhilarating experience to watch it get caught in the trap and to be able to hold it in my hands. While driving home, I kept thinking, *What am I going to do with this hawk?* It didn't matter; I was determined to take the challenge and turn it into a hunting hawk.

There could not have been a more receptive time in my life to tune into training hawks. I had just gotten over a long four-week cold and flu, and during that awful, depressing month, I had had several remarkably horrible dreams. Each nightmare occurred somewhere in the early hours of the morning. I would see something move across my room and hover directly over my bed. It had no shape, but it had a wicked and dangerous presence. This dark, cloud-like, moving shadow would surround my body. My body would become paralyzed, and I could not move. As it came closer, I could smell a pungent, almost rancid odor. All I could do was watch in horror. If I tried to open my mouth to scream, I could taste the most god-awful substance forcing itself into my mouth. Somehow, I managed to conjure up the image of my parents or one of my brothers. Just the thought of them or something good would make the thing move away, and then I would snap out of the dream and it was gone.

This type of dream occurred at least once or twice a week. Sometimes it would come back two or three times in the same night. Each time I woke up, I would toss and turn until I fell back to sleep again. In my weakened physical state, I just laid there helplessly suffering one attack after another every night until the sun came up. I dreaded going to my room at night, but I had no choice but to obey my parents.

One night, right when I sensed the return of this ugly, spiritual intruder, I woke myself up and sat straight up in bed. Like a vigilant soldier on guard, I watched to see if I could somehow fight this thing off. I was at my wit's edge; it was do or die. Afraid of lying down and falling asleep due to fatigue, I gently rocked myself back and forth singing songs and praying prayers I had learned from my old Catholic school days. I kept this up for an hour or two. It didn't matter how long it took, I was going to wait until it showed up.

As I sat there determined to do battle with my eyes wide open, an amazing thing happened. My room started to fill up with a faint, undulating light. My eyes scanned the strange light until I noticed it seemed to be coming from thousands of tiny dots. These tiny dots would brighten and dim simultaneously, gently changing from one color hue to the next. I found myself fascinated with this vision until I noticed a sensation coming from the pit of my stomach. Next thing I knew, my body felt like someone had turned on a gentle heat lamp inside of me. The warmth expanded up into my chest and spread through my arms, my legs, to the top of my head, and to the tips of my toes and fingers. The sensation was so soothing that I felt as if something very loving was embracing me all over my body.

This experience was so reassuring and invigorating that I knew without a doubt I could go back to sleep with no fear of being attacked by any more nightmares that night, so I carefully lay down, closed my eyes, and fell sound asleep. When I awoke that morning and opened my eyes, I instinctively knew that I was healthy again. Upon rising from the bed, I felt strong. My nose was unplugged, I had no muscle aches or coughing, and the usual feeling of nausea was completely gone. I looked out the window and saw, for the first time in what seemed like ages, a beautiful ball of golden sunshine. I smiled and thanked God for whatever He had done for me the previous night. I could not explain it, but I knew something very special happened, and I was well again.

All throughout my high school years, I learned and practiced the art of falconry. I became a skillful hunter of small game birds, squirrels, and rabbits. In order to feed my hawks, I had to get up early before sunrise to hunt for their food. Taking care of wild birds forced me to discipline myself and take on responsibility for their care and management. I got into the habit of organizing my day so that I had enough time to spend walking and hiking several miles up into the hills above the town. The hunting, walking the hawks, hiking in the hills, and training birds of prey kept me immersed in silence and in solitary places. My parents noticed that I had grown a little more independent and responsible for myself, especially in my schoolwork and chores. They trusted me and gave me more freedom to be on my own.

The further I distanced myself from the city limits, the harder it was to stalk wild animals. A successful hunt depends a lot on being able to sneak up on the prey as quietly as possible so as not to be sensed by the animal. Stalking a wild animal requires patience, stamina, and perseverance. I liked the challenge, so I kept going back into the foothills. The frequent immersion into the silent hills isolated me from the world and all its distractions. The quiet solitude also set the stage for the quiet, inner animation of my soul. Something deep inside me was coming to life without my knowing it.

I remember how peaceful it was to gradually learn how to track animals and discern their movements. Watching and listening to the animals in their natural order filled me with a sense of awe and admiration. Little did I know that these frequent exposures to God's creation threatened the rule of worldly and evil spirits who had some control over me. The long, lonesome hours in the woods had awoken my soul, and it wanted to grow stronger and become freer too. This spiritual awakening to know more about the Creator and His mysterious creation disturbed the Prince of Darkness and his realm.

Lacking in healthy spiritual direction, the world, the flesh, and the Devil took me for a joy ride. After high school graduation, I took the liberty of youthful zeal to indulge myself in an unhealthy amount of parties, pleasures, and passions over and beyond the call of obedience. Except for an occasional disconcerting dream, I did not pay much attention to church teachings, sacraments, or prayer. I was too busy making a spectacle of myself.

Much to my spiritual demise, I did a lot of much to do about nothing. I remember commenting to one of my drunken friends that we were living in a teenage wasteland. It is true; I wasted many days sleeping in late, watching TV, listening to rock music, drinking beer, smoking pot, stealing gas, tires, liquor, and money, playing cards past midnight, looking for parties, playing with my girlfriend, laying on the beach, and loafing my life away until I met a man who gave me a little book called *The Christ in You*.

After reading this little book, I remember looking up and spotting an old Bible my mother had stored on a shelf. I took it down and started reading it from the beginning. As I read the words, I could visualize gardens, animals, scenarios, faces, and even personalities of the characters involved in the stories. Enraptured by the biblical stories, I could not read any other book for an entire year because that's how long it took for me to get through it. I did not just read it . . . I walked through it. I lived it. I sensually perceived people, places, and events as if I were historically present. There were times when I laughed, cried, gasped, cringed, and sang while traveling through the pages of that book. When I finished it, I felt as if I had read God's own personal diary. I decided from then on that I wanted to get to know more about God, myself, and what the heck life was about.

From age eighteen until I was twenty-four years old, a sequence of fate, family and personal problems, trials, and tribulations occurred one after another. My parents divorced. Both my grandfather and my father died, one shortly after the other. One of my brothers moved away, and my mother barely made rent. I went to jail for unpaid traffic violations. My driver's license went into probation, and I had to go to court and got sentenced to sixty days of mandatory community service. Work was scarce. Heavy rains flooded our house several times, and we lived in the cold and damp because we fell below the poverty level. In spite of all that, we survived because my mother kept our spirits up. My mother, my brothers, and I grew closer to each other, mutually helping and supporting each other with our joint efforts and sense of humor. Observing our mother's persistent work ethic inspired us boys to get out and find jobs.

Even though I found two jobs and went back to school, life seemed like a drag. At first I could not understand why life was so difficult. I was trying hard not to do any more bad stuff and stupid things. I cut back on unhealthy indulgences, curbed bad habits, and stayed away from friends caught up in the party lifestyle addicted to harmful vices. But things just seemed to get worse. Deep inside, my heart felt like it was stuck in a rut. I went for walks by myself, only this time I was not carrying a gun or a hawk to entertain myself. Instead, I went carrying around difficult questions. Who am I? Why am I? And what am I here for? I would go into the woods searching for answers to the meaning of life, existence, love, and answers to an assortment of mysteries. Is there life after death? What is beyond the solar system? Does the universe have an end? My soul yearned for peace and tranquility, but at the same time, my body craved old habits, and my mind was frustrated and wanted quick answers.

The daily struggle to know myself coupled with serious values and personality clashes between my girlfriend and me made me wonder in what direction was my life headed. On top of that, I would wake up morning after morning exhausted from swimming all night long in dreams. In these weird dreams, I found myself going through endless mazes and tunnels of liquid clogged with floating sponges looking for a way out. In one dream, after being flushed along what seemed like miles of tubes, I passed through a couple of large chambers that made a rhythmic, loud thumping noise that reminded me of waves crashing on the beach and receding back into the sea. Some days later, while sitting in a biology class watching a documentary film on the functions of the human body, I saw how food went from the mouth, down the esophagus, through the stomach, and into the intestines. Then the video showed footage taken by tiny fiber-optic cameras inserted into large arteries and veins to show how blood platelets traveled to various destinations in the body. That is when it dawned on me. Those recent dreams were experiences of my self, or my conscience, passing through the inner tubes and blood vessels of my own body! If that was not scary enough, I also remembered passing through dark areas in various organs and other places that looked like dead tissue and burned-out nerve and brain cells. "That's it," I said to myself as I walked out of the class, "no more drinking and smoking for me."

Before my father died, he saw that I needed a change of atmosphere and suggested to me to get the hell out of Dodge. He called his brother in law to see if he needed any help on his ranch somewhere in Nevada. I had worked for this man one summer drilling a well for water in the desert of Southern California. It was a hot summer, and it was hard, dirty work. He was a tough guy to work with, but I liked his style and admired his strength.

The Lady of the Desert: a Place of Love (Jer 2:2)

As far back as my memory serves, I enjoyed being alone and still in quiet solitude. Sometimes I would sit up for hours to listen to the sounds of the night before falling asleep. There was no problem for me spending all day immersed in solitude. As a child, I could entertain my thoughts with a swing, a rocking chair, or wandering alone through orchards and empty lots and places outside the city limits. Hiking the foothills above my hometown was commonplace. Solitary places gently called me out to get away from spending too much time in a teenage wasteland filled with inner chaos and meaningless boredom. I thought maybe some hard work and isolation would do me some good, so I decided to take the job and go to the high desert of Nevada.

From my mid-teens to early twenties, I would drive to the high desert of Nevada every summer to work for my uncle who owned a ranch some twenty-five miles from the nearest town. It was a desolate and lonely place well over one hundred miles away from any large city (Elko). Every time I drove out there, my body would react as if this was going to be my last trip. It was not from the thoughts that arose from seeing stereotype images of people starving or dying of thirst under a hot desert sun. It was more from a spirit of fear generated by false illusions coming from people ignorant of the desert. These illusions always tried to make me turn around and run back home to my old life where it was safe and secure. Something deep inside, however, would always nudge me onward to the ranch. Unbeknownst to me, my soul yearned to get another opportunity to grow. My foot seemed to obey a higher command to keep a steady pressure on the gas pedal while my eyes stayed fixed on the eastern horizon.

At first I was afraid to go out into the desert, especially at night. But the more I wandered around outside the ranch area in the desert after work, the more something inside me yearned to wander further out into the unknown among the sagebrush. One morning my uncle told me to load up the truck with a bunch of stakes and barbwire and then to head out several miles into the desert to dig holes and build fence. The other ranch hands were busy, so I had to go out there alone.

Hour after hour, I kept my mind focused on the job, but my eyes and ears slowly got caught up in the sights and sounds of the surrounding wilderness. I heard a strange noise, as if some large object was rushing through the brush about fifty yards behind me. Upon turning around and to my surprise, a twister swirling dust and sagebrush roared right toward me within close range with such swiftness, my body automatically jumped back and ducked to the ground. Clutching on to the trunk of sagebrush, the twister hissed and whistled as it moved over me. The powerful whirlwind rose several hundred feet into the sky as it churned over the desert floor. After that little taste of raw desert power, something inside me liked that awesome show and felt like it wanted to learn more about what goes on in this wild and scary place.

Dazzled by the twister, I sat down on the desert floor to watch it spin away. The funnel cloud slowly churned its way through the open valley. As it faded into the distance, the stillness and silence returned to normal. While sitting there trying to play back the sights and sounds of that event, my attention became keenly aware of a silence never before perceived in my life. I closed my eyes to focus my full attention on the surrounding quiet.

Submersed in tranquility, I actually heard my heartbeat for a few moments until some bird, a stone's throw away, made a high-pitched, shrill sound. Then my ears perked up to the sound of coyotes yapping in the distance. My attention then shifted to a sweet smell coming from the surrounding sagebrush. My body could sense a gentle breeze gently rolling over the area. Several subtle fragrances wafted into the area. I was so caught up in all these hidden smells and sounds that I had lost all track of time. Next thing I knew, the sun was setting, and the sight above the western horizon was breath taking. The soft, separated pastel shades of tequila sunset colors were striking and mesmerizing. This final majestic display of natural beauty beckoned my soul to adore the Creator of the universe before returning to the ranch house.

That night while lying in bed, I felt as if I had been under the influence of some powerful drug. I could not sleep. The feeling can be compared to someone falling in love. A venomous snake had bitten my soul—only the venom did not deaden my senses or put me to sleep. Instead, it invigorated my sense of curiosity. My soul had been introduced to a tantalizing and beautifully serene creature—the lady of the desert. From that night forward, I would be drawn to her silent whispers like a wistful lover for the rest of my life. At every chance available, I would wander out past the ranch boundaries to wander aimlessly into the wide expanse.

There is a certain freedom one feels when one can walk in any direction with no expectations and no goal in sight. My wanderings would last for several hours. In the early stages I feared getting lost, but as my familiarity with the terrain grew, so did my self-confidence. As the days passed, the distances lengthened. Sometimes I could go all day from one side of the valley to the other. It slowly dawned on me that after being exposed to so much time in the desert, the intense silence no longer bothered me. On the contrary, I got used to it. As a matter of fact, I reveled in her quiet, still, and eerie mysteriousness with delight. This desert spirit enraptured my soul and filled it with reverential love, so I wrote a poem about her:

The Lady of the Desert is tall and long like the desert's vertical and horizontal vastness. Her hair is black like the night, and her eyes dazzle with stars. Her hips sway like the wind making waves in the sand. Her voice carries a long distance like a lonely bird calling for a mate. Her heart is single, like a pure virgin land that waits in the midst of eternal solitude for her true lover to come and make his home in her land.

I fell in love with this Lady of the Desert, and that is probably why I never got married because I was always looking for a woman with this type of spirit: wild, free, innocent, and pure. The only woman who possessed this kind of spirit, which I discovered many years later, was Mary, the mother of Jesus, and still is.

Uncle Ron's Wild Flight into Darkness

One of the more revealing dreams of the soul's flight after death was the night of my uncle's departure from this world. On the night of his death, I had a dream where I recognized my uncle under great distress.

The dream went something like this: I heard a voice calling my name. I looked around. The voice sounded familiar but far away. Then it called again and sounded much closer. It seemed like it was in motion and traveling at a high velocity. Next thing I knew, my Uncle Ron's face was right in front of me. I tried to greet him, but something pulled him back with great force and he went hurtling back out of sight. Within seconds, he came back and stopped in front of me again, but with a desperate expression on his face. I reached out my hand, and away he went off again. This time I could see him being flung way out into the dark sky. I watched as he kept coming back and forth like a yo-yo on a long string. Each time he stopped to say something, his facial expression looked more frightened and grotesque.

The anguish in my soul became increasingly severe as my vision saw him being chased or whipped around from one end of the universe to the other. The rate of speed he traveled was amazing. It was quicker than the speed of light because he came and left my presence faster than my thought process could keep up with. Whatever was happening to him, the experience was causing his appearance to become less and less recognizable. Eventually, the extraordinary movements and transformation of my uncle's soul was too overwhelming to both my mind and my own soul. I woke up out of the dream saying to myself, "My God! Did my uncle die?"

I got up out of bed because I could not get back to sleep. It was about 6:00 a.m., so I put my clothes on to go down and get some coffee at the donut shop. As I was about to leave the house, the phone rang. *Who could be calling me so early?* I thought to myself. Right away I recognized the voice of my cousin, one of my uncle's two sons, on the other end of the line. He called to tell me that he had just got off the phone from speaking with my aunt in Nevada. "Steve, my dad died last night."

Shivers went through my body, not because of the news of his death but because God answered my question before anymore thoughts came to my foggy morning mind. Later that day, the recollection of the dream brought more light on its content. The dream kept playing over and over in my mind as I searched for spiritual clarity. The Holy Spirit must have helped because my mind could not fathom the meaning of such a confusing dream. While going about my business, I recalled all the years of living on and off with my uncle. I remembered his mannerisms, his personality, his moods, his ego, his pride, his weaknesses, his strengths, his recklessness, his hard work ethic, his quick temper, his callousness, his emotions, his foul language, his lust, his drinking, his smoking, his evasive eyes, his wild spirit, his shallow practice of faith, his smile, and his laugh. Many other images of my uncle kept flashing back.

Each one of these images brought with it a spirit of its own that formed a pattern, a pattern that revealed a possible eternal truth. "The proof is in the pudding," as the saying goes. Well, the proof (the existence of good and evil) is in the person (the pudding). The truth, according to Christ, is something that will set you free. But if a person is not fully in Christ (the truth), then that person becomes a slave to something (evil) binding him or her. Who was my uncle bound to in that dream? Why did my uncle's soul come to me? Could it be that I was one of the few people he knew in his life who was not afraid to talk to him about Jesus Christ? Maybe he could see that I was not bound to anything in the world, the flesh, or any evil spirit.

Whatever it was, he knew I loved God; he knew I read the Bible; and he knew I liked being alone in the desert to pray. Perhaps his soul knew that my soul would understand what he was going through and would be able to help him. The more I remember the dream, the more my spiritually informed soul understands the frantic expressions and the wild actions that took place that night of his death. I am 99 percent sure that evil spirits or powers in a spiritual zone were chasing his soul between heaven and hell. I prayed for him then, and I continue to pray for him to this day. I also can't help but wonder where he is now.

One time my uncle caught me in a lie, so I confessed the truth to him. He expressed to me how deeply he hated and despised liars. Ever since I made that confession, he gained respect for me and would confide in me things that he probably didn't tell anyone else. My uncle was not a politically correct man. As a matter of fact, in his own words, he repeatedly repudiated and despised liberal "hippy" types, especially the save the planet "environmentally retarded" types. He also rejected "n_____s," "queers," "thieving wet-backs," and "lazy effers" for various reasons. It took me many years to eventually understand why my uncle harbored so much anger and hatred toward certain groups of people. He was not afraid to let anyone know what he thought of him or her. He respected hard workers, and he had a passion for women.

This man's influence opened a new chapter in my life because his independent, rough, and rude personality was intoxicating. As uncouth as he was, what I admired most about the man was his extraordinary admiration of silence and solitude. He lived in isolated areas for the bulk of his adult life. He was one of the most innovative people I have ever known in my life. His independent spirit was contagious, and many local farmers and ranchers envied his wit and charm. If it were not for my uncle, I would not have had the early opportunity in life to be introduced to the lady of the desert. It was his crude and wild spirit that drove me into the desert. It was in the high desert above his ranch where I learned not to fear the unknown. It was in this desert where God's provocative Holy Spirit, not far from my uncle's ranch, would someday whisper in my ears one of the most challenging propositions in my life.

Indestructible Spiritual Beings

Until demons or evil spirits are condemned to hell, they are constantly on the prowl, looking for a place to stay. Evil spirits cannot stand being alone in the shadows and empty space, so they look for some human being to reside in. All human beings have a spark of God that faintly glows within the person's body. It is this light that attracts these ugly, spiritual moths to a soul's flame. Like bugs that crawl all over a light bulb looking for a crack into the source of its light, evil spirits crawl all around a person's heart looking for holes into the source of its light—the soul. They look for cracks into our consciences, the innermost sanctuary of our selves.

The Catholic Church teaches that the Holy Spirit of God the Father and Jesus Christ is written on our hearts, and that God's voice emerges within our consciences. "For man has in his heart a law written by God. To obey it is the very dignity of man: according to it he will be judged. Conscience is the most secret core and sanctuary of man. There he is alone with God, whose voice echoes in his depths."[17] God is constantly trying to guide us through our consciences, but if we do not attend to this voice deep within us, we avoid God's direction, and we become spiritually vulnerable and lost.

Evil spirits generally enter and inhabit spiritually weak people, conscience-less people. A spiritually weak person is easier to sneak into. These people have little protection because they have little faith in God. God's light is not very strong and does not burn very brightly within people of little faith. A spiritually strong person is harder to squeeze into because his or her soul has grown in brightness due to a healthy dose of faith and religious practices. For example, a strong person is someone who prays, confesses his or her sins to a priest, and receives frequent communion in a Catholic liturgy compared to a weak person who practices none of the above. A soul that has been nourished with God's light or grace maintains a glow—a brightness—that overpowers the strength of evil or dark spirits.

Most evil spirits cannot handle too much interior light emanating from a soul feeding on the grace of God. Sin blocks the flow of grace from the soul's nourishment. A soul that is not nourished by God's grace will weaken and corrode. Some physical sickness is connected or results from a sinful or weakened soul. Death of the body cannot be stopped, but it can be restored to new life by a healthy, vibrant soul (resurrection). People who have not nourished their souls with God's grace will cause their souls' brightness to lose their vitality, and their souls begin to breakdown. At the death of the body, the weakened soul, due to spiritual corrosion, will not be able to overpower the powers of evil spirits. The powers of darkness will envelop the corroded and weak soul and drive it further into spiritual oblivion.

Based on personal experience, I would venture to say that people are in more spiritual danger than ever before because they have little faith in the only one who can shield and defend them from infernal spirits. How many demons or evil spirits swarm around the average human being today? Thanks to the liberating effects of Jesus Christ and the church, a number of these fallen angels have been cast into hell. The light of Christ protects and strengthens the holy soul during its encounter with the Devil at death. However, the evil spirits that roam within the shadows chase the darkened and unprotected soul into deeper darkness at death. Perhaps when we crack

---

[17]   Vatican Council II, *The Church in the Modern World*, (paragraph 16).

our holy and healthy surface[18] with sin, we allow these demons to penetrate and infest our bodies with spiritual and physical disease.

Could this be the answer to the question why so many of the world's inhabitants are so full of disturbance and discontentment? It only takes a little intelligence to see that few people live in true peace in our neighborhoods. I would venture to say that many or even most poor souls living in the modern, first-world countries today are clueless and ignorant of God. Many people seem to contain driven souls within their bodies. Personal experience leads me to believe that perhaps many people possess souls driven by evil spirits who prevent them from unlocking the interior doors of their hearts to the mysteries of the knowledge of God because they have not taken the time to discipline their minds and bodies to be still, to be pure, to be quiet, and to wait on God. They do not know how to put themselves in the presence of eternal peace because they have built their lives on the suggestions and foundations of evil and distracting spirits that do all they can and use every means possible to block the soul's desire to learn and build on the Holy Spirit and words of God. Jesus mentioned the following to His disciples:

> Everyone who listens to these words of mine and acts on them will be like a wise man who built his house on rock. The rain fell, the floods came, and the winds blew and buffeted the house. But it did not collapse; it had been set solidly on rock. And everyone who listens to these words of mine but does not act on them will be like a fool who built his house on sand. The rain fell, the floods came, and the winds blew and buffeted the house. And it collapsed and was completely ruined. (Mt 7:21, 24-27)

The light or essence of God that comes from the heart of God is so real, so alive, and so sublime; it cannot be described in mere human words. His light or essence must be experienced. We can only compare the essence of God in a metaphoric way, such as: the essence of God is sweeter than honey. You can try to explain the taste of honey until you are blue in the face, but the only way a person can truly know the essence of honey is by putting it in his or her mouth. They must experience it. The same goes for conveying the actual experience of God. One must submerge himself in the light of God before being able to attempt any explanation of such an experience. It

---

[18]   "Surface" refers to moral barriers protecting our innermost person.

is extra-worldly. It is extraordinary. It is heavenly. It is indestructible. It is lovely. There exists no power greater than God. The soul that builds itself on the Word of God and feeds on the body and blood of the Christ of God eventually grows so bright that its power and brilliancy could be said to even cause the sun to cast a shadow through the universe.

What happens to the person who refuses to build his or her soul on the foundation of God and builds on the sands of evil instead? Souls can be ruined, but they cannot be totally destroyed. We are indestructible spiritual beings. Evil spirits are eternal, just like holy souls are immortal. Evil spirits roam in the dark, in the vast, empty lifelessness of eternal rejection. They are not wanted by anyone or any living life form. The only way they can find any comfort or satisfy their existence is to steal into and hide in another person's body. Then they find the hate-filled opportunity to undermine the person's moral foundation to make another soul fall into the same miserable condition the evil spirits are in.

An evil spirit's only compensation in existence is to drag another person's soul down to its level of deplorable ruin. Evil spirits are so jealous of the light in a soul that they will go to any extent to put it out before it grows brighter. What these pitiable ruins fear the most is watching another soul grow stronger than they are because a grace-filled soul can eventually learn to pull them out of hiding and expose these evil spirits in plain view of all holy souls. They dread to be recognized as the cause of evil, pain, and suffering to the holy ones and others in God's creation. This exposure brings to light on the eternal stage more shame on them for all to see.

Imagine what it would be like if you or I had to show a recorded video of all the bad thoughts and evil things we did to all we encountered in our lifetime. Imagine the shock and horror you and I would experience if everybody who loved and respected us could see what we really thought and did toward them. Evil spirits suffer for all eternity this exposure of who they really are: the horrible face of ruin and hatred. That is why these damned souls remain in hideous darkness and despair. As the old saying goes, misery loves miserable company.

Dreams as Instruments to a Higher Calling

If the Spirit of God is within us by virtue of baptism, then why are we rejecting God? Why is it that most people don't express to each other on a daily basis their love for the Holy Spirit? Instead, we want the spirit of the world. Instead, we prefer to love things and people above God. We prefer excitement and doing wild and crazy things with wild and crazy company. The answer boils down to the fact that evil spirits do everything in their power to hide God and keep people doing wild and crazy things. God knows their trickery, so God uses the spiritual medium to communicate to us, to warn us, to guide us, to direct us, to soothe us, and to encourage us to come closer to knowing Him.

All of us—at least everyone I have ever talked to—have had dreams. I have yet to speak to someone who has never dreamed. And I am not talking wishful thinking. I am talking dreams that come to us during the hours of sleep. Can human beings who sleep an average of one-third of their daily lives away find any meaning in it? Is sleep limited to resting the grey matter of the brain only? Or is there another reason or function for sleep? I would say there is. Granted, most dreams a person experiences in a lifetime do not amount to any real significance, but some dreams count and can make a significant difference to someone's course of action in life if heeded.

Out of all the dreams I can remember, only about 2 percent of them contained any value or meaning in them that could be applied to help or change my life's circumstances. But one thing I learned from that 2 percent of significant dreams is that spirits exist, and they are real. As a matter of fact, these dreams, which I will call *extraordinary dreams,* put me on roads that sobered me up, body and soul, from all my foolish indulgences in life. Alcohol and drugs are not the only indulgences people use to escape a world full of problems, competition, difficulties, and pain. No, people can spend their entire lives watching TV, staring at computers, playing games, or living in a fantasyland. These and many other indulgences distract and disconnect a person from coming in contact with a world that is far more real than the objective, material world we live in every waking day.

It is important to note here that not everyone has the same kinds of dreams. There are certain kinds of dreams given to the kind of temperament suited to the type of character a person has developed for him or herself. Some dreams can be very beautiful and prophetic, given to those who have gentle, humble, and loving hearts. For example, there are characters like the prophet Daniel of the Old Testament who received many dreams or visions of heavenly beings because he loved God above all else. The holy prophet Isaiah envisioned and prophesied that someday a "virgin shall be with Child, and bear a Son, and shall name Him Immanuel" (Isa 7:14). No one had ever dreamed that this prophecy meant that a virgin would conceive a child without any sexual relations. Nonetheless, over seven hundred years after the prophecy or dream, the humble and gentle Saint Joseph of Nazareth received informative, directional, and visionary type dreams from an angel concerning the virgin birth.

> "Behold the angel of the Lord appeared to him in a dream and said, 'Joseph, son of David, do not be afraid to take Mary as your wife into your home. For it is through the Holy Spirit that she has conceived this Child" (Mt 1:20). After Mary, Joseph was probably the first one to understand and believe Isaiah's ancient prophecy. After she conceived, Mary no longer had to believe in Isaiah's prophecy. She knew for a fact that she had conceived without sexual relations. However, Joseph knew this only by faith. Throughout his life, only he believed that Isaiah's prophecy was literally fulfilled in the pregnancy of his wife and the birth of his Foster Son. Joseph did not have the Church or the New Testament to confirm his belief. He had *only a dream*, his relationship with Mary, and primarily his relationship with the Lord. [19]

Then you have proud and vicious biblical characters who received cautionary dreams or visions that appeared to be very frightening and diabolic in nature, such as those received by King Saul in the book of Samuel and King Belshazzar in the book of Daniel. As a priest, I occasionally hear desperate stories coming from certain personalities who have revealed very ugly and shocking dreams to me. After listening to their life's history, usually full of aggression and dangerous indulgences, the hideous dreams or visions they suffer from fit the kind of lifestyles they have chosen to live.

As a young man, my life was like a spiritual tossed salad. It was full of school work, games, jobs, sports, parties, friends, drugs, alcohol, trips to the desert, Bible, beach, thinking, girlfriends, immoral acts, and so on. It was mixed up and messed up at the same time. God must have felt sorry for me, or someone was praying for me, because He started slamming me with a whole range of dreams. When these 2 percent of extraordinary type of dreams took

---

[19]   One Bread, One Body, www.presentationministries.com Advent (Dec. 19, 2010).

place, I tried to disregard them because they were too overwhelming and frightening for my mind to grasp or understand, let alone try to interpret. The more these confounded dreams occurred, the more I indulged myself in certain bad habits. Why?

I would ask myself in my lonely and depressed state of mind after another wasted night of doing something stupid, why did I find myself retreating into stupid and meaningless habits? The truthful answer to this question slowly dawned on me in painful time. I indulged in the dumb things of this world because I did not want to admit that there was something more powerful than me and myself in control.

How can I begin to put what I just said in other words that make sense? The best I can say is that these unusual dreams turned everything upside down. They revealed truths about myself and the world I had constructed around me. Before these amazing types of dreams came along, my understanding about who I was, what life was about, and where I fit in this world was fine, dandy, and right on. But since the advent of these extraordinary dreams, everything I thought I knew and understood about who I was, what life was about, and where I fit in this world was sick and wrong. Therefore, to escape from the hard truths, tortures, and frightful realities revealed to me by these dreams, I indulged in whatever I could to avoid remembering or thinking about them. The problem with indulgences is that they only cover a festering wound; they do not heal a person at the source of the wound. The indulgences always led me down, path after path, to a mental complacency and spiritual dead end.

I feared the extraordinary dreams because they shattered my whole existence; they tore apart the veil of my false personality that I had so carefully constructed since my adolescence. These dreams showed me that I was not in control of myself. As a matter of fact, the spiritual beings that came at me during these dreams had far more control and power over me and whoever I thought I was. These dreams opened up cans of worms that were responsible for the rotten kind of person I had become underneath the surface of my skin. They put a light on the diseases eating away at both the flesh of my body and the beauty of my soul.

As horrifying as these dreams were, in hindsight, I thank God for them. Like the dreams that St. Joseph received in times of danger to himself and his holy family, these dreams saved me from earthly and eternal destruction, and they continue to do so. As they did to several biblical characters, some of these earlier dreams have been fulfilled in my life so far. Many of them acted as warning signs preventing me from choosing to go down bad roads, while others led me on good ones. I owe my road to the priesthood to responding to the suggestions and directional signs of these dreams. Some of these dreams lifted me up out of the poisonous ponds of worldly pleasures and settled me into the cleansing rivers of the Catholic Church and her sacraments.

One person from the Old Testament Scriptures who comes to mind who greatly benefited from dreams is Joseph, the second to the last son of Jacob, the patriarch of Israel. As a young boy, he experienced very profound dreams that revealed things that would save himself, his family, his tribe, the baby Messiah, and eventually the whole world. Salvation by means of a Redeemer promised to expiate mankind from its sins and ultimate destruction. God sent the world its Redeemer to be born among threats to the child's life. But the father, whose name was also Joseph, Joseph of Nazareth, was warned by an angel in a dream to pack up the virgin mother and the incarnate child Redeemer and go to Egypt. Both Josephs were guided by providential dreams.

> God provided the Joseph of the Old Testament the gift of interpreting dreams which foretold his own destiny. And the Joseph of the New Testament was also provided via dreams the directions God wanted him to follow. Both Josephs were led into Egypt foretold in their dreams. Both Josephs had two extraordinary dreams apiece. And both Josephs had pairs of dreams that were later fulfilled according to God's plan of salvation. *"Now Joseph had a dream, and he told it to his brothers... Listen to this dream I had. We were binding sheaves in the field; my sheaf rose up and remained standing, while your sheaves gathered around, and bowed down to my sheaf"* (Gn 37:5-7). This first dream of the Joseph of the Old Testament came true when his father [Jacob] with all his family came to Egypt and prostrated themselves before him who had become the prime minister of the country, the provider of all peoples of the earth.[20]

---

20   Griffin, Michael D. *Saint Joseph and the Third Millennium*. Teresian Charism Press: Hubertus (1999) 63.

"He had another dream which he also told to his brothers . . . The sun, the moon and eleven stars were worshipping me" (Gn 37:9).

The second dream of the Joseph of the Old Testament came true when Jesus, the Son of God and Mary, the woman of the Apocalypse, and the Church would place themselves under the authority of Joseph of Nazareth in the New Testament as head of the Holy Family. The sun represents Jesus, the moon Mary, and the eleven stars the Christian Church.[21]

Both dreams that the Joseph of the Old Testament had came true immediately after their occurrences. The dreams that Joseph of Nazareth experienced were more urgent, more powerful, and more amazing. Look how quickly he responded and how Mary went along without a mention of doubt. These passages describing the dream experiences of two prominent figures in the Bible provide a valid reason that some dreams matter in life. It demonstrates that God can use dreams to convey important things and messages to the "righteous"[22] that can profoundly change or alter someone's life or community, including the whole world.

Like the extraordinary dreams mentioned above, through dreams, I have had wonderful and dreadful experiences with occupants from both heaven and hell. Hell's occupants are not friendly. As a matter of spiritual fact, your worst earthly enemy is friendlier than any spirit from hell. And when you have had an experience with a creature from heaven, you do not mind suffering the assaults from hell. When talking about my dreams to others, I often hear something in their response that says, "Hey, come on, let's get real," meaning let's get back to the only real world we physically live in. If they only knew how mistaken they are.

This is not the only real world that exists. Reality does not cast shadows. The real you has the capacity to make shadows. The real you can touch hearts, either in a good way or in a bad way. The real you can free or imprison a neighbor. The real you can make someone truly laugh or cry. Those who think that going to work every day to make a buck in life is reality will someday discover that they will not be able to take a single cent of their so-

---

[21]   Ibid.

[22]   Doze, Andrew. *Saint Joseph: Shadow of the Father.* Alba House: New York (1992) 126.

called real money into what they thought was an unreal world after death. Let me try to illustrate to you what the other real world appears to be like through the window of what I call a real, extraordinary type of dream, not a typical dingbat dream full of vague scenes and confusing sequences that do not add up to anything worth remembering.

PART II

THE SEARCH

To the Moon over Chile

At age twenty-four, possessed by an insatiable quest to know God and my own destiny, I paid a visit to the Lady of the Desert and remained with her alone. My life in California seemed meaningless and empty, so I drove to Nevada and went out into the desert canyons high above my uncle's ranch to pray and fast for three days and two nights. In the middle of the night, I heard a familiar and at the same time unidentifiable voice tell me to go to an unknown and distant land. I was not sure if I was awake or asleep; all I knew was that I was sure to leave the United States. When I went back to my home in Aptos, California, my mother told me about a man she met in San Francisco. He was an ex-missionary priest visiting places in North America. He gave her his name and address in some foreign country. When I wrote him a letter, he wrote back inviting me to come to South America and visit his agricultural center designed to teach native Indians new techniques in farming. In less than three months, I departed to go on my first foreign adventure that started a five-and-a-half-year journey to over forty foreign countries spread throughout three continents.

My first extraordinary dream beyond US borders occurred while I was living in a small town called Nueva Imperial in southern Chile, South America. This extraordinary dream took place in the middle of winter after nearly six months of adjustment into the Chilean culture. I had been struggling with learning the Spanish language, getting used to a very slow pace of lifestyle, high unemployment rate, living in extreme poverty, and experiencing homesickness from family and friends. My days were filled with long walks, solitude, and boredom.

One day while I was standing around on a street corner in the town plaza, a man came up to speak to me. He had taken notice of me walking around the town and asked if I were interested in coming to his home for a meal. I said yes in my broken Spanish and went to visit him. While sitting at table, I could see through the side door off his kitchen a room full of simple cutting tools and bamboo shoots stacked up in neatly stacked bundles. I asked him if he knew how to make baskets and he said, "Yes. I'm the town basket weaver." I got up and asked if I could take a look at his work.

He showed me around his little shop, and after a little more discussion, he offered to teach me how to make baskets. Something in me jumped at the opportunity and said, "When?" For the next couple of months, I buried myself in learning how to make baskets. The time went by slowly, but I was at peace. To my relief, I was able to stay focused on one thing instead of being scattered all over the place in mind and heart. I found something constructive to do with myself. The baskets kept me from wandering around aimlessly and from feeling sorry for my lonely self. I started pondering on things like life and God again. Some of the verses I had read from the Bible ran through my thoughts as I carefully weaved away the hours making baskets. While my fingers grew stronger and more confident in the art of basket weaving, the simple work helped to soothe my anxieties and slowly melted away deep insecurities.

One night while lying on my back fast asleep, my eyes opened and stared up at what looked like a large hole in the ceiling above my bed. The next thing that happened can only be described as if someone had launched a rocket and I was strapped to it. I shot up out of the bed straight up through the ceiling, through the attic, and then the roof. I could see the town below me fade away and disappear out of sight as I gained height. I remember picking up speed as I continued to watch the earth below me grow smaller in size the higher I rose. Finally, I looked up to see where I was headed, and to my shock and surprise, the moon looked as if it were a couple of miles away to one side as I rushed past it.

I did not know where I was going. All I knew was that I was moving at an incredible speed and that everything in this atmosphere was extremely intense. My vision, my hearing, and my thought processes were super excelled and incredulous. I could not believe this was happening. It seemed so unreal. Suddenly, it sounded like someone back on earth said, "That's enough," and with one swift jerk at what seemed like a rope tied around my waist, my body snapped right back down into my bed like a slingshot.

In an instant, I sat up and reached for the light. After turning on the lamp, I looked up at the ceiling to see if there was a hole in it. There was no hole, so I got up and walked around in the room asking myself what had just happened. Was it just a dream, or did something else occur to me that deserved attention? I tried to make sense of the dream but soon fell back to sleep without any conclusions. For several days afterward, I reasoned that the everyday challenges and preoccupations of living in a foreign land must have brought on such a wild and crazy dream. Little did I know that it would take several more dreams and many years later to learn just how real that dream was.

On the Road with Eternal Spirits at My Heels

Winter in Nueva Imperial turned to spring, and I turned from a beginner of Chilean dialect and bamboo splitter to a more fluent Spanish speaker and skilled basket weaver. Like sap that begins to rise in the thawing trunk of a tree, the spirit of exploration began to rise from the depths of my frozen soul to warm the outer veins and arteries of my eager body to move on to something beyond the horizon.

Every once in a while I would get a chance to accompany some of the Agric-Co-op technicians in the field. They would drive hours through dirt roads to reach indigenous farmers living on their ancestral lands far outside the Chilean towns and city limits. These Indians still live on their original tribal territories where the Spanish conquistadors never completely coveted. To this day, they have managed to secure ownership without paying taxes to the Chilean government. The particular tribe, to which the charity based Farm Co-op ministered, was called the Mapuche Indians. They were members of the Araucano heritage of native peoples. The Mapuches are one of the few tribes never fully defeated by the Spanish invasions. They were very strategic in the use of guerrilla warfare tactics. I took a special liking to these people because they were very calm and quiet. They seemed to blend into the atmosphere. Their movements and mannerisms made the Chilean technicians look awkward outside their societal fishbowls. I felt a growing desire to break away from my Chilean hosts to go and live among the Mapuche people.

Back in town and busy at making baskets, I would ponder what it would be like to be totally self-sufficient and on my own. Time passed, and in the middle of the night, I heard a noise of someone coming into my room. He moved so swiftly that I did not even have time to turn to see who it was when suddenly I felt two powerful hands pushing hard down on my back trying to crush the life out of me. My body froze to the point that I could not breathe. The pressure mounted every second, as if tons of bricks were being dumped on top of me. I somehow managed to suck in a deep breath of air and screamed something out at the top of my lungs. The intruder backed off, and the pressure was gone.

I woke up, quickly turned on the light, and looked toward the door. The door was shut, but I went to open it and see if I could spot the invader. Nobody, not even a mouse, stirred in the house. All was quiet. *Was it just a stupid dream?* I thought. I was afraid to go back to sleep, so I stayed up replaying and pondering the event. Somehow, I fell back to sleep and had another dream. In this dream, I was walking at a fast pace on a dirt road in the direction toward Repocura, a territory I had become familiar with on several visits with the co-op. It was a bright, sunshiny day, and it must have been springtime because the flowers were in bloom. There were Mapuches dressed in colorful robes working in their fields. I felt strong and healthy striding along, as if I lived there, and the people seemed to know me and greeted me as I passed by. When I woke from this dream, something in me said, "It's time to go."

The Agric Co-op where I stayed in town was going through some political and financial problems. The owner, who was an American from Washington, DC, area, made frequent trips to the United States to do fundraisers. One day after returning from one of his trips, we had lunch together, and he asked me how I was doing. I told him everything was good but that I felt like I needed to move on.

He asked me, "Where?"

I said, "I would like to go live with the Indians in Repocura."

He stopped eating, looked at me, and smiled. "Really?" he asked.

"Yeah," I said.

"What are you going to do out there?" he inquired.

"I don't know. I'll leave that in God's hands."

After that, he looked at me and somehow knew I was serious, so he reached out, shook my hand, and said, "God be with you." In less than a week, I found myself with a backpack on my back and my feet taking their first steps on the road to Repocura with no strings attached to Nueva Imperial.

At first, I was a little nervous, but as the miles wore on, my heart was encouraged by the serenity and natural beauty of a land not dominated by motorized vehicles, electric power lines overhead, and shouting vendors asking for money. The deeper I entered into Indian territory, the deeper the silence grew. There was a certain mystique that filled the atmosphere. By evening of the first day abroad, I reached a small Indian village called Chol-Chol. I knew a man who worked for the co-op who lived there. He was half Chilean and half Mapuche. I paid him a visit, and he invited me to stay the night. I had dinner with his family, and afterward I told him where I was headed. He gave me the name of a person he knew who lived in the heart of the Repocura territory. The next morning we had breakfast; I thanked him and then said good-bye to return to the road.

From the time I left Chol-Chol to the time it took to reach the river that separates the region of Repocura from the Dueco region, the sun was already setting. The little dirt road shrank down to a footpath that wound down to the bank of a good-size river. Three people were crossing over to my side when I reached the bottom. The rowboat looked as if it had been hewn from a large tree.

When the boat came to rest on the bank where I stood, I asked the man rowing the boat if he knew where a man named Don Oscar lived. "A friend from Chol-Chol told me to go see him."

The man looked up and said, "I am that man."

In my astonishment, I introduced myself and told him the name of the man in Chol-Chol. He quickly waved me into the boat and rowed us back with enthusiasm to the other side of the river. It only took a few minutes on foot to arrive at the door of a little two-story, wooden house hidden under thick trees. After fixing me something to eat and telling me stories about his life, Don Oscar took me upstairs by candlelight and told me that I could stay in the house as long as I wanted. *"Mi casa es su casa."* He then gave me some blankets, a candle, and a pot to pee in during the night. I thanked him and said good night.

My first night in the heart of Repocura was suspenseful. You would think that no one lived out there because it was so quiet and still. All I could hear were a few frogs and insects singing down by the river. After a few days in the company of Don Oscar, I began to catch glimpses of human faces peeking through the forest brush. At first they were careful and hidden, but after a while, human native faces became more visible. Soon, the younger and braver ones came out of hiding. Don Oscar would call them to come over and greet me, but they would just stand and stare at me. Their blank expressions were a little unnerving but not hostile. As they stood there staring at me, full of curiosity in their eyes, they reminded me of surprised deer, curiously staring at me way back in the canyons behind my uncle's ranch in the Nevadan high desert. Their faces were smooth and showed no signs of stress; it was hard to tell their age, except the younger ones were easier to spot because they smiled easily when my eyes met theirs.

Those first days in Repocura passed slowly, and the news of a strange, white man in the forest spread through the region. I soon discovered that I was living smack in the middle of a couple hundred Mapuche Indians concentrated within a three—to four-square-mile section of forest. I was amazed at how quietly so many of these people could live and function together in such a small area. The younger natives would follow me around because they got a big kick out of watching my awkward movements within the forest. The kids would show me the different medicinal plants and fruits that grew there. They laughed at my facial expressions as I bit into the fruits they dared me to try.

Eventually, the kids would bring me to their huts, and I got to meet the parents of the young natives. The parents and elderly adults always seemed a little embarrassed or timid when I greeted them. They would immediately busy themselves fixing some kind of herb tea and start baking me some kind of fresh bread cakes. After serving me, they would sit and stare in silence for what seemed like hours at a time. It was uncomfortable at first, but the more I frequented their huts, the more at ease they became in my presence. Some of them knew some Spanish and would break the silence with a mixture of Spanish and Nahuatl, their language.

I made friends with a couple families closest to Don Oscar's house. One of the kid's fathers was about my age and took a liking to me. He would send over his son early in the morning to wake me up and invite me to accompany him and his father into the forest. I enjoyed going with them and learning how the Mapuches lived off the forest. I was amazed how much they knew about every plant and animal, and how they could benefit from so many things that I always thought were nothing more than no good weeds, worms, and rats. The more I learned about the forest, the more I felt like it was not such a harsh and scary place full of dangerous snakes and animals. As a matter of fact, I felt safer in the forest with the wild Indians and animals than I did in the modern civilized cities and towns full of beggars and crime.

Groups of Mapuche men would take me to work with them during the harvest season up into the higher elevations where they had planted fields of wheat. After working several hours, they would all sit down to take a break in the shade. We would eat dried meat and fruits. We would then sit and stare at the majestic scenery of forest-covered valleys below. The views were beautiful, the air was pristine clear, and you could hear life in the forest for miles around. The combination of the splendid sights and sounds of the forest mixed in with these indigenous people engaged in subtle conversation and their gentle songs put me in some kind of state of contemplation that filled me with a certain type of joy and appreciation for a wilderness never experienced before in my country or the desert of Nevada. My days were filled with work and this exquisite form of Mapuche contemplation. But it did not take too long until the enemy caught up with me.

El Diablo Visits el Extranjero, the Stranger in Repocura

Life was too good as I grew more knowledgeable of the Mapuche way. My nights were full of rest and healthy sleep until the dark intruder caught up to me to wreak spiritual havoc in Repocura. One warm day, a couple young Mapuche men and I were on our way to take a swim at the bottom of some waterfall the youths wanted to show me. We were casually walking along the main dirt road connecting the only two villages in the territory when we spotted a middle-aged Mapuche woman coming toward us. Out of the corner of my eye, I noticed one of the young men whisper something in the ear of the other one walking beside him.

The woman was about to pass by, when suddenly she waved a hand and said something to one of my Indian companions. They stopped to greet her with a few words in their native language. She also stopped and exchanged a few words with him and then turned to look at me. She smiled and said something in broken Spanish that I did not understand. I smiled back and sort of waved at her. She lifted her hand and made a gesture as if she wanted to shake hands. I shook her limp hand; she smiled again and then turned and slowly proceeded on her way. We also continued on our way to the falls.

We must have walked several minutes in silence when the older one of the two, named Arturo, spoke up and said to me, "You just met the Macchi."

I asked him, "What's that?"

They both looked at each other and laughed. Then the younger one said, "I think she likes you."

They chuckled again and I said, "Okay, but who is she?"

Arturo said, "She is *la cura* or the witchdoctor of the region, and she is single."

They both busted out laughing, and so did I. Their laughter was contagious, but I didn't really know why I laughed. It just felt good to laugh. We soon arrived at the bottom of a large waterfall. The sight and the sound of it were breathtaking. The water cascaded down from high above and landed in a wide, shallow turquoise pool, nestled amongst smooth rock formations on all sides. The water flowed out between two towering stone formations forming a spectacular entrance to the pool area. We spent the whole afternoon enjoying the water, loitering, and basking ourselves on the sun-warmed rocks.

Before I fell asleep that night, I sat up on a stool made of wood from the forest with a seat made of thick woven grass. Visions of the waterfall cascading down the mountain and remembering the splashing sounds of the water showering the pool filled me with wonder and admiration for God and His creation. I sat still in the chair, letting all the things, places, and people I had encountered so far on my journeys engulf my soul. A wonderful spirit that seemed to belong to the forest enraptured something deep inside me. As I lay in bed, somewhere in the distance I could hear someone chanting a song while rhythmically beating a drum. The voice seemed to blend in with the shrilly, chirping sounds of the forest night creatures in chorus with one another. My eyelids grew heavy as I drifted off into a deep sleep.

The violent speed of the attack caught me by total surprise. Whoever was on top of me applied so much pressure that it flattened the bed to the floor. My thoughts ran wild with fear as I desperately tried to breathe. The weight and pressure per foot pounds was increasing at a rate so fast, I felt as if I were going to explode and blow out my insides all over the floor like a squashed rabbit run over by a two-ton truck. I tried to open my mouth, but it was smashed shut, face down to the ground.

The next thing that seemed to occur so instantly, so spontaneously and so powerfully, came from somewhere way down inside of whatever was not squashed out of me, an audible, loud voice of someone I once admired in my past that yelled, "Get off!" The creature, the thing, or whatever it was on top of me flew back with a bang and was gone. I did a push up off the floor that sprung me right to my feet. Scrambling for the matches, I lit the candle. After feeling my body with my hands, I searched my room and the whole floor for any sign of some foreign object moving around.

Tip-toeing down the stairway, I listened for any peculiar noises down below, nothing but silence. I went back and stood by the bed and saw that it was not broken or smashed up. My mind was confused; nothing made sense of what just happened. I could swear to God that something came into my room and just tried to kill me. It was no dream, and yet I was sure I was asleep when it caught me off guard. I sat up on the stool for a long time, afraid to go back to sleep, but somehow the dawn snuck into my window and woke me in the morning. I had fallen back to sleep.

For the next three months or moons, because I had no calendar, this dark intruder paid me several more midnight visits. The attacks were always exceedingly violent and overwhelmingly frightening. My body would always go into some kind of paralysis until some image or voice from somewhere inside of me shook me out of that horrible state. At one point, I thought the Indians were slipping some kind of weird drug into the herbal tea drinks they would serve me. My mind began to play tricks on me, making me convince myself that perhaps I was under some kind of trance where my body would sneak out at night to go visit the woman witchdoctor down the road to smoke some kind of bad, hallucinogenic weed.

The seasons were changing, and winter was around the corner. In order to keep my wits about me, I made it a daily habit to go for a walk down to the riverbank and pray to God in any way I could to help me deal with these nightly attacks. One day while walking along the river's edge, my eyes focused on a familiar reed that none of the Indians brought to my attention—*la mimbre* or wicker plants! To my satisfaction, I found several patches of bamboo plants growing along the riverbanks. I grabbed my knife and cut several stalks to take to my room. I made a make shift tool to split the reeds and set to work making baskets at night. The work got my mind off the nightmares and focused again on making baskets. At the same time, the weaving helped me fall asleep exhausted from physical and mental fatigue.

The days grew short, and the winter came in cold and hard over the land of forest and forest people. A few of my Mapuche friends took notice of my carrying bundles of bamboo reeds to Don Oscar's house. They grew inquisitive as to what this lone American white man was doing with a bunch of sticks. The young ones were always the first to come over and investigate my antics. Both boys and girls would come over to sit and watch the maestro, craftsman make baskets. There was a little creek that ran by the house during the wet season, so I would lay the cut reeds in the shallow water to keep them fresh.

One young brave man took a reed out of the water and started peeling the skin off with his knife. When he had finished, I showed him how to split the reed with the splitting tool. The others watched and heard him giggle as he successfully split it into three slender pieces. Before long, another took a reed and joined in on the action. By the end of the day, several young people were learning how to make baskets. An average of three Mapuches would hang around long enough to get halfway finished, but then they would lose interest, usually because of teasing each other. Others gave up because they would lose patience and quit. A handful of diehard, apprentice Mapuche basket makers and I weaved our way through the autumn and early winter months. The news spread throughout the region that el *extranjero forastero*, the foreign woodsman, knew how to make *canastos*, baskets.

Mapuche adults, usually women, would come over to check out the baskets. If they liked what they saw, they would make orders for baskets in exchange for wheat, beans, and other goods they would yield from their lands. One woman gave me *una manta*, a wool poncho made from the goats she raised. I remember watching the women make ponchos and rugs out of hand-spun goat hair. It was fascinating to observe the long process it took to make a five-by-six-foot piece of cloth.

The women would first dip burlap sacks full of shorn goat hair into large pots of boiling water mixed with dye extracted from certain flowering plants. Then the hair was dried out and carefully finger spliced and twisted into strands that were spun tightly together around a stick rubbed between the palms of their hands. Next, they would take the balls of yarn off the stick and weave one end of horizontal strands in and out between a series of vertical strands tied to a frame of long thin wooden poles mounted on a makeshift loom outside the hut. The women would continue threading and splicing different-colored yarn back and forth between the poles. After every two or three strands, she would slide a long, smooth, flat, sword-like stick in between the vertical strands and pull down tight against the recently woven strands to pack the work together.

She would continue doing this operation hour by hour, day after day until she reached the top of the loom. Finally, she would carefully interlock the ends together all the way around in some fashion that firmly secured a border, enclosing the finished product. For this weathered, little Mapuche woman to give me an awesome poncho for a couple of measly baskets was quite a deal. I remember looking at her with an expression on my face that probably read, "Are you sure about this?" She looked back with an expression of gratitude that said, "I'm glad you are here with us." She then reached out and shook my hand with a big, bright, toothless smile on her round, wrinkled face, and then turned and walked away.

The basket business and visits to indigenous farms around the region took my mind off the dark and horrid midnight intrusions. Several months went by free from spiritual disturbance during sleeping hours. Things were looking up again for me in the land of Repocura until I got sick. Whatever I caught, it would not clear up for days. One of the Indian neighbors closest to Don Oscar's house got wind of my illness from her kids, who liked hanging out with me. She was a fairly young Mapuche woman who had three children and another one on the way. This kind mother paid a surprise visit to my room one day while I lay in bed. She asked me how I felt, and I told her not too good. She told me she was going to prepare some medicinal drink for me and have one of her daughters bring it over. I thanked her, even though

I really didn't feel like drinking anything because it would only pass right through me. Her gestures and smile made me feel better than her bitter herb tea. The days passed painfully slow, and the nights were worse. In my state of physical weakness and mental depression, the Devil paid his visits too.

One thing I learned about evil spirits in my travels and years of encounters afterward with them is that they are cowards. They always wait until a person is feeling down, weak, vulnerable, afraid, or sick before they strike. They never really came at me when I was feeling strong and secure in mind and heart. This time they came at me at all angles and with a ferocity that could drive a spooked horse crazy, making it run wild and out of control. The problem was, I couldn't run any further than back and forth between the outhouse and my bed. But my spirit went totally out of control.

The nightmares took on a slightly newer tactic this time around. There was like a series, a slough full of dreams where I experienced death in several different ways. Years before I journeyed to South America, I remembered having several very distinct dreams of being chased by people threatening to kill me. They were very scary and awful dreams where no matter how fast I ran or how well I maneuvered away from the pursuer, the assailant always seemed to catch up to me. Right before he delivered the deathblow, I would wake up just in time. Well . . . not this time.

In one of my sickbed dreams, I was back in the house my family lived in when I was in high school. After coming home from school, I went into the kitchen to get something to eat as we kids used to do. The house was quiet. My mom was not home, and neither were any of my brothers. My father usually came home later sometime around 5:00 p.m. I walked around calling out for my mom and brothers, but there was no response. Something in my gut sensed danger was afloat.

We lived in a split-level house. I stood in the kitchen between the basement and the upstairs. What I saw next was, like an x-ray vision through the ceiling and the floor, several men hiding in our rooms with rifles in their hands. My instant thought was to head for the front door and go call the police for help from one of the neighbors next door. Halfway to the door, about a half dozen men emerged out of the shadows and surrounded me with guns raised. I tried to say something to them like, "Don't shoot," but before the words came out of my mouth, they proceeded to blast my body full of bullet holes. I felt like a statue in the middle of a fountain where little streams of water gush out all around it falling into the font. I remember looking down while watching my blood cover the floor, and then I woke up.

Feeling around for the candle, I managed to get it lit. I stood there next to the candle, carefully checking to see if I had any bullet holes in me. There were none, but that did not make me feel better. The nights were cold, and I could not go back to sleep for fear of another dream, so I would wait for the dawn by gently rocking back and forth on the stool.

In the next dream, I was walking along a wide riverbed with one of my brothers named Dave somewhere back in California. It was a hot, sunshiny day. We used to go fishing together in this river for crawfish. My brother is one year younger than I, and we were always close to each other in our youthful days. We were walking along the shore on the rocks just meandering around doing nothing. He drifted upstream as I went downstream. I heard a familiar noise somewhere up in the sky above me, so I turned and looked up. There was a hawk gently soaring high above my position. *Cool!* I thought.

I kept my gaze on it as it circled the sky. It looked like a beautiful, large, female adult red-tailed hawk, but I was not sure. I hoped it would come a little closer so I could identify it. I looked over to see if my brother spotted it, but he was busy doing something else. When I looked up again, the hawk had come down closer and was still circling overhead. *Wow, great! It's getting closer.* But I still could not tell what kind of hawk it was.

To my delight, it kept circling down closer and closer. My neck started getting sore from staring up at it, and it was hard to keep my eyes on it because it circled faster and faster around me. I decided to sit down on the beach and spin myself on my seat to keep up with the circling hawk. *This is so awesome,* I thought. The bird came within a hundred feet above my head with tighter and faster circles. I could not keep up with it until suddenly I felt a strange, inner voice warning me, *You blew it again, idiot, it is not a hawk!*

It was too late. The hawk dove down, and in an instant, it slashed at my throat and ripped it open. Blood came spurting out all over the rocks. I stood up and looked to yell for my brother, but he was too far away as I weakly tried to scream. I remember falling to my knees looking in his direction and then laying on my side as my blood and life drained out of me onto the rocks and sand. It felt as if my *self* leaked out and slid on top of the rocks and seeped into the sand. My vision disappeared as I sunk below and underground. This time I woke up holding my neck, as if someone had just slashed it with a knife. I lit the candle and found my little wallet-sized mirror to look at my neck. It was fine—no gash and no blood. "Whew!" Back on the stool I went to wait for the dawn.

When the rains came, it seemed like it would never stop. The river was flooding its banks in certain areas of the lower territory. Several families were forced to abandon their valley huts and to climb up into the mountains where they built lean-to shelters in the wheat fields. Thank God Don Oscar's house was built on a grade above the river. I also thanked God for no mirrors in the house because I knew I was a frightful sight. I was going on three weeks, and still no sign of relief. Whatever I ate went right through me. My Mapuche neighbors kept bringing me tea but to no avail. I didn't want them to worry so much, so I would lie to them about how I felt.

The wet, cold, and long grey days put a damper on my spirits. Don Oscar was in bad spirits also. He liked the summers but hated the winters in Repocura. He was originally from the city. He was born and raised in Santiago, Chile. He worked in the theatre and retired to live the country life because he got tired of the phony lifestyle of acting. He had moved out to Repocura eleven years before, but he never got used to the wet and cold seasons. We would sit in his kitchen at night because it was the only room that had a little wood-burning stove in it. His conversations grew a little strange by the night. He seemed to suffer from depression and loneliness. Hardly anyone would come to visit him.

One day, when the kids came to visit me, I asked them to tell me what the local Indians thought about Don Oscar. They tried to conceal it by putting their hands to their mouths, but when I looked at them with a funny, inquisitive look, they started to laugh. Rosita, the older daughter next door, came right out with it and said they considered Don Oscar to be *un pajaro raro*, a rare, crazy bird. Then in unison, they all busted out laughing. Since I spent a lot of time in bed, I soon discovered they were right. Almost every day, I could hear him conversing with someone outside my window who I thought were nearby neighbors. I came to find out, after peeking out my window, that he had been talking to his pigs grazing beside him as he raked the ground or chopped wood. He told me himself that he did not have much faith in God, so he probably did not pray much. All of this put more darkness into my situation, and sure enough, the attacks continued.

Almost every other night, some dark being would wait until I was nearly asleep before it would grab some part of my body, usually one of my feet, and try to pull me out of the bed. I instinctively learned to suck in a breath of air as fast as I could before going into some form of hyper-paralysis. Other times, if it got to me before I could breathe, I learned to call out someone's name that was dear to me. That usually backed it off. But the shock of it touching me always stunned me into a catatonic state of submission until something in me would explode to my defense.

One night my stomach and bowels were both moving at the same time. The rain was pouring, and I had to get up several times to run to the outhouse. As I sat over the hole, thoughts of my body shrinking away made me envision falling through the hole into the sludge and sewage below. Somehow that morbid thought was so stupid that it made me start laughing there in the pouring rain. The image of falling through the shit hole made me laugh and crap at the same time. There I was sitting on some God-forsaken crapper in a place full of evil spirits ten thousand miles away from home with a body slowly shrinking its way to death. Of all the places, a beautiful voice rose from nowhere and straightened me up because I was all bent over from abdominal pain; it seemed to come somewhere out of heaven and said to me, "Take courage, I am with you." I actually felt a little better, so I got off the bum hole and went back to bed. I fell asleep, only to die again. Oh, what fun it was.

At least in this dream I died a sudden death. People or animals were not after me this time. I was in a car driving on a freeway somewhere in California. It was nighttime, and there was a lot of traffic on both sides of the freeway. My car was in the fast-lane moving about sixty to sixty-five miles an hour. Up ahead, I could see a car swerve over from the oncoming side past the center divider into my lane. The car was still way ahead of me and had lots of room and time to swerve back over into his lane. I figured he would do that, but instead he kept coming straight down my lane. He was not even slowing down, so I flashed my lights on and off to get him to move back over. He would not do it.

We were fast closing in on each other, so I swerved to the lane to my right and he did the same. *What the hell is this guy doing?* I thought. I quickly swerved back into the fast lane, and he did the same. Now it was too late. I let out one last shout and boom! It felt like I ran into a solid brick wall because all I could hear before I woke up was a dull thud and ringing noise somewhere in my head while my body was crushed dead upon impact. My eyes flew wide open. This time I felt so weak, I didn't bother to get out of bed. I just brushed my hands over my body to make sure it wasn't all smashed up and went back to sleep.

Don Oscar was beginning to get on my nerves. His weirdness increased as the rainy days drummed on. He would not come out with it, but I could tell he wanted me to leave. I tried to tell him that I was too sick to leave right then. My sickness probably bothered him and wore on his nerves as well, but he would not tell me. Our nightly conversations in the kitchen grew thin, and so did his generosity. Instead of serving me two slices of his fresh-baked bread, he would offer a piece of old, stale bread. I didn't really care because his food was blah and my appetite was zilch. Cabin fever was worse than my physical fever, so I forced myself to sit outside under a porch that faced the river during the rainy days.

The young father of the family next door came up from the river one day and spotted me sitting alone. He had gone to Chol-Chol for some staple supplies and to sell charcoal he and his brothers would make locally. He came over with an expression on his face that read, "What are you doing out here? You're sick." I smiled and shrugged my shoulders. He read my mind and smiled too.

"You are tired of sitting inside the house, yes?" His smile and inquiry were kind and warm.

"Yes, Ignacio. I am."

He sat down next to me and stared out toward the river. It was the first time a man came by to see me. There was something about his concern for me that opened my heart. I told him everything how I was feeling and the situation with Don Oscar. He listened very attentively while nodding his head from time to time. When I had finished my confession, he told me how the practice of his belief helped him get through difficult times in his life. My ears perked up when he mentioned his faith. I thought he was going to let me in on something about the mysterious Mapuche religion and its spiritism that has been kept off limits to foreigners for centuries, so I prodded him, "Tell me Ignacio, who or what are your beliefs?"

As he started describing how once a month he and a bunch of local Indians would gather together in some out-of-the-way spot in the woods, I began to envision a circle of Indians in their tribal gowns dancing and chanting to the forest spirits. But to my surprise and amazement, he went on painting me a verbal and hand gesture picture of a gathering of indigenous peoples praying the rosary and praising the Lord Jesus Christ. *You gotta be kiddin' me!* I thought as I sat there gazing at his animation.

Here I was, a baptized and raised Catholic, listening to someone who I thought all along was a pagan that practiced some kind of old, native sorcery, preaching to me about his faith in Jesus! He probably saw the dumbfounded expression on my face, as if he was talking to me for the first time about Christianity. To avoid a long explanation of already being a Christian, I gave him a handshake and thanked him for enlightening me. He seemed very happy to spread the good news to a white man! As he got up to leave, he told me to go to Chol-Chol and talk to the owner of Don Oscar's house.

"He will let you stay here as long as you want," he said.

"What? Don Oscar does not own this house!" I exclaimed.

"No, his brother does. He is a good man and rich too." Ignacio then winked at me and walked home.

After pondering my Indian friend's advice for a few days, I decided to take him up on it and go see Don Oscar's brother in Chol-Chol. Going back to Nueva Imperial was too far away to walk to in this condition. I needed more time to heal; besides, the idea seemed like a good incentive to get out of this dismal house for a while and go visit my half-Chilean, half-Indian friend Joel too.

The trip to Chol-Chol was a pleasant one, even though my stomach felt like crap. There was an old school bus that would come half the distance from Chol-Chol to Repocura to pick up the kids in the region every day. Ignacio rowed me across the river, and I managed to make it on foot in the nick of time to catch the bus. The bus driver took a double look at me and waved me on with a grin on his face. The kids would turn to look at me with their smiling and giggling faces as we bounced down the road. Their little, innocent spirits gave me a good feeling about this journey to town. Somehow, I intuitively knew this trip was going to do me some good. When I stepped out of the bus, I asked the driver if he knew where Don Villareal lived. He pointed to the only big house in town and said, *"Alli esta!"* Right there! He lived right in the center of town.

Don Villareal answered the door, I introduced myself, and he invited me in. "You came just in time for lunch. Please sit down." He was amazed to hear my story about living out in Repocura, especially for someone like myself coming from such a rich and modern country.

"Those people are so poor. Why are you living out there?" he asked.

I did not know how to answer that question. The only thing that came out was, "I'm a country boy at heart."

He laughed and asked me how his brother was. He seemed like a well-educated man, so I told him the truth about his brother's strange, stingy behavior and how he talked to pigs. He looked at me and chuckled to himself as he got up to fetch a bottle of good Chilean red wine. While uncorking the bottle and pouring me a glass, he said, "I don't want you to worry about a thing. You are welcome as my guest here and in my house in Repocura for as long as you like." I thanked him and enjoyed his wine and his company as we shared each other's history.

It was late afternoon when I knocked on the little shanty door of my friend Joel's house. A little girl with big brown eyes answered the door and ran back inside. Moments later Joel came to the door. With an expression of joy and amazement, he opened the door and grabbed one of my arms, pulling me inside the house. His thin wife, tall for a Mapuche woman, shyly greeted me. Joel introduced her and their three little children to me. After a few minutes, he motioned something to them, and they all left the room.

"You don't look so good," he said.

I looked at him and said, "I don't feel so good."

After telling him about my stay in Repocura, he asked me how long I had been sick. I told him for about a month now. "Oooooh," he groaned. He got up and told me to sit still and that he would be right back. Several minutes went by before he came back. He sat down opposite me and said, "My wife is preparing some medicine for you, but the treatment takes three days to work. You need to rest and stay here for three days. In order for it to work right, you can't walk around or do any kind of physical labor."

I could tell by the expression on his face that he was serious and hoping that I would trust him. I said, "Okay, what have I got to lose?" Little did I know what I had just said.

The three days went quickly as Joel's children entertained me day and night in between meals and teacups full of a strange-tasting herb drink. They wanted me to play with them all kinds of little games. They learned I could draw, so we did lots of drawings too. By the end of the third day, I noticed the stomachaches were gone. My appetite started to come back, making me feel like I could eat something without worrying about bolting out the door for a run to the outhouse. That evening Joel's wife served me a delicious dinner made from fresh meats and vegetables. I ate heartily and hoped that I would not disappoint them for all their care. Both of them seemed confident and content to serve me.

The next morning, I felt like new again. I had slept the whole night without waking up once. It was the first time I slept like that in months. After breakfast, Joel took me outside and around the side of his house to a garden full of a variety of plants and vegetables. He showed me one in particular and said, "This is the herb my wife prepared for you to drink three times a day. It is the only medicinal plant in the country that can cure what you had. But it is so powerful that if a person drinks too much of it, or even too little, it would kill him." He looked at me, and I looked back at him with chills going through my body. He started to laugh and said, "That's why we wanted to keep a close watch on you, because if a person drinks this stuff and gets busy doing something, he could forget to take the drinks at the right intervals. You'll be fine now. It worked."

On the way back to Repocura, I somehow felt as if God were putting me through all kinds of endurance tests. For the life of me, I was not sure what for, but one thing was for sure—I was grateful to Him for my friend Joel. Every time I thought of how close I came to death, a chill would go up my spine. To my surprise, the sun was out and the air was so clean. I had missed the bus, but that didn't matter. What mattered was that I had my strength back and it also felt good to walk again. The sun was setting by the time I got back to the river. Ignacio's son spotted me and came running to get me in the rowboat. He told me to come over to the hut as soon as I could. When I arrived, the whole family greeted me and invited me to eat dinner with them. Their excitement encouraged me to stay, so we spent the evening eating and talking while the kids entertained us adults. I told Ignacio and Trancita, his wife, what happened in Chol-Chol. They seemed very content to hear the news. Ignacio told me that when I was feeling strong again he wanted me to accompany him to the hills to cut down trees to make charcoal. "I'm ready when you are," I said.

"Good, I'll look for you in a couple of days."

As I grew stronger by the day, the ugly dreams seemed to fade out of sight for a while. Ignacio, his brothers, and I were busy cutting wood and preparing the tree trunks for the earth ovens. Early signs of spring were in the air and in the trees. The nights were still and silent as we sat by the ovens keeping watch on the fires.

Making charcoal out of wood was a complicated thing. The logs inside the ovens had to be smoked, not burnt. In order to make sure they would not burn up, a man had to uncover a basketball-size earthen plug to let in a certain amount of fresh air or wood. This meant the person keeping watch had to be vigilant, because if he fell asleep, the fire could be choked out or burn up the logs from a leaky plug. To keep awake, I learned to pray in a way that kept my body warm and full of vitality until morning. I noticed the other men doing this with ease. Those nights were silent and tranquil. No sickness. No evil attacks. What a gift.

Time for a Wannabe Indian to Move On

The leaves started to unfurl as the days lengthened, the clouds pulled out of the Indian sky above Repocura, and old Don Oscar carried on with himself in the garden talking to the trees and the animals as if they were in a conversation together. To their delight, the Mapuches learned that the Gringo Americano survived the winter, and they were wondering what he would do next. It was kind of nice to learn how popular I was, even though I didn't do much except visit them. Maybe it was because I did not come to teach them anything like so many other foreigners have done historically but gave them a chance to teach a white man something instead. Whatever it was, I started pondering if I could do this.

This Indian lifestyle was attractive and non-complicated. Yeah, it was dirty, poor, and simple, but a man could make it on his own without the stress of paying bills and driving to work every day. He would be free from worry and crime and from all the unhealthy habits of modern city life. The thought of staying there more permanently kept crossing my mind, especially after visiting my many Indian friends and observing their genuine, sincere desire to have me around. I would take long walks to the south along the river where the valley opened up to broaden my knowledge of the terrain and to contemplate the direction I should choose ahead. As much as I wanted this life, something in me fought against it. I prayed, "God, You need to help me. Where can I go? I don't want to live another winter in Don Oscar's house."

One day while walking along the river to the south, I crossed paths with a Mapuche man I had not seen before. He was tall, thin, and gaunt. We greeted each other with a few words in passing, and then I noticed he stopped to turn around. I stopped and looked back at him. He waved and made a motion with his arm to beckon me to come closer. I walked up to within a few yards of him and stood still. He asked me if I was the foreigner from America. I smiled and said yes. He pointed over to his left toward a small, thatched wooden hut out in the open with two large trees next to it. "That's my house," he said. "I invite you to come by tomorrow for lunch." He then smiled and waved good-bye as I agreed to be there.

That night, I had a nice dream where I saw a young Chilean woman who worked as a secretary for the Agric-Co-op back in Nueva Imperial. She was always very pleasant to talk to and helped me learn Spanish when I first arrived in Chile. She looked different, and it seemed like she was living in some big city instead of her hometown, called Temuco, situated about twenty miles north of Nueva Imperial. She was a hard worker and had a joyful spirit. It was the first dream I had had of someone living in the modern world since my stay in Nueva Imperial.

Upon awaking, I felt unusually refreshed and ready to greet a new day in Repocura. Little did I know that this day would be a day fraught with unusual decision-making. After my morning café and dry bread, I decided to hit the familiar path to the river and make my luncheon appointment with an Indian whose name I did not know. I had forgotten to ask him for his name. *Oh well,* I thought.

On the way, I meandered along the riverbed thinking about the things, places, and faces encountered so far on my South American journey. *What I am doing here? What am I looking for? As much as I like living in Chile, where is my life going from here?* Reflections of my past flooded my mind with memories of significant people and events in my life. Did God want me to stay here and make a living among these Indians whose culture was so different from the one I came from? When I lifted my head to look up at the sky, a childlike memory flashed in my mind as I watched a flock of birds swirl down and land on the beach. Certain anguish filled my gut as my eyes looked away from the birds and down the valley, searching for the hut of my newfound host. There it was, about a quarter mile to go. "Okay, here we go. Time for lunch."

From about five hundred yards away, I could spot the tall, thin Indian and someone else standing outside his hut. Judging by the colors of the clothing, the other person was a woman. *Oh, he has a wife, good,* I thought. *It'll be a tastier lunch.* We greeted each other with smiles and a handshake as I walked up to his front door. He had been cleaning around the outside of his hut because the ground had been swept and sprinkled to keep the dust down. His face was beaming with delight as he showed me his property and animals. He had a lot of land, but most of it was rocky and treeless.

When we entered the hut, I noticed a little wooden table had been set up with plates and silverware. A fire was burning at one end of the hut, and the smell of cooked food filled the air. He pointed to a little stool for me to sit down as he took one for himself. We sat there looking at each other in silence, as was the usual custom. After a few minutes of sitting and waiting, a young woman appeared from behind a woven partition near the back of the hut. She brought over a little wooden tray with two plates of food on it. While setting the tray down on the table, I looked up and caught a glimpse of her face. She looked to be anywhere from fifteen to nineteen years old.

She also took a quick glimpse at me, shyly smiled, and then moved back to the kitchen.

We ate heartily without saying a word, for the food was good. *His wife is a good cook,* I thought. Then I found myself marveling at how young his wife was when he seemed so much older than her. Next, the woman appeared again to take our plates, went behind the curtain, and came back with two cups of herb tea. As she put down my cup, I thanked her and watched her shyly smile again and retreat into the kitchen. In between sips, the Indian and I engaged in some small talk about the weather and crop damage due to the long rainy season.

About halfway through the cup of tea, the man slowly drew my attention to his keen observance of my daily activities. He had been watching me from a distance working in the fields and in a garden below Don Oscar's house near the river. I was a little taken aback at how much detail he knew about my daily routines. He suddenly sat up straight and called for his wife to bring in some more hot water. She came in with a small teakettle covered with soot and poured more hot water into our cups. This time she didn't go back into the kitchen. Instead she stood behind him a little off to the side.

He then went on to tell me in a very polite manner how he admired my independent spirit and that he wished he had a son like me. He pointed in the direction to the east of his hut where he had several acres of untilled land. "All the land to the east of my hut I want to give to you. I will build you a hut and give you some animals to raise. Here is my daughter." He reached over and gently pulled her over next to him and while mentioning her name. "I give her to you for your wife."

The expression on his face was dead serious, while I can only imagine what my expression must have read as I went brain-dead. The rest of my body went into shock, as if I was having one of those paralyzing dreams. The only thing I could hear was the sound of my heartbeat growing louder by the second. In a near coma, I remember looking at her face, grinning even more shyly as she blushed and shook from a nervous laughter. The sound of her childish laughter, however, broke me out of my catatonic state of mind-paralysis. Listening to her giggling voice gave me time to recollect my thoughts.

They were both smiling at me as I regained consciousness. His stunning proposition came so quick that I had no time to think of fancy words to buy time to think about his offer. I responded with such gut-felt spontaneity that it reminded me of when I was a kid caught for doing something wrong and having to own up to the truth.

I reached for the cup, took a sip, and looked at the Indian man in the eyes, whose name I still do not know to this day, and said, "Thank you very much for your generous offer. Since my arrival in Repocura, I have been asking myself if I could live *como los Mapuches*, like the Mapuches. In the past few months, I have been looking for a sign, something from the Spirit of God to tell me what to do with my life. Today, God has spoken to me. As much as I wanted to be a Mapuche, I now know that this is impossible. I am an American, a man from a different culture that is branded deep within my soul. For me to force myself to be one of your people would only be pretending to be someone who I am not. You and your daughter have made me realize, at this very moment, the hard truth that I was not willing to admit to myself. I know now that I must leave this beautiful territory and its peoples and culture alone."

When I had finished saying this in my broken Spanish, with a little Indian dialect thrown in, something in me was both relieved and a little sad because what came out of my mouth was the sword that cut the cord to my life in Repocura. The man got up and motioned me to follow him to go outside the hut. We stood there looking over the land toward the east for a moment. He then murmured, "I understand. You spoke well. You spoke the truth from your heart. Thank you for coming."

We shook hands and smiled at each other as I parted and headed back toward the river. The walk back to the house started out on a heavy foot, but the closer I got to Don Oscar's, the lighter grew my step. Deep down inside, I knew it was time to move on beyond the horizons of the Araucano lands. As much as I wanted to have an easy life, living on Indian land, having a good, simple *mujer*, wife, kids of my own, and all the Mapuche trimmings to boot, the truth set me free. I knew enough about myself and the promptings of the Spirit of God to know that this lifestyle was not meant for me. And from hindsight, all I can say is, God truly had other plans for this wayfaring dreamer.

Leave the Low Ground to Take the High Ground

My decision to leave the Indians and the Agric-Coop can be compared to a fish jumping out of the lower stream to climb to a higher level upstream to reach its rendezvous with destiny. The fish takes an upstream course in its life to swim against the current, jump over raging waters, and risk being caught and eaten by dangerous animals like hungry bears, hawks, and humans to reach a place where it can safely mate, spawn, and die after completing its journey.

The struggles a fish takes against all odds offers a spiritual metaphor I use to illustrate how God beckons His human creatures to take a risk and jump up out of the lower, mediocre streams of the world we live in and to allow our natural selves to be pulled up by God onto a higher level to gain a special, spiritual knowledge of our hidden, immortal selves. Thus, God and His Spirit enables the now-wiser human being to gather more knowledge and strength to jump to an even higher elevation where a person gains more of God's divine power in order to fend off dangerous spiritual powers, diabolic entities, or demonic attacks that come against the person. The higher a person climbs in the knowledge and wisdom of God, the more a person can avoid all kinds of harmful indulgences and dangerous temptations. Such a person can even defeat evil spiritual powers until eventually the perfected and purified human being reaches the ultimate quest of spiritual union with God—a love so transforming and so divine that all the struggles and pains of life's upstream climb, fraught with spiritual difficulties, are worth the physical, mental, and emotional suffering, including death itself.

My journey and eventual life in Los Farellones, the Cliffs, a small town high in the Andes mountains above Santiago, enabled me to go further away and to be more alone with God. Cut off even more from all family ties, friends, and American contacts and living so far above the world, the city, and people I knew, I literally discovered greater heights of both the spirits of the world and the Spirit of God within me. But my eagerness to climb a higher spiritual ladder and to shun the temptations of the world brought on new spiritual attacks as well. My prayers and contemplations, however, also increased and intensified with every attack as I gained more knowledge of God. God took pity on a sinful dummy not afraid to give up the fight against evil spirits. He came to my rescue to protect and strengthen me from the evil enemies lurking within the dark, silent hours of the high mountain nights and among the shadows of the lonely Andes Mountains.

Within a week, I arrived back in Nueva Imperial. The American in charge of the Agric Co-op Foundation was not there, so I waited for a few days until he returned from a fundraising trip to the United States. He was both surprised and glad to see me. We had lunch together, and after the meal, we conversed a little. He was curious to know how things were going in Repocura. To make a long story short, I told him about Don Oscar, my Indian friends, and some of the spiritual lessons I learned during my stay in the forest. When I told him about the Indian man who wanted to build me a house, give me some of his land, and his own daughter to boot, his eyes grew wider.

"What are you going to do? I mean, what are your plans?" By the sound of his voice, he was amazed to hear of my adventures among the Indians he knew so well.

"I can't be an Indian, so I left Repocura, and now I'm planning to go somewhere north," I replied.

He understood and told me that Ninoska, his secretary, had quit working for the foundation and moved north to Santiago. Suddenly, I remembered the dream. I asked him if he had her address. He answered, "No, but her parents can tell you."

The next day, after saying good-bye to the Agric Co-op in Nueva Imperial, I went to Temuco to see her parents. They gave me Ninoska's address, so I bought a one-way train ticket to Santiago and climbed aboard to go another level upstream.

The trip to Santiago was at night, but my body could sense the different terrain and climate change as the train moved toward one of the driest deserts in the world. When the train pulled into the station, the sights, the sounds, the hustle, and the bustle all indicated that I was in a major, modern city. On first impression, downtown Santiago reminded me of some familiar cities back in the States. While walking around the streets looking for her address, my body quickly tired from walking on hard, concrete surfaces. What a relief it was to find her apartment, but she was not home. Her mother had given me her work address, so I decided to go there. The receptionist at Intel told me she would be right down. A few minutes went by when an elevator door opened, and out came Ninoska. She was smiling as she walked toward me, but she motioned for me to go outside. We went outside to sit in a little courtyard. She was obviously surprised and a little nervous. After greeting each other and catching up a little on where we were at in our lives, she looked at her watch and told me to come to her place after 5:00 p.m.

It was 5:30 when I returned and knocked on her apartment door. She opened the door and let me in to a small one-bedroom flat. The nice thing about Ninoska was that she spoke good English. We sat down and discussed things about each other. I told her about my time out in Repocura, and she told me about her move to Santiago. We stayed up talking for several hours until she noticed my eyelids were closing from the long train trip. She got up to get some blankets and said, "Go to sleep now. I'll see you in the morning for breakfast before work. Goodnight." At breakfast, Ninoska gave me the directions to the US Consulate building. It had been almost two years since I left the States, so I figured on paying a visit to see if anybody had sent me anything from home.

Inside the building there was a long line of American citizens waiting for assistance. Next to me in line was a family speaking an animated mixture of Spanish and broken English visiting from New York. They were Chileans waiting for a marriage license. One of two sisters in their early twenties had just married a young man in New York. He was here in Chile to get married again in the Chilean tradition. The older sister asked me if I spoke English, so I said yes.

She grabbed my arm, pulled me over to the side, and said, "Oh, please, speak to my husband. He is going crazy because he is so bored and he does not have anyone who can understand him."

I looked at the desperate expression on her face and said, "Sure, where is he?"

She called out to a big, stocky-looking guy, "Tomas! Come here!"

Her audacious outburst cracked a smile on my face as he came over. After a brief introduction by his wife, he went on to tell me how happy he was to meet someone who was from the USA. "Yeah, now yo talkin' ma language!" He was an Italian American with a Brooklyn accent. We must have talked for about a half an hour. He dumped enough-drug related stuff on me about himself that would have filled a large dumpster full of trash. By the time we were done with our business at the American Consulate, Kika, his wife, the older sister, begged me to come over and join them at her aunt's house for their wedding reception. This was the start of a three-month mixed-up fiasco, living between metropolitan Santiago and the surrounding ghettos.

Ninoska was always busy and my newfound Chilean, half-ghetto friends were going nuts with their American *cunado*, brother in-law Tomas. He was a recovering alcoholic and drug addict who would lose it in the presence of his Chilean in-laws. If it were not for Tatiana, the younger of the two sisters I met at the consulate, I would have long disappeared from their turbulent son-in-law and his co-dependent family. She liked me and kept me entertained by taking me to different places of interest all around the Santiago area. She was street smart and had a good sense of humor. When Tomas was not around, she would teach me Spanish grammar and Chilean *dichos*, wit. One day she told me she had an uncle that knew someone who worked up in a ski resort high above the outskirts of Santiago. He told her there were Americans up there, so she arranged for him to drive me to the foot of the mountain. People who worked up in the small town called Los Farellones would hitchhike for rides from some bus stop at the bottom opening of the mountain pass.

The next morning, her uncle came and picked me up and dropped me off at the empty bus stop to wait for a ride. Someone going up the mountain stopped and offered me a ride. The road wound zig-zag up over eleven thousand feet to a tiny little town made of stone houses. When I got out of the car, my body chilled from the cold, crisp air, but my eyes were delighted to see such grand views. My ears basked in the soft, silent wisps of gentle high mountain breezes. Something in me said, "Stay here."

I asked the driver if he knew where Andacor Ski Company was. He told me it was about another two miles up. "Just follow the road. In twenty minutes you'll be there; you can't miss it." It turned out to be a good half hour until I reached a turn off with a little sign that read, "Welcome to Andacor de Los Farellones Ski Center." The place looked abandoned until a man in overalls drove up in an old jeep to a little garage made of stone. He looked over and waved at me as I approached him.

"Are you looking for someone?" he asked in Spanish.

"Yes, I'm looking for the owner of the ski resort."

He pointed towards a wooden A-frame house about a hundred yards away. "He's over there."

I thanked him and walked over to the house. It was a very nice, modern-looking structure that I imagined people in the European Alps would live in. As soon as I knocked on the only door I could find, a tall, balding, white American-looking man opened the door. He stood there staring at me as if I were someone from another planet. I introduced myself and told him I was looking for a job. His blue, gringo eyes scrutinized me for a few more moments, and then he said, "Come in."

After about an hour of telling him of my origins in California, my work in Nueva Imperial, and a little about the Mapuche Indians, he interrupted me and asked, "Do you know how to weld?"

"Yes," I said.

"Do you know anything about diesel engines?"

"Yes."

His eyes started to light up a little. "Follow me over to the shop. I have something to show you."

We went back over to the little stone garage where the man driving the jeep parked. He opened the door with a handful of keys that swung open to a room chock-full of tools and parts to machinery. He then pulled out what looked like a homemade arc-welder. Next, he handed me two pieces of half-inch rebar and told me to run a few beads to join the two iron rods together. He handed me a helmet, flipped on the machine, and I proceeded to weld a three-inch pass of molten iron between the rebar. When I finished the weld, I took it out of the vice and handed it to him. He looked at it and said, "Damn, you're good."

I whispered to myself, "Thanks, Uncle Ron."

I learned the basics in school but practiced welding to perfection on my uncle's ranch. Next, he showed me various diesel engine parts and wanted to know if I had rebuilt engines. Once again I said yes. He then took me back over to his house to fix me something to drink. "You're hired. Come back here in two weeks to go to work." We shook hands, and I headed back down to Santiago. As I passed by the town of Farellones, I smiled knowing that God was providing me the opportunity to climb up another level in the river of life.

The next two weeks were nearly unbearable listening to constant complaining and gossip among the families I lived with. Tatiana had gone back to work, so she was not around much. The stress of noisy city life and the anticipation of actual employment for the first time in over two years drove me batty. For two weeks I must have walked enough streets to cover five hundred miles. When the day came to report to work, I said adios to my Santiago families and hightailed it to the mountain. The sun was out, and the morning was fresh when I made it to the bottom of the mountain. While waiting for a ride, I remembered that it was around the same time a year ago that I walked to Repocura for the first time on foot. While pondering my time in Repocura, a car with a young couple drove by and slowed down to ask me if this was the way to Farellones. I said, "Yes it is."

Then they asked, "Are you going up?"

I replied, "Yes."

"Vamonos! Arriba!" they shouted.

"Let's go up!" I echoed back.

This time going up, I paid more attention to the terrain. For most of the steep climb, the mountain carried a sheer wall angle from forty-five to fifty-five degrees. It was the first time I had ever been in a mountain range so steep. The excitement of living in such a high altitude sent a chill through my body, while at the same time the anticipation of not knowing what to expect could be felt in the pit of my stomach. My inner gut feeling was optimistic and filled with high expectations. The more I observed the massive rock formations coupled with the majestic beauty of these mountains, the more I admired its Creator.

My young Chilean chauffeurs took me all the way up to the ski resort and dropped me off under the Andacor Ski sign. The boss was waiting for me and let me in as soon as I knocked on the door. He had been interviewing another American applying for an administrative position. We introduced ourselves and then sat and listened to the boss brief us about our duties, schedules, and living quarters. He then drove us down to the town of Farellones to show us the house where the secretary and I would stay during the ski season. The house was one of the few wooden structures in town built on a stone foundation. The boss walked us through the dwelling, gave us some basic instructions and the key to the front door. Before shutting the door he said, "See you tomorrow for work."

Deborah, the newly hired secretary, immediately claimed her room and got down to business unpacking her things. Me, I went outside for a walk around town. There was no time for thoughts because my mind was overwhelmed by the soaring joy within my heart. God had provided more than what I had anticipated. It was like a good dream come true. Here I was, on top of the world in one of the most serene and majestic-looking places on earth. The surrounding glacial peaks glimmered in the sunlight like giant golden watchtowers looking down on earth's inhabitants below. The silence was intense, and so was the echo. The whole atmosphere prompted my soul to praise the greatness of God. While standing in the middle of a large open area just outside of town, I slowly pivoted around on one foot to observe what looked like a huge open cathedral inviting me to spend some time to contemplate and adore the maker of these natural, monumental wonders.

Early the next day, we set off to hike up one of the dry slopes to reach our first day at work. As we drew closer to the top, I soon discovered how the town got its name. It was built on a large plateau with cliffs dropping straight down hundreds of feet on three sides. The secretary, being a little on the heavy side, was not a fast hiker, so to give her time to catch up, I would drift over toward the cliff to look over the edge of a sheer drop down the north side of the slope. I could barely see the bottom it was so far down. Upon our arrival, she went to her post and I went to mine. All the men working for Andacor were Chileans. I was the only American working on the maintenance crew. There were eleven ski lifts powered by large, diesel-fueled engines. My job involved routine motor inspections and repairs. The power plants for each lift line were spread out covering up to six hundred acres of ski slopes. The mechanics got around in old four-wheel drive vehicles during the off season, but when snow covered the mountains, the only way to get tools and engine parts to the power plants was by ski and backpack.

After work hours, I got into the routine of taking walks outside the ski center. The views from the slopes were fantastic, especially if I hiked up on some of the peaks. On a clear day from the peaks, I could see Santiago to the west of Farellones. Even though it was over fifty miles away as the crow flies, it looked only a few miles away through the clean, crisp mountain air. For the first two months, I spent several hours a day after work walking and hiking my way around the mountains above Farellones. Not only did I enjoy the exercise and the views, but I also enjoyed the intense silence of the high altitude. Sometimes I would find a spot to just sit down and listen to the sounds reverberating off the distant mountain ranges.

My ears learned to pick up sounds coming from rocks falling several miles away. Certain high-altitude birds would make their calls that would echo all around me. It was hard to judge from which direction the bird was flying because its voice bounced all over the area. One day while hiking close to one of the cliff edges, two large condors floated up from below the cliff edge and hovered within twenty yards from where I stood. They were riding an updraft of wind rising from the abyss below. They caught me by surprise, so I froze to watch what they would do. Both of them remained hovering in the same position in flight for several minutes, checking me out. We were so close to each other that I could see their eyes blinking in the wind. It was the first time in my life to be so close to such large birds. For as big and clumsy looking as they were, I was amazed at how easily they could steady themselves in such strong drafts of wind.

The snow fell late in the ski season, but the boss kept me busy with repairing things that had been broken for years. He liked my work, so he did little things to keep me around. I think he was worried that I would get bored living up in the middle of nowhere and would miss the excitement of city life. Little did he know just how content I was being up there far removed from the loud, smoggy city below. The nights were generally quiet because people came to ski, not party. There were no hotels, only cabins. This quiet setting put me in the mood to meditate on good books and do silent prayer.

About halfway through the ski season, my boss hinted at giving me a higher position of employment if I decided to stay. We became good friends, but I really didn't have any plans for the future. Up until the time the snow started melting, the work was consistent. The days passed swiftly immersed in work, learning how to ski, and long hikes. Sometimes I did not get down off the mountain until way after dark because the joy of being in such a mystical setting invigorated my soul. While high up over the world at night, my eyes grew accustomed to spotting light coming from cities and towns beyond Santiago.

One night while staring at the city lights below, I looked up and saw an amazing display of stars in the northern sky. Countries like Peru, Ecuador, Columbia, and Panama came to mind, so I thought to myself, *Why not spend a little time and money to go see other countries in South America?* For the first time in years, I had money to travel. When the ski season ended, the boss asked me if I had any plans for the summer. "Yes, I'm going to do a little traveling." He looked down and nodded his head with a solemn expression, and then I said, "But I'll be back in the fall." He lifted his head up, smiled, and said, "Good, have fun. See you then."

The summer months flew by from visiting hundreds of small towns and places of historical interest in several Latin American countries. The desert of Atacama in the northern end of Chile was like walking on the moon. There was no vegetation, no animals, only little oasis-like towns scattered here and there. I spent several days wandering about in that desert wondering about the mystery of life. Where does God come from? And where do we go after death? A deep desire came over me to visit mysterious places hoping to find clues as to who we are and why we exist.

My search for more clues to life's questions started in Peru. Peru is a country rich in mysterious sites and ancient ruins. The lines in Nasca were a sight to see. I rented a plane and flew over an area full of large, mysterious drawings telling us something extraordinary once happened there years ago. The Peruvian and Bolivian Andes mountain ranges were full of ancient ruins, many of them hidden under thick vegetation. I spent several days hiking old Incan roads deep in the heart of Peru. The Incans set stones in the ground along the mountain ridges so they could run faster between high mountain villages.

Most tourists went to places like Machu-Picchu because of modern roads and transportation. Thanks to the Mapuches, I learned how to find small footpaths that led to other ruins way off the beaten paths of tourism. Some of those ruins had not been visited by anyone for a long time, so I had the pleasure of occupying them all alone day and night. At night I wondered, *How did such ingenious people disappear? If they were smart enough to build such amazing structures and irrigation canals, how could they not figure out a way to survive the boring, tea-slurping European invaders?*

In the Bolivian Alti-Plano, high plains, I visited several ancient stone monuments and sights built to align doorways and other openings to rising celestial bodies in the eastern horizon. Whoever built these things knew a lot about the four seasons in relation to the position of the sun, the moon, and the stars. For example, the ancient architects calculated precise moments when and where on the horizon, the sun, the moon, or some star would rise at the peak of the summer solstice or winter solstice. Lake Titicaca, the highest body of sweet water in the world, still has people living on floating houses made of some type of reed. These Indigenous people are the remnants of an ancient civilization and are unique in South America. Ecuador is covered in jungle with coastal towns teeming with little farms and fishing villages. When I arrived in Bogotá, Columbia, a family took me into their home to stay a couple of days. They were Christians who wanted to show me around the city, but I kindly talked them out of it. "Thank you but I need to go now," was my usual line to avoid eating, sitting, and talking for hours and sometimes days with city people.

My exploration of the Central American countries went by in passing because the villagers were involved in civil war. There were several rebel groups fighting drug-related wars for political reasons. Without knowing what was going on, I could not understand why there were so few people on the streets in some towns. One day while walking around in one little Guatemalan town, I noticed people coming out on their porches waving me to come closer. Ignorantly, I thought they wanted to sell me stuff, so I would say in passing, *"No gracias."*

Finally, a Guatemalan man and woman stepped out of their front door after watching me pass by alone in the street and yelled, *"Oiga! Venga aqui!* Hey you! Come here!" There was a tone of urgency in their voices as they made me sit down on a couch. They then proceeded to explain to me that the people would hide in their houses at certain hours of the day because rebels would come through the streets looking for food or someone to rob.

They informed me the best hours of the day to travel. One man suggested I go into Mexico because the border was close by. With a little help from good people, I crossed the border into southern Mexico after spending a few cautious days in Guatemala. Sometimes, it pays to be dumb.

Other times you lose to be dumb. Somewhere in the 1970s a guy named Carlos Castenada wrote some impressive books about a Yaqui Indian from northern Mexico who possessed certain divine powers. Well, being a semi-liberal, gullible, young fool from Santa Cruz, California, I figured maybe if I went to the northern deserts of Sonora and Chihuahua, Mexico, I might find a wise Yaqui Indian like Don Juan and learn from him secrets of how to bi-locate like he did in Castenada's books. Unfortunately, the only thing I found was thousands of square miles of vast, empty, inhospitable land. After a few weeks of gallivanting around the northern deserts of Mexico, I grew discouraged, disappointed, and drained for going on a wild goose chase looking for some Yaqui wonder Indian. My money supply was draining too, so I decided to head back to Chile.

The cheapest way I learned to get back to Chile was to catch an international bus line from Mexico City. Mexico City sits on top of what once upon a time used to be floating gardens loaded with exotic plants and animals. Today, it is loaded with congested traffic, smog, and noise. The trip to Mexico City was hot and exhausting. When I got off the bus, I got lost trying to find my way around. A taxi driver took notice and gave me a ride to a cheap hotel just outside the city. While reaching into my pocket, the cab driver told me to keep it. "I am Christian," he retorted. He led me through the doors of the hotel, paid for my room, and didn't charge me for the ride. Grateful for his generosity, I wanted to shake his hand but I could hardly lift my arm, so he smiled and opened the door to my room. Finally he said, "Adios amigo," and left. I took a warm shower, first one in several days, and crashed in the bed. That night, somewhere around two or three in the morning, for the first time in over a year, a visitor from the shadow world disturbed my sleep.

This dream, or vision rather, was different from the other extraordinary shocker dreams because it involved some visible, animal-like moving object. When the vision occurred, it seemed like I was half asleep and half awake. The room was pitch black, still, and quiet when suddenly I became intensely aware of an evil presence in the room. My eyes automatically opened wide. But without moving a muscle to look back, as if I had eyes in my feet and backside, I could see a large, weird, rat-like creature run from a far corner of the room and jump on to the end of the bed. Next, I could feel it immediately run up and down over my back while lying on my stomach.

As soon as it ran over me, I instantly swung around with incredible speed to watch where it would go. It jumped down off the bed and ran zigzagged across the floor as if it were desperately trying to dodge my sight. It made a strange, hideous little noise as it scampered out of sight somewhere in the far corner where it came from. Immediately, I turned on the light and ran over to the same far corner to look for a hole. After a thorough investigation, I found no hole, nothing, not even a crack. *What the hell was that? Where did it come from?* My mind went haywire with questions. The funny thing was, something in me seemed to know what it was and where it came from. It was no ordinary rat. Back on my uncle's ranch, the barn and the chicken coops were crawling with rats. Sometimes I used to sleep in the barn, and I never had rats come at me or try crawling on me at night. This thing was not natural, but I refused to admit what my sixth sense was trying to tell me. One thing was for sure—whatever it was, it was real and it was dangerous.

The quest for answers to the mysteries of life was put on a shelf for a while. My Latin American exploration lasted about six weeks, and I was worn out from so much travel. It took five days to get back to Farellones by bus. It also took a few days for my body to soak in the quiet and stillness of the mountain heights in order to restore its vitality in all aspects: body, mind, and soul. The boss was glad to see me again, and I was eager to return to work. He asked me if I wanted to work on the tower maintenance crew. This work involved checking the conditions of the pulley wheels, from top to bottom, at each tower of the ski lifts. There were six low mountain lifts and five high mountain lifts. This gave me an excellent opportunity to be exposed to some of the highest peaks in the world. When he asked me if I wanted the job, as difficult as it was, my response was an immediate yes.

For the next several months, I found myself climbing to some of the most remote places on earth. My workdays started out at daybreak and ended at sunset. After visually learning the lay of the mountain passes and topography from the tower heights, I would hike down the mountain after work hours. It took a good two hours to reach Farellones by foot from the high mountain ski-lift towers. This gave me the chance to explore several passageways within a wide range of territory. There were places that trapped the sunlight warming up an area to a temperature suitable enough for a body to sit still without freezing. Sometimes I would rest in this setting, basking in the warmth and amplified silence of the deep canyons for a good hour. On an average day, I would spend several hours alone in the mountains before returning to Farellones. The nights passed quietly in reading and doing minor chores and repairs. But for the most part, I enjoyed reminiscing on the more significant events that took place in the day.

The high mountain exposure to such spectacular views and tantalizing silence had a way of reviving my curiosity to ponder on the secrets of the universe. There were times when the mountain seemed to echo my thoughts back at me. Other times, I would ask an interior question and an answer would bounce back at me. At times, it seemed as if the mountains were haunted, like someone was watching me from afar and knew when and how to interrupt my attention to draw me away from useless thoughts into a more meaningful, inner dialogue.

While I was home in the still hours of the evening, my mind would retreat to dwell on the nostalgic past or race wildly into some speculative future. It was not until I started reading the Holy Bible again and meditating on its words that I discovered a deeper answer to life's most troubling and confusing questions. For example, there are several incidents in the Scriptures where the main character meets an angel of God for the first time. The angel usually has to say something like, "Do not be afraid." Why did the angel have to greet the person with an order to have no fear? What was he afraid of? There is another scene where three men were thrown into a fiery, hot furnace but did not burn to a crisp. How did they survive?

These questions defy common sense, but they gave me food for thought. Instead of daydreaming away the hours of the day and night, I found myself in deeper thought and meditation on certain events in the Bible. To my delight, these events would unfold certain truths, especially if I suffered physical and mental difficulties with patience and perseverance. These truths, when understood, unlocked closed doors to timeless secrets that every person in every generation can learn from. Such as, "A wise man learns to trust in God, whereas the foolish man can never understand."

"Do Not Be Afraid. I Am Here" (Jn 6:20)

"Come near, my children, do not be afraid. I am here to bring you news of the greatest importance." These were the first words spoken to two surprised children from the mouth of a strange lady seated on a rock high in the mountains above a small town in the French Alps called La Salette. Two little shepherds, an eleven-year-old boy and a fourteen-year-old girl, while tending their cows alone in the mountains, saw a brilliant globe of light coming from on top of a rock stuck in the ground. Within this light, the form of a beautiful woman spoke to them. It would take fifteen years from my stay in Farellones, Chile, for me to fully comprehend what the initial greeting coming from this extraordinary woman meant to those two poor children in the mountains above La Salette, France.

At this stage in my spiritual quest in life, my mind and heart hungered to learn and understand more about the Spirit of the Bible. My sincere desire to meditate on God's Word set off a flashing red light down in the caverns of hell. Satan responded to this alert and ordered some of his dark angels to go and frighten me away from further pursuing holy, spiritual knowledge. Like a scared child, I ran and hid from prayer and meditating on the Bible; however, a part of me despised such cowardice. So, in spite of such fear, I continued to endeavor in deep prayer and meditation.

As the days shortened, the nights lengthened. The daytime flew by occupied in work, but the nighttime dragged on in loneliness. There was something intense about the nights in the high altitude. As the days and weeks went by, I could not help but wonder what was going to happen to me. The same old questions kept coming back to me, demanding answers: Who are you? Why are you here? And what are you supposed to be doing with your life?

There were times when I was tempted to go down to the city to get drunk and party, but I had been there and done that. So I kept reading and meditating in the silence of the long, cool mountain nights. As the winter nights lengthened, the cold and darkness steadily crept into Farellones. Trapped inside because it was too cold to go outside, cabin fever and feelings of isolation and loneliness slowly crept into my heart also. Stir craziness became overwhelming at times, but I forced myself not to get discouraged by these things. Then work slowed down because of the weather, so it was hard to get to sleep at night because I was not tired. Not only that, the clear, clean, high mountain air invigorated my body, allowing insomnia to keep me up for long hours until I would manage to drift into a half-asleep, half-awake state.

One early hour in the pitch-black stillness of the high Andean night, while in a half-asleep, half-awake state, another strange visitor came to *not* knock at my front door. All eyes and ears suddenly opened to what looked and sounded like a fast-moving jet dropping out of the distant sky above. My spiritual radar picked up on this thing moving at an incredible rate of speed headed straight for my little house in the midst of Farellones. It seemed as if every cell in my body had eyes and ears to watch and listen in on this fast-approaching target originating from above the northeastern mountain peaks. As it slowed down within moments of hitting the house, it emitted a sound I had never heard before. The strange noise sounded menacingly powerful.

The extraordinary audiovisual effect caught my complete attention as it came to a dead stop on the front porch. Without much hesitation, it then slowly drifted right through the front door while transforming itself into some indescribable shape. It floated directly toward me and grew into another enormous, fluctuating, dark, hideous-looking thing that remained hovering over my bed. The intensity of fear gripping my body was beyond comprehension. The only thing that comes close to describing how I felt at that moment would be comparable to someone plugging their fingers into a 220-volt electrical wall socket without letting go. It felt like every cell in my body was accelerating to such an intense vibration and rising pressure that at any given moment, my whole body would explode into a million pieces.

Every hair felt as if it was sticking straight up off my scalp when I noticed my body instantly take on the appearance of a TV character I knew from my childhood. My face suddenly changed into the image of that person's face whose hair would blow straight up in the air whenever something frightened him. The character was Moe of *The Three Stooges*, a popular show my brothers and I would watch almost every afternoon when we returned from school. With no time to think, my instant reaction to this menacing invader above me was to take a deep breath and shout out, in full force, a sound Moe would make when he saw a ghost: "Nyaauh-uh-uh-uhh!" Somehow, the power of that sound knocked the intruder back with such force that it blew right through the front door, over the mountain in the same direction it came from, and hurtled it out into space beyond the galaxy. My super-hyped vision and hearing was able to catch all of this action before I woke up.

The first thing I did, as usual, after going through another extraordinary dream of this type was to turn on the lamp next to my bed. *What in the world just happened?* was the first thought that came to mind. I looked at the door and saw that it was shut. In the dream, the door looked like it had been wide open. To make sure it was locked, I got up to check it. The door was locked, so I opened it and went outside. After walking up and down the only main street in town, I stood still and looked toward the northeastern skyline. My eyes could trace the exact location between two peaks where the illusive intruder came and went. As shook up as I felt, there was an odd, slight sense of delight or triumph felt deep within my gut. Once back inside, I sat down in my chair and tried to make some sense of what had just happened. For some reason, I found myself feeling rather exhilarated, instead of frightened by such a powerful and dangerous intruder, afraid to go back to sleep right away.

After pouring myself a cup of tea, I sat contemplating the whole event. Like the dreams in the past, my body did the usual things: it went into a paralytic trance; it could not move; it stopped breathing; it could not speak; it . . . whoa! Wait a minute, how was it that I was able to spot and watch a thing, while lying on the flat of my back, move from hundreds of miles away across the mountains descending upon my house through a closed door and a windowless wall? In the usual paralyzed state, I was never able to see much of the intruder's coming or going.

Then I remembered being able to take a deep breath, something I usually was too frightened to do in past dreams. Next, I meditated on the voice of the Stooge Moe who screamed in a familiar voice something that did not belong to me. The utterance that came out of my mouth was uniquely his. It was as if his spirit was in me. Then I remembered my ability to see my face change into the face of Moe. How I was able to see his facial expressions and image on my face was impossible to explain.

The unique thing about this dream or vision was that something deep inside of me fearlessly took control of the situation. It was as if something in me was savvy to this evil spirit's tricks and refused to be bullied around. My brothers and I enjoyed watching *The Three Stooges* together. All four of us knew every show they made and would laugh every time, no matter how many times we saw their reruns. Before falling back to sleep, I was laughing to myself while replaying over and over in my mind Moe's goofy facial expressions and his funny utterance of fear as he came to my rescue and blew the dangerous intruder out of my room.

When morning came, I woke up refreshed and ready to go to work. There was a sense of security and confidence in my gait as I walked up the mountain. Work took my mind off the previous night's strange, mystifying event. And because the ski season was fast approaching, there was more work than usual. Official weather reports predicted a wet winter in Santiago while local mountain authorities warned major storms were on the way, so the maintenance crew and I found ourselves scrambling to get all the machinery ready for the first snows. Several weeks slipped by without giving much thought concerning the extraordinary night visitor until it paid another startling call.

Due to a heavy work schedule and physical fatigue, this next encounter caught me in the middle of the night fast asleep and off guard. It was during the same early hour as the last encounter when my eyes suddenly flew open. This time the same dark, hideous thing had snuck back into my room without any advance notice. There it was hovering right over my paralyzed body, bigger than ever. There was no time to think, only react. My first reaction happened so fast that it surprised me as much as it did the intruder. In one swift gulp of air, my face transformed into the shape of a large wolf. The bark that proceeded from my mouth was so powerful that it vibrated the walls of the house. Within an instant, I was able to see the muzzle and teeth protruding from my face. At the same time, I was able to see my eyes. They glowed a faint fluorescent color as they focused on the floating enemy above. Within the same instant after the horrendous bark, the dark intruder was thrown into a high-speed retreat through the opposite wall and out of sight.

When it was gone, I immediately jumped up and ran to the door. On the porch outside the house, I stood scanning the entire area and listening with ears peeled; nothing, not a sight nor sound of anything unusual. Before going back inside, I walked over to the wall to check for any damage. There was none—not a mark—so I went back to make some tea and ponder the event.

What was going on here? For as disturbing as these visits were, why did I feel so strangely good about what just happened? My mind was confused, but my heart was not racing, and something deep inside me felt safe. For a long time, the event played itself over and over in my mind. Where did the wolf come from? I have never seen a live wolf. Coyotes, foxes, and wild dogs, yes, but a real, wild wolf, no. The breath! The breath of air that I sucked in just before the bark! The wolf helped remind me, or maybe it made me take in the air.

There is something about remembering to breathe in as much fresh air as possible during these terrific dreams. It was still a mystery as to how I was able to see my face and eyes turn into something else. After a while, my inner-gut told me there was nothing to fear. "Now go back to sleep."

On Top of the World

The ski season started up early thanks to two large storms, back to back, dumping more than six feet of snow in less than four days. Many of the men complained about the cold, but I was delighted to see so much snow compared to the previous year. *Maybe I'll get more practice in skiing this season,* I thought. In the previous season, I was always in the shop doing repairs.

A couple days later while I was busy welding metal fence stakes, Richard, the boss, came into the shop one afternoon and told me that one of his more-skilled engine mechanics was injured and could only drive the snow plow this season. He asked me if I wanted to take his position.

"Sounds interesting," I said. "What do I do?" He took out a map and traced out with his finger the entire scheme of ski trails to all the power plants on the mountain a man could reach on skis. "You will have to learn how to carry tools and parts on your back. Can you do that?"

My feet almost jumped out of their shoes, and my mouth wanted to open and shout out, "Yeah!" But I coolly turned and said, "Sure, I think so. What do I use to carry the tools?" He then pulled down off his back a large backpack and gave it to me. I didn't even notice he was wearing it. "Here, take this and go fix the fuel pump on the Embudo lift." Things were looking up as I prepared for my new highland assignment.

Joy and excitement pumped through my body as I rode the highest chair lift in the center. My body was ready for this, even if my mind was saying something quite the opposite. "Who cares? I'll learn as I go!" was my gut reaction as I took to the slopes for the first time carrying nearly fifty pounds of metal on my back. In a few weeks, my legs grew accustomed to skiing with extra weight on the skis. At first I was very cautious and I would snow plow most of the way down to the engine wheel. But the more my body adjusted itself, the stronger it got. By mid-season, I was able to parallel ski my way down without having to snow plow. Instead, I learned to parallel break carrying over sixty pounds of weight on my back.

The days were filled with thrills and chills as I learned to ski faster and harder. Once in a while my skis would catch, and I would flip over and bury the pack, including myself, in the snow. Even though the freezing snow would get under my clothes, I didn't feel a thing because I would be laughing at the thought of what it must have looked like to another skier watching a big buffoon eat it in the snow with a large backpack strapped to his tumbling body. Every day was a challenge between staying dry on the slopes and keeping those diesel engines running smoothly. The days went by fast at work, and the nights passed swiftly at ease.

One morning, late in the season, my boss invited me to go on a little excursion with him beyond the limits, high above the ski center to one of the glaciers. The glacier was located about ten miles behind the highest slope in the center. It took us a good hour to ski across a ridge and then hike up the north side of the mountain with skis on our shoulders. When we reached the point where the snow stopped and rock jutted into the open sky, we stood and gazed around us at the immense Andean mountains. It looked like we were standing in the midst of a frozen, stormy sea. To the west, there were waves after waves of towering peaks for as far as the eye could see.

"Argentina is over there," said my boss as he pointed toward the eastern horizon. As I gazed over this range of endless snow-covered peaks, a sense of sacred awe rose up and filled my soul with an admiration for God that I have not felt since childhood. The vast, pristine beauty and power of being up so high above the earth filled me with joy that gave me a desire to immerse myself in God's mystery. All I could think of for the rest of my time in Farellones was how can I get closer to understanding the mysteries of God, creation, and life?

Down and Out of Argentina in Two Months

The ski season was ending when the desire to explore what lies east beyond the Andean horizon was beginning to spring up from the depths of my heart. One day while storing equipment away for the dry season, I went to the only market in the town of Farellones. There was a man talking to someone interested in horses. Apparently this man owned horses and was looking for buyers. My ears perked up as I overheard him talking about a horse he had bred for high mountain use. To make a long story short, after talking to him, I decided to buy a horse with the idea of crossing the Andes Mountains and go into Argentina. It was a far-fetched idea, but after a few invitations offered to me by some of the maintenance workers who lived in small towns bordering Argentina, the idea turned into a reality. In less than two months, the trip to Argentina on horseback began.

Halfway up the mountain to a town called Illapel, I stayed a night with one of the workers. He gave me a few pointers on how to maintain the horse in good physical condition for such a long trek. The climb to the highest peak would take a good four or five days. About two days from the peak, I stopped and lodged with the family of the skiing mechanic who was injured. His father was a goat shepherd who was very familiar with the territory on the other side of the Chilean border. He spoke about the mountain trails and the passes most accessible on horseback. His son, Jose the mechanic, drew me maps of how to get to a pass that would take the least time and wear to reach.

Both he and his father told me stories how they would sneak over the pass to pasture their animals because the grass was much better on the Argentinean side than on the Chilean side of the mountains. They also warned me to keep a sharp eye out for Argentinean rangers. The Chileans and the Argentineans never got along well. They told me many of their fellow countrymen never returned to Chile and are believed to be dead or in prison. For some reason or another, all their stories went in one ear and out the other. Worrying about the Argentineans or the rangers was the least of my concerns; I just wanted to be all alone with God in one of the most extraordinary mountain ranges on earth.

The climb from Illapel to El Paso de los Helados, Frozen Pass, was extremely steep. It took the horse and I nearly two days to climb ten thousand feet. About an hour's walk before going through the pass, I spent the night in a shepherd's dugout full of dried goat dung. The night sky was filled with stars. Never have I seen light from the stars dominate the dark spaces in between them.

It was about an hour before dawn when I learned why they named the pass *Frozen*. My body was stiff all over from the cold. It took several minutes to rub heat back into my limbs. When I got outside to saddle the horse, the blanket I left on its back had a sheet of ice on it about an eighth of an inch thick. The horse looked like a statue in the moonlight. As soon as I jumped into the saddle, the horse took off at a fast trot without a kick-start. It climbed the steepest part and made it to the entrance of the pass with no sweat.

By the time we got to the summit, the sun broke the dawn, and the colors over the eastern frontier were breathtaking. The rays of the sun slowed the horse to a stand-still. Looking down, I noticed the descent from the pass down to Argentina was long and gradual compared to the steep ascent from the Chilean side. At that moment in my life, I learned why eagles like hanging out in the mountains. As cold as it was standing on a frozen pass at nineteen thousand feet, my heart was warm with an inexplicable joy of being perched on top of the world. No words can describe what it feels like to see such grandeur.

The grass was greener, there were more wild berries, and the horse and I were in hog heaven on the Argentinean Andean mountainside. Water was abundant and more accessible than on the Chilean side. About three days down from the summit, off to my right, my eye caught a mother mountain lion and her cub perched on a rock. They sat calmly basking in the late-morning sunshine on a large boulder about twenty yards away. The only thing dividing the horse and I from them was a small creek in between us. One thing I learned about wild animals in general is if you don't bug them, they won't bug you. So with eyes straight ahead, I walked right by the big cat and her little cub, watching them through the corner of my eye. After a few minutes, I turned to see if they were still there. They were there big as life, gleaming in the sunlight, watching me go down the mountain. It was a majestic sight, one I will never forget.

The descent was long and confusing because there were so many boxed-in canyons to get trapped in. Sometimes I would lose up to half a day backtracking to take another route. It was harder to judge which draw to follow, especially when two or more canyons would all meet at the end of a narrowing valley. It made it difficult to choose which canyon would open up to another.

Finally, after three days of winding through a giant maze, I came upon a large river. It was a good sight to see because I could spot a small dirt road on the other side. The river was moving pretty fast because of the snowmelt. There was about twenty-five to thirty yards of river to cross to the other side. I nudged the horse ahead. It got about halfway across when it started to slip. The current was strong, and the water was deep. Suddenly, it stopped and tried to back up. I spurred it on to a depth close to its head. It got spooked by the rushing water and lunged backward, pulling hard to the left. It was stronger than I, so it pulled itself back up on the bank from which we came. I walked the horse back and forth at the mouth of the canyon looking for a lower spot to cross. We tried again in a spot that looked a little shallower, but when the water came up to its shoulder, it would rear up and spring backward, nearly throwing me into the stream. It was the same depth no matter where I went.

After numerous tries, the horse refused to go in the water. It was getting dark, and the night would be cold if I did not get out of wet clothes. After finding a small niche on one side of the canyon wall, I built a fire and made camp. The night passed in slight agony because I did not know how I was going to get across the river. To turn back would mean several days of backtracking and climbing steep canyons. Despite the dilemma, it was another beautiful night in God's majestic mountain backyard.

When morning broke, I could hear the river. By the time I finished breakfast, it sounded even stronger and faster than the day before. After waiting for the sun to get a little higher in the sky, I saddled and mounted the horse. My strategy was to give it a good kick-start and keep it moving strong. It cut the current to about halfway across, and then it started slowing down again. I raked my spurs hard against its shanks, but it only reared up and spun around in the middle of the river on its hind legs. Unfortunately, it came back down facing the bank where we came from and bolted to the shore, nearly bucking me off into the river. No matter how much I tried spurring it back in, it refused to go more than halfway.

For several hours, I sat on a large rock set back from the river, cold, wet, and exhausted from the struggle. *Now what?* I thought. Here I was trapped at the mouth of a narrow canyon with no way to get across a fast little river because the dumb horse was too scared to cross it. About another hour passed as I visualized the agony of going back the way I came when suddenly two ducks flew up from the descending canyon on the other side of the river. They turned into my canyon and flew right over my head and kept going up the canyon behind me. At least I knew which direction to go if I got on the other side. Ducks always fly up canyons where there is least resistance from boxed-in canyons.

Something in me told me not to move but to be patient. Not more than fifteen minutes went by when my ears picked up a low roaring sound coming up the road. A small truck appeared clambering over the rocky road. I jumped up and waved to the driver. He stopped and got out of the truck. I yelled, "Do you have a rope?" He pulled out a rope, but it was too short. He looked like he was going to leave, so I jumped in the water and swam against the current. It was fast and strong; I could see why the horse freaked out. But there was no way I was going to let this guy go without me. He pulled me up the bank, half in shock. I don't think he ever saw anybody jump in a river that fast and deep and live to tell. The driver told me he was on his way to deliver some supplies to an army post a few miles away. I replied, "Good! Maybe they can help me get my horse to the other side."

When we reached the post, several men in dark green uniforms greeted me. One of them, who looked older than the rest, came up to me and asked,

"Where did you come from?" I told him from Chile. "Which pass did you go through?" I then gave him the name of the pass. He looked at me with a stern look and said, "You are under arrest." I said, "Okay, but I need you to help me get my horse across the river!" He nodded his head and dispatched three men on mules to go get the horse.

One of the men was ordered to watch and contain me to a certain area. He was a curious, young private from Bolivia who took an interest in my travels from the United States. After listening to my origins and some of my life stories, he wanted to confide some vital information to me. He was a foreigner himself serving in an Argentinean army, so he knew how the military was going to treat me. We talked for over a couple of hours before the three soldiers returned with my horse. All three of them were wet and tired looking. The horse had pulled all three soldiers into the water as they fought to push and pull it with their mules across the river. It took all I had inside of me to keep a straight face.

Early the next morning, a military truck arrived at the mountain post to take me down to a town called San Juan for detention and interrogation. It took most of the day to drive down the mountain to a military fort located on the outskirts of town. Inside the fort, they locked me in a small room with old, buzzing fluorescent lighting and a radio blaring. They left me in there all night without turning them off. I was unable to sleep while in this room.

At daybreak, I was taken outside by a guard and ordered to do various sorts of manual labor. When I was not working, I was ordered to stay inside a four-by-eight-foot area marked with chalk on the ground. This area was located in an enclosed courtyard between two large army barracks surrounded by iron fencing. An armed guard sat in a booth opposite the courtyard. Whenever I needed to relieve myself, the guard would follow me into the latrine. Every once in a while, the fort sergeant would come to take me into a small room to interrogate me. The advice I learned from the Bolivian soldier in the mountains paid off. He tried to trick me into saying something stupid.

Day after day, the confinement was bad enough, but the empty monotony grew unbearable, so to pass the time, I recalled all the prayers of my childhood. The noise from the radio blaring all night long started doing things to my brain. Sleep deprivation put me into a depressed and irritated mood. All I could do to avoid the buzzing, mind-drowning noise was to learn to concentrate on something else instead of the constant drone coming from the lights and radio.

While standing in the courtyard one afternoon, I pushed myself to try to remember old prayers the nuns made us kids memorize back in my Catholic school days. By sunset, my memory slowly brought back the words to some of the prayers like the Our Father, the Hail Mary, and the Glory Be. For the next several nights, since I could not sleep, I was amazed how many prayers came back to me. Prayers like the Confiteor, Hail Holy Queen, and even the Apostle's Creed, which I could never recite on my own, all came back to me. Somehow, while praying these prayers, I would fall asleep for at least a couple of hours. My body began to feel rested, and during the monotonous day, my attitude and mood went from feeling like crap to feelings of compassion toward the soldiers who had to watch me. They were not happy-looking guys; besides, they were stuck in a job that bored them to tears.

About two weeks had passed, and to my relief, the radio and lights were turned off at night. The silence and stillness were welcome, but the confinement and not knowing when and if I would ever leave this place started to chew on my heart. A deep sense of loneliness and isolation crept in and tried to fill my soul with self-pity and self-loathing. How long would it take to get out of here? Nobody knew where I was. The stories of Chilean goat herders locked in Argentinean prisons never returning to their homes flooded into my mind, haunting me at night.

One night, I had a dream where I was taken in a van to some undisclosed place. The van suddenly stopped, the back door swung open, and a man holding a gun reached up and pointed it at me. I stood up and walked toward him to make a plea that I had not done anything wrong. He pulled the trigger, and in slow motion, I watched the bullet hit my forehead. I felt it go through my brain and out the back of my head. Then my knees buckled, and I fell forward, lying on the floor of the van. My head hung over the back bumper. There was a rushing sensation as my blood drained out of the bullet wound.

Once again, I could feel my *self* pouring out of the hole in my head, sliding down over the bumper, and flowing out on the surface of the street. My vision seemed to go in front of the flow of the blood. Next, I remember seeping down into the cracks in the street. There were tiny little bugs in the cracks running to escape from me, from drowning in my blood. I could see how the roots of tiny little blades of grass grew down inside the cracks searching for moisture and nutrients in the scant soil. The frightened insects looked as big as me. Everything was so clear and up close until the blood went deeper into the ground. Then everything went dark.

Suddenly, I became conscious of a voice from somewhere yelling, *"Levantate, levantate! El sargento quiere hablar contigo."* "Get up! Get up! The sergeant wants to speak to you." The guard took me to the small interrogation room. The sergeant came in and told me the captain of the fort wanted to speak to me. He then ordered me back outside to wait for his call. The day drug on as I stood and waited in my four-by-eight-foot spot. Finally, the guard got up from his post and waved me over to a door in the middle of one of the buildings. He led me into a room, where a doctor gave me a quick physical checkup. We then went down a corridor to an open doorway.

The guard saluted the captain and then let me in. The captain said something to the guard and then personally shut the door. "Sit down," he said. The captain was a middle-aged man with a mustache. He sat down and lit up a pipe full of tobacco.

"Do you smoke?" he asked.

"No I don't," I replied frankly.

He could tell by my reply that I was not a man of small talk, so he went on to tell me that I had crossed over into Argentina through an uninhabited pass. "You were arrested because you snuck into our country like a spy or a drug-runner." Then he went on to tell me they found no evidence of any drugs in my possessions or on the horse. "You can speak Spanish. Are you a spy?" he asked.

"No," I responded.

The look on his face grew curious as he relit his pipe and sat back in the chair staring at me. And then with a slight grin on his face, he leaned forward and asked, "Then why did you come into this country through a God-forsaken pass so far away from a border checkpoint?"

I looked him straight in the eye and said, "Look, all I wanted to do was ride a horse through the Andes Mountains and explore Argentina. Now I want you to give me my horse back so I can be on my way through Argentina and into Brazil."

He sat back and took another drag on his pipe while looking out a small window. He then turned to me, looked me in the eye with an expression of amazement, and said, "I can't let you go through this country. But I will send you back up to the mountain post where you were arrested. You will then be escorted back to the Chilean frontier. Come back to Argentina with a visa." When he finished saying that, he stood up and shook my hand. Then with a grin on his face he said, *"Vaya con Dios."* "Go with God." The guard came in and escorted me back to the yard.

The day after my meeting with the captain of the fort, I was sent back to the mountain outpost in the back of another military truck. The road back did not seem half as long as it had going down to the fort. It must have been the joy to know that I was free again. Back at the post, my Bolivian soldier friend was delighted to see me. He could not get over how quickly they released me. He gave me a minimum of three months in detention with a rare possibility of ever seeing me again. It was unheard of among any of them there that an illegal alien was ever released and freed to go back home so early.

The next day, the sergeant detached three soldiers to escort me back to the Chilean frontier. These men were ordered to take me through a different pass where the same river ran slower and the crossing was shallow. It took three days to reach the foot of the mountain where the pass was visible. It looked like a huge saddle between two towering, snow-covered peaks. The soldiers decided to dismount and camp down for the night. The soldiers made a fire and roasted some meat from an animal they had shot two days earlier. They started drinking wine they had packed also. In a couple of hours, they were feeling pretty good and started talking about food and women in a crude way. They offered me some wine and meat, but I politely refused. While they laughed and carried on with a bunch of stupid talk and jokes, I planned out a way to make an escape.

The three of them did not quiet down until the moon had traveled halfway across the night sky. I made sure my horse was tied up to a log about ten feet away. The soldiers had forgotten to secure their mules, so they were grazing nearby. About an hour before dawn, I quietly slipped out of my bedroll and packed my horse. The mules had drifted a good fifty yards away from the camp. Gently pulling the horse by its leash, I quietly walked it about fifty yards away from the sleeping soldiers. With one swift jump, as soon as I landed in the saddle, the horse broke into a gallop. Somehow it knew what I was up to.

When I turned around to see what they were doing, two of the soldiers were chasing their frightened mules, while the other one was hopping around his mule trying to put his pants on. It was a sight that brought shouts of laughter and tears to my eyes as the horse and I peeled away in a clean getaway. Even a good half an hour away from their camp, I could still see their half-drunken bodies trying to catch and saddle their spooked mules.

Within three days, I found my way back to Illapel, Chile. My friends and their families were glad to see me, especially after hearing about my imprisonment. Jose gave me a piece of paper that contained a name and address of a man who needed a diesel mechanic somewhere off the coast of Brazil. "You still have time to get the job if you leave now by bus from Santiago," he said with a cigarette in his mouth.

"What about the horse?" I asked.

"We'll take care of it for you."

As I looked at the horse for the last time, it looked back at me with an expression that read, "This was the wildest two months I've ever had in my life."

Brazilian Bats in the Human Belfry

The song, "What a Difference a Day Makes," went through my mind as the bus left the Aduana, the customs building in Chile, to enter Argentina. What a difference a piece of paper makes when crossing foreign borders was also on my mind when the border patrol agent stamped my visa and welcomed me to Argentina. As the bus traveled through Argentina, Paraguay, and Uruguay and onward to Brazil, my mind meditated on the many borders there are in South America. For two months, I had been incarcerated for border reasons.

My eyes gazed at the many different birds that flew over land as the bus drove, and I wondered why people limit each other's freedom. The birds didn't have to check in with some customs agent to enter another country. Yes, birds are dumb, but men are dumber for not learning how to get along with each other. Why? When it comes to relationships, why do we put up barriers between each other individually and between nations collectively? It would take a few more years of traveling and a few more amazing dreams to grasp the complexity of such a problem. One thing that did flash a hint of an answer was when I recalled my dream back in the military fort. There was something in the expression on that man's face who shot me that registered pure hatred. Why did he shoot me? What did I do that deserved a termination of my life? As I sat and tried to recall all of the bad things in my past, none of them really deserved a death sentence. Was it the Devil? Was it because I was free and he is not? Maybe because I love life and he is restricted to death?

Suffering frees us from restrictions. The reason I had so many dreams of dying was because my past sins restricted me from the knowledge of God. God knew I wanted to get closer to Him, so He allowed sufferings like prolonged sickness (the flesh), jail time (the world), and evil spirits (the Devil) to test me and to purify my heart. The suffering broke barriers that enabled me to see how sin limited my vision of God and from experiencing true freedom. Sin puts walls between God, who is real love and freedom, and us. The Devil does not want us to learn this, because he hates the fact that he is eternally condemned to restrictions whereas men still have a chance to become free of all spiritual restrictions if they know and understand how God works.

It is one thing to know the concepts to freedom that Christ taught, but it is another thing to put those Christian concepts into practice. Jesus did not spend thirty years in the kitchen baking cookies with His mom. Jesus disciplined Himself to pray, fast, and work on developing a deep relationship with God. Jesus would not have walked on water if He had just talked about praying. Jesus walked the talk. He learned how to go to the Father for the wisdom, grace, and power to be able to do things like walk on water and transfigure His human self into His divine nature in the sight of men.

The bus pulled into the terminal in downtown Rio de Janeiro around late afternoon. The nicer part of the city sits right on the coast of an inlet facing the Atlantic Ocean. When I called the telephone number my friend gave me, I was surprised to hear a person speaking in perfect English on the other end of the phone.

"Oh! We have been expecting you!" said a pleasant-sounding female voice. She gave directions on how to find an office building not far from where I was. After walking the streets of Rio for about a half an hour, I found the place. The woman who answered the phone was the wife of the man who needed a diesel mechanic. She seemed very delighted to see me. *Jose must have called them,* I thought.

"The season has begun, but you're here! No problem!" she blurted with enthusiasm in both her voice and hand gestures. Then she led me by the hand to an office where her husband was talking with another man. "Excuse me, dear, he's here—the mechanic from America." She broke into laughter as I turned to look at her for making such a surprise announcement. The man got up from his desk with a loud welcome and came over to shake my hand.

"We thought you'd been shanghaied!" he shouted.

With a shy laugh I said, "No, almost, but I made it, thanks." His loud American accent cracked me up. Little did he know how close he was to the truth.

They invited me to stay at their house in Rio for the night, and in the morning they would take me to the island. The man's name was Bill, and the wife's name was Diana. Diana casually informed me about their business in Rio de Janeiro. They were co-owners of a tourist agency that ran a twenty-four-acre cabin complex and restaurant on an island about two hours south of Rio. Most of their clients came from European countries and Canada. They had three sixty-five-foot wooden sailboats powered by marine diesel engines, and one large diesel-fueled electric generator powered their island facilities. My job would be to keep them running smoothly and maintained during my stay. Bill said he would take me to the island tomorrow to show me to my own cabin, the boats, and introduce me to the island staff.

"Are you game?" asked Bill.

"Sounds good to me," I responded.

"Good! Let's go home and eat!" Bill exclaimed.

After a pleasant evening meal, my hosts brought out some wine. While Bill opened the bottle, I asked him how they heard about me. Once he got the cork out of the bottle, he said, "A couple from Chile came to stay on the island for a week vacation and recommended you as a good mechanic."

Diana went on to say how much the wife of my boss in the ski center trusted my work over the Chilean mechanics. Both went on to tell me how difficult it was to find a good Brazilian mechanic. "Most of them barely make it through grammar school," said Diana. "We can't trust them either. They say one thing and do another," she added.

"And I no *entiende* their language," said Bill. "Things are always breaking down or going wrong . . . and no one knows why. It gets a little frustrating around here," Bill continued as he stopped to sip on his wine glass.

Then Diana added, "The Brazilians are sweet but very superstitious. They have a tendency to blame things on evil spirits when things go wrong." We talked for about an hour about Brazilian culture before they showed me to my room. As I lay down to sleep, I had forgotten what a mattress felt like. It was the best sleep I had in months.

Itacuruca was the name of the island, about an hour south of Rio de Janeiro by road and another hour southeast by boat. Bill and I reached the port around mid-morning. One of the boats was scheduled to dock carrying passengers from the island in less than an hour. There were two staff members from England waiting for the boat to arrive. They worked on the island as tour guides and facility managers. They were a young couple living in Rio de Janeiro who worked as private English teachers during the off-season. James had a funny sense of humor. His wife or girlfriend Amanda was more serious but pleasant. They were both from London, England. Both were glad to see me because they were well aware of the desperate situation the island was in without a mechanic who knew how to troubleshoot an engine problem. This was their second season working for Bill and Diana's vacation resort.

The trip to the island was the first time I had ever been out to sea in a large sailboat. There were several islands visible about a half hour out. The big island, Itacuruca, was hidden by a series of little islands seen from the boat's bow. When we came close to the island, the water had a turquoise tint surrounding beautiful white beaches. Looking down into the water, I could see the bottom twenty feet down it was so clear. There were tropical trees everywhere, with little hut-like cabins spread throughout the jungle. On our arrival, Bill showed me the reception room and office; he then assigned James and Amanda to take me to my hut. We took a walk through jungle footpaths to get to the cabin. It was a nice little furnished two-room cottage with a little bathroom. *Wow! A real bathroom,* I thought to myself.

James and Amanda enjoyed telling me about their time in Brazil, especially island life and the native islanders. When I was not working on boats or the main power plant, I would venture out into the jungle to observe the many fascinating creatures on the island. The vast amount of insects, moths, and butterflies enraptured my attention. In my junior high school days, I had a large insect collection, but I never saw so many different bugs in one place like this island. There were birds galore, tree monkeys, tree frogs, and several colorful species of snakes. At night I could hear the big snakes slithering over the roof.

The most amazing thing about the island night was listening to the grand chorus of singing insects, tree frogs, and spider monkeys. Their concert was deafening and could last up to two hours before quieting down. Without being able to sleep, I would sit up in a chair on the porch and be entertained by a giant surround sound orchestra of shrills, clicks, whistles, humming, and buzzing sounds all blended together. Certain species would sing at a lower pitch, while others at a higher one. Some would alternate between bass and sopranos like singers in a choir taking the lead spot. This immense concert would fill the air with a mysterious sense of something eerie and dangerous lurking in the darkness.

Late one night, I woke to the sound of a horrifying scream. Not sure what it was, I got up and crept outside to get a better earshot if it happened again. Nothing happened, so I fell back to sleep. In the morning, James and Amanda joined me for breakfast, so I asked them if they ever heard anybody screaming at night. They both looked at each other and grinned. Then Amanda turned and with a very serious expression on her face, proceeded to tell me about some of the native belief systems on the island commonly practiced throughout various jungle tribes and villages in Brazil.

"Many natives on the island practice a certain type of voodoo rituals," she said.

James described things they would not do at night. "They will not walk on certain paths after nightfall. Evil spirits can use an animal to kill human intruders walking on footpaths that don't belong to them."

Apparently, each tribe or village had sorcerers or black magicians that could protect their community by putting certain spells on another person, tribe, or village, especially if they were hostile. Now I understood why I had run into so few natives walking the various footpaths around the island. "They will hang certain items like what we would call good luck charms over the entrance of their huts. This is to prevent certain types of bad spirits from coming into their domain, especially if they were fearful of a black spell cast on them by a magician." After listening to their lesson on black magic and voodoo stuff, I grew curious and decided to take a walk around the island to check out some of the villagers. Besides, I didn't have anything else better to do in my free time than to wander into the jungle.

While walking the footpaths around the island, it occurred to me that James and Amanda never answered my question about if they heard screams at night on the island. Oh well. It didn't matter. After passing through a few villages, I learned that most of the native people seemed pretty normal—a little shy but content with my presence. Their huts were very close to each other, without any fencing or barriers between them. Most of the men were fishermen, while the women were busy preparing food and tending animals in wooden pens and cages. Banana and mango trees were abundant on the island. Their lifestyle reminded me of the Indians in Repocura. It was very simple, slow but practical. They did not engage in a lot of talk. If I greeted someone, they would invite me in to eat something or have a cup of herb tea and then sit and stare. But these native people seemed a little more nervous than the Mapuches. There was a certain agitation in their eyes that I didn't see in the Chilean forest people.

The captains of the boats and their crewmembers liked the way I kept their engines running smoothly. They enjoyed having the spirit of an

American man in charge of the welfare of their boats. These men, especially the captains, treated their boats as if they were sacred. They would talk about their boats as if it were a special person, like a wife or a beautiful woman. They would get all emotional if something went wrong with them. The boatmen would give me a beer after work and talk about Carnival. According to them, it was approaching. They also liked making jokes about an American boat mechanic (me) who needed a woman. The captains invited me to go with them to other islands to go swimming in hidden pools where I could find a beautiful woman. It was funny to see how much they enjoyed heckling me. I didn't pay too much attention to them because most of the time I could not understand Portuguese mixed with their native language.

James and Amanda invited me to accompany them for a week in Rio de Janeiro. The famous Carnival was about to begin, and they wanted me to see the Samba dancers. There were several schools of dancers that would prepare and practice up to nine months of the year for these huge parades through the streets of Rio. We all stayed in an apartment belonging to some friends of theirs. For all their promotional talk about the wonders of Carnival, this would be the first and last time I would ever go to one of these events.

In the first three days on the streets of Rio, in broad daylight, I witnessed several hit-and-run robberies where young men would knock people down, steal their wallets or purses, and then run through the streets, followed by ten to twenty people chasing and shouting behind the thief.

"Where are the police?" I wondered. As a matter of fact, I did not see a single peace officer for six whole days in the city of Rio de Janeiro during Carnival. The streets were so packed with people and garbage that everywhere you walked you were constantly bumping into someone or tripping over trash. People would stay up all night long walking in the streets drunk or high on something. There was constant shouting and noise of glass breaking from empty beer bottles crashing into the street. Many over intoxicated people were sitting on the gutters weaving and heaving their guts out. I kept a constant eye out for thieves while wandering street after street filled with perspiring human bodies due to the humidity.

On the eve of the sixth day of Carnival, my English hosts, a friend of theirs, and I were passing through streets on the outskirts of Rio. James and Amanda used to work in this particular neighborhood. It was a poorer section of the city, and there were a lot of cheap bars in the area. James wanted to stop in and buy us a beer in a tavern he used to frequent after work. While seated inside, a young man came up to our table and shook hands with

James. They were carrying on shouting things in Portuguese and laughing for a few minutes.

The rest of us were relaxing and drinking our beers as they engaged in a discussion that lasted about ten minutes. Suddenly, the man got up and left the table. James took a sip of beer and winked an eye at me. Five minutes later, the man reappeared and said something that sounded a little heated to both James and Amanda. James said something back that made the guy blush, put his head down, and leave our table. While we were finishing our beers, I watched the young man go to the back of the room, where he got into an animated conversation with a few other guys. There was something about his body language that told me he was not happy. After finishing our beers, Amanda asked James if we could go for a little stroll. She wanted to leave.

We all stood in the middle of the street adjacent to the tavern, discussing in which direction to go, when suddenly the young man who had been talking to James came bursting through the front door of the tavern with an empty beer bottle in his hand. He ran up shouting and swinging the bottle at James in a semi-rage like manner trying to hit him, but James managed to dodge his swings. Then he went into a fitful rage, swinging wildly. James managed to knock the bottle out of his hands. It fell and broke the back end of the bottle off against the pavement. The man then picked up the front end and started slashing it at James. Amanda ran over to distract him, but he then turned on her. He grabbed her purse, and she got into a tug-a-war with him. Their friend and I came around and flanked him. He then dropped the broken bottle and ran down the street.

James was bleeding a little above one eye and from a scratch on his right arm. We decided to walk back to the apartment. He kept insisting it was nothing and that he wanted to go to another bar to have a drink. Amanda did not like the idea and insisted that we get back to the apartment. We all walked in silence through the packed streets of Rio de Janeiro making our way through the drunken, raucous crowd. Looking at the people's faces as we passed through the staggering bodies on the streets of Rio, reminded me of horror movies I saw as a kid full of zombies, the walking dead, and evil clowns. Some of the expressions on their faces made shivers go up and down my spine. Their eyes were totally black, as if a non-life force possessed them.

My feet ached like never before. My shoulders and back got increasingly heavy, as if I were carrying a hundred-pound sack of cement on my head and shoulders. By the time we reached the apartment, I could hardly breathe, let alone walk another step. Amanda felt the same way, and after tending James's wounds, she said, "Let's go to bed." We all agreed and crashed out in the apartment. *Carnival is one big drag. Carnival is one big drag*, kept drumming through my mind until I drifted off into a deep, morbid thought—filled sleep.

As soon as I woke up next morning, all I wanted to do was get out of this hellish city and go back to the island. There were still two days remaining to celebrate Carnival in Rio, but my English hosts were tired and fed up with the city madness as well. During breakfast they all decided to return to the island, which brought a sigh of relief from me. The streets were packed with litter and a heavy smell of spent alcoholic beverages and smoldering tobacco butts. The littered city streets looked like a war-ravaged zone. En route to the island, we saw people passed out in the streets, sidewalks, and gutters. Some of them were sifting through the trash heaps; maybe they were looking for stuff they lost the night before. Anyway, I kept asking myself, *Is this what the people look forward to every year? What's so joyful about Carnival?* The effect it had on me was the complete opposite. Those six days immersed in that atmosphere of sheer decadence put me in one big psychological downer. It was a depressing drive back to the docks. All I wanted to do was go for a swim, lay down on one of those beautiful beaches, and soak my mind in the sounds of the island's insect and animal noises, not human noises.

Carnival was over, but its hellish spirits seemed to follow us to the island. James and Amanda were not talking to each other, the tourism business dropped on the island, Bill and Diana were talking divorce, and to top it off, the demons were keeping me up at night again. Only this time, they were going after some of the native neighbors down the path a ways from my cottage.

One night, in the dead silence of the early-morning hours, I heard what sounded like a man screaming for mercy at someone threatening to kill him, so I got up and snuck down below my front porch to listen to see what was going on. A few minutes went by as I stood in the quiet jungle. Suddenly, a man shrieked and then uttered some words in a loud voice, as if he were begging to be left alone. There would be silence for about five to ten minutes before he would repeat the same thing over and over. What I did not hear was anyone else responding or yelling back at him. The shrieking noises were hair raising.

Finally, after about a half an hour of standing there listening to this weird ordeal, I went back to the cottage and sat on the porch. The frightful sounds coming from that tortured victim made me think of my past nightmares and evil visions. Was this man having the same kinds of dastardly dreams? Were evil spirits attacking this poor guy too? What I didn't know while living on the island was that Christianity was the dominant institutional religion in Brazilian culture mixed in with all kinds of native pagan worship.

The Choice between Two Solitudes

The first snows had already fallen by the time I returned to work for a third season at Farellones Ski Center in the Chilean Andes. Because it was late and the ski season well underway, the boss was not happy to see me.

"Why didn't you call me?" he asked. "The house in Farellones has been rented because I didn't know if you were coming back."

I made some lame excuse, but the expression on his face was not buying it. "You can stay in an old, broken-down house below the parking lot. That's all I can offer to you for now." At least I got my job back as a roving mechanic.

The old house used to be an old mining barrack. It had holes in the roof and no heat or running water, but it had lots of beds. The good thing about it was I had the whole place to myself. After choosing a bed, I went to work in the snow. It took several days to get acclimated to the cold after having been in a hot, humid climate. The nights were extremely cold and quiet. I missed the sounds of the bug-and-frog nightly concert back on the island. When it snowed, snowflakes fell through the holes in the roof and made little piles on my covers during the night. During working hours, I would join the workers in their barracks for meals because it was warmer inside their barracks.

The boss had hired several new ticket checkers and lift assistants from Santiago. During the summer months, he had the maintenance crew build a new barracks. All the new personnel stayed in this new building. To my surprise, one of the new ticket checkers was a girl from the family I stayed with on the outskirts of Santiago. She told me her cousin Tatiana made her apply for a job up in the ski center. It was good to see her, but I kept my distance from her because she liked me too much. She was nice but too emotional and gossipy. Besides that, she was too young for me.

One of the higher-level ski lifts was having engine problems one day, so I took the highest ski lift to ski down to the lift losing power. There was a long line of impatient people waiting for the operator to let them on the chairs. He was being heckled for his inability to get the lift moving. While working on the engine above the bull wheel, I could hear two ticket checkers heckling back at the crowd. At first I didn't pay attention, but then people in the crowd started laughing.

My eyes scanned over the crowd and found two tall new ticket checkers acting out some little scene and cracking jokes to each other. The laughter from the crowd grew louder at the performance of these two girls. After putting the last nut on the valve cover and before testing the motor, I watched their performance. They were genuinely clever and funny too. When I shouted down for the operator to give the motor a try, one of the ticket checkers looked up and shouted, "*Damelo!*" The engine fired up back to normal again, and the whole crowd cheered and laughed at the same time! It was a rare moment to see so many Chileans in a public setting laughing in unison. For a few moments, I stood there looking at their faces as they jumped on the chairs. The people's facial expressions spoke as if their day had been made. Then I looked over at the two ticket checkers, and they both smiled back and blew kisses at me while waving their hands like two excited children.

While making the rounds on the slopes, I couldn't get their faces out of my mind. There was something different and electrifying about those two new ticket checkers. Out of all the years I had spent in South America, it was rare to see a city dweller, a native, or a woman much less, over eighteen years old wear a smile on her face and express so much joy in public. Children were the only ones that I saw smiling and laughing in public, not adults. No matter which station these two were working, they had the people in line singing or laughing at something to pass the time. On one occasion while waiting to catch a chair, I asked if they were sisters. They both turned and looked at each other at the same time and blurted out, "*Ninguna manera bebe!* No way, baby!" Then they busted out laughing. My face turned a little red as I laughed. They noticed that I was blushing, so they quickly grabbed my arms and invited me over to their barracks someday for empanadas and coffee.

A couple days later, I paid a visit to the new barracks to see if the two vibrant ticket checkers were in. They were both in the common kitchen making something to eat. When they saw me walk in, they screamed with muffled voices as they grabbed my arms again and pulled me into their room. They were obviously overjoyed to see me and that I had come to visit them.

One of them came up to me and asked, "Can I take your order sir?" with a big, goofy smile on her face. She quickly went off and came back with some toast and coffee. The other one grabbed sweet jams out of her drawer, and we ate, talked, and laughed. Both of their names were Soledad, which means solitude. Las Soles, as I called them, were from the same side of town, and it was their first time out of the city. They were both in their early twenties. When I got up to leave, they put an expression on their faces that looked like a couple of teddy bears ready to cry. "I'll come again," I said. They both laughed and jumped up and down as they clapped their hands. Walking out the door, I involuntarily shook my head, which made them laugh even more.

It had been years since the town of Farellones had seen such an unusual amount of snowfall. There was a lot more activity on the slopes this season that included an international racing event. Foreigners from European countries were all over the place. The boss hired an Englishman, a Swede, and two men from the United States to help out during the races. They were all good skiers. After hours we would ski together in the upper slopes. They liked me because I would turn on the lift lines to ski the slopes all to ourselves after closing time. We did our own races out of bounds down the steepest sides of the mountain. The snow was deep and bouncy. It was exhilarating to ski down unchartered territory way outside the center. This ski season I spent more time flopping around in the snow than at work.

The nights were longer and colder than usual this season, so I found myself frequenting the workers' barracks more often to warm up a bit. The two Soledads were always glad to entertain me in the evenings with their nutty charm. One night, as I was putting on my jacket to leave, the younger Soledad told me to stay until the older one came back from the bathrooms. She jumped up on the top bunk bed and waved me up to join her. I hesitated, but she made a face at me and said, "I won't bite, get up here."

She took out a book written in English and started reading it to me. Her facial expressions and broken accent made me laugh. She made me lay down next to her so I couldn't see her face. It didn't work because there was something about her accent that cracked me up. After a few minutes, she sat up, turned toward me, and then leaned down to peck me gently on my lips. I was shocked for a moment, but then she put the dumbest expression on her face as she batted her eyelashes so cleverly fast that it made me laugh to tears. She started to laugh at me and then bent down to give me another kiss. This one was a little longer where I could taste her lips and smell her hair as it fell over my face. She quickly laid down and grabbed her book to read a few more lines in English.

We lay side by side as she read. My inner reaction was to get out before things got a little hotter in there. Could I risk opening myself up to this woman who I hardly knew, or should I get up and go? But there was something so inviting about her moves that they allowed me to be vulnerable, so I turned toward her to watch her read. She then turned toward me with such a beautiful smile that it made me drop my defenses to return a little kiss to her lips. We both turned and locked each other in an embrace that lasted several minutes. Her warm body against mine felt so good. I could not remember the last time when I held a woman so close. Her lips were so sweet and her skin so soft, for a moment I felt like I was having a dream.

Then we heard a voice. It was coming from the mouth of the other Soledad. *"Vaya! Vaya! Que hacen muchachos?* Come! Come! What are you kids doing?" The Soledad in my arms started laughing and told her to be quiet before the security police came in. We all laughed because there were no security police at the ski center. That was a good moment to make my escape, so I jumped to the floor, saying goodnight to the two Soles, and headed back down to my frozen barrack.

The physical relationship between Soledad and I was reaching a critical point. Temptations to use her body for pleasurable purposes were growing by the day. Images of the face of my old girlfriend back in Aptos, California, reminded me of my old, selfish way. We ended up psychologically hurting each other because we used each other. We acted irresponsibly and did wrong. If I kept playing with Soledad the way I had with my old girlfriend, there would come a time where I would not be able to stop. The Lord knows I did not want to commit the same mistakes. "Dear God, help me. What do I do now? She's such a good girl."

A Sorrowful Fall into the White Glove of God

The snow was melting and turning to ice on the slopes because the long ski season was finally coming to a close. The only places to find good snow to ski in were on the northern side of the mountain out of bounds in the shade. The lifts were running at low capacity, so I had a lot of spare time to mess around. On one particular morning, I decided to make a downhill run all the way down the northern edge of the mountain to see how fast I could make it from the highest peak to the bottom of the ski center in Farellones.

After checking my watch, I launched myself straight down from the highest point on the mountain. Crossing the sun-parched slopes was fast and hard on my knees, so I headed toward the shaded snow out of bounds. The snow was much more manageable in the shade, but it was harder to see where I was going. My speed would vary according to the snow. I was so busy looking for good snow immediately in front of my skis that I failed to take notice that I was fast approaching an open cliff about ten yards in front me. Suddenly, I looked up and saw empty sky in the near future. "My God, I'm a dead man . . ."

My body instinctively knew it would not be able to brake in time. With only a couple seconds left to the point of no return something inside me said, "Jump!" so with full force, my legs lunged off the edge of the cliff into the open air. All I can remember was freefalling down into a deep canyon and catching glimpses of skiers resembling tiny specks at the bottom of the mountain. The experience of falling reminded me of an old cartoon I used to watch when I was a kid. In the cartoon, a stupid coyote would chase a roadrunner. The coyote would always run too fast before stopping in mid-air past the cliff, only to find itself plummeting straight down like a whistling bomb crashing into the desert floor below, and end up in a puff of smoke.

A strange thing happened. During the free-fall, my body started to go into slow motion. The next thing I became conscious of was that everything seemed to slow to a stop, a sort of suspended animation. Faces of people from my past came toward me.

The first face was that of a man I had never met. Even though we did not know each other, I knew he was the owner of a lawn mower I had stolen out of his front yard one night while driving around some strange neighborhood. The next face was of a girl from my seventh-grade class. The last time I saw her was when I angrily called her names and pushed hard against her chest, causing her to cry. She turned and ran away from me in tears. I never saw her again, but her crying voice haunted me for a long time.

Then another face appeared and another, and another. Every face belonged to someone I had offended through the years. It seemed like there were hundreds of them, one after another. Each one of them triggered an instant replay of the actual event as if I were watching a video playback of all my life's sins. It was so real that I tried to say something to them, but they moved away too fast. I was overwhelmed with a deep shame and sorrow that seized my entire being. I felt so ugly inside that all I could say was "sorry" repeatedly.

All three parts of me—my heart, my mind, and my soul—were all united in the most profound distress and doleful grief ever experienced in my life. It was unbearable; I just wanted it to end. I just wanted to die.

Time and space seemed to disappear, and I did not care what happened next. Suddenly, in an instant, everything went still, and a white light surrounded me. No more faces flashed before me. There was utter silence. The first thought that came to mind was that I had hit bottom, I was dead, and God was coming to get me. Then I slowly felt something cold against my face. I felt the same sensation around my hands.

For a moment, I was not sure where my hands were. I could not move. Somehow, I was still breathing. My lungs were still working, but how? My mind was racing, trying to comprehend the situation. I started to move my head from side to side. My neck was not broken. I moved my hands and feet as well. That's when I noticed they were above my head. In a flash, like a flickering light bulb going on in my head, my brain reconnected all its loose circuits to learn that I was buried in snow.

To my great relief, I realized I was alive, but how in the world did this happen? Familiar with that cliff, I knew the drop was more than five hundred feet down, so I just lay there full of wonder and amazement. Then the thought of no air to breathe put me in a near-panic mode. I quickly pulled my arms close to my chest and began pushing the snow to the side. I noticed my feet were almost straight above me, so I pulled them in close also. It took several minutes to push and kick myself upright. I then proceeded to dig my way toward the faint light filtering through the snow over my head.

Finally, I broke through the surface and could see the blue sky above. It took another few minutes of digging to manage my way out of the deep hole. On my hands and knees, I stared down that hole while catching my breath. When I straightened up, my eyes slowly focused on a pinnacle-shaped rock standing about two yards in front of me. My head slowly turned to my left and then to my right. I then turned completely around to see that I had fallen smack dab in the middle of an out cropping of tall, pointed rocks jutting from the side of the mountain, forming an enclosed terrace. The winds had blown and filled in this ringed enclosure with snow. I stepped close to the edge to look over. There was nothing but a sheer wall of rock dropping to the canyon floor at least five hundred feet below.

Then I looked up to see where I went off the cliff. The top of the mountain was too high to spot the edge, but if I had not jumped, my body would have taken a serious tumble down all kinds of exposed rock. I must have fallen between eighty to a hundred feet before landing in this bed of snow. I was totally dumbfounded. What happened to my skis? They had snapped off my feet upon impact and were buried in the snow also. When I dug them out I noticed they were damaged a bit. Then I took noticed that not one of my bones was broken, and I had not a scratch in sight.

I carefully climbed out of the rock enclosure and stood above the terrace. There was nothing but rock. The only place that had snow in the vicinity was the eight-foot diameter terrace my body had dropped into. The fingerlike rock pinnacles made the terrace look like a giant hand reaching out of the mountainside, palm up. It looked as if it were waiting to catch something from above. I could feel my stomach cringe and my heart sink and break. God had heard my sorrowful cries above, so He commanded His angels to spare my life. Tears fell from my eyes as I broke into a prayer of thanksgiving. I sat on the edge of the terrace for quite a spell thanking God over and over in my mind, telling Him how much I loved Him and that from now on, I would never again doubt His presence. I spoke to Him all the way down the mountain. Even though it was dangerously steep and sheer, it didn't matter; I had a grip with the strength of three men in one. I also felt as light as a bird, and I softly sang like one too.

As I lay in my frozen barrack that night, it came to me that my romantic involvement with Soledad had taken me away from my evenings alone with God. Sleep evaded me most of that night as what should have been a deadly flight off the cliff kept repeating itself over and over in my mind. The chances of my body ending up where it did were one in a million. I ruled out luck, but why did God spare my life? He must have something in store for me, but what? I sat in silence and waited for the sunrise.

The Swede came to my barrack in the morning looking for me. I had fallen asleep with my clothes on in a chair, and the sun was up. "Hey, hey!" he said. "Are you going skiing?"

Stepping outside to stretch and yawn, I said, "Yeah, let's go."

On the way up to the center, we stopped in the machine shop to see if the men had made any coffee. They did, so we drank a cup before catching a lift. I was still in a daze from my spill off the cliff the day before. The Swede and I grabbed a chair lift together and started our way up the mountain.

"Where are you going when the season is over?" he asked.

"Oh, I don't know," I replied without thinking.

"You told me your grandparents came from Sweden right?"

"Yeah," I said.

"Have you ever been there?"

In a daze I asked, "Where?"

"To Sweden," he repeated.

"No," I said.

He looked at me with a broad grin on his face and said, "Why don't you come to Sweden? You can stay at my place, and we will look for some of your relatives, your roots. Plus, there are a lot of good ski runs nearby my home." He was serious, so I told him I would think about it.

The next day the Swede caught me on the slopes taking oil to one of the engines. "Hey man, I'm going to that island you talked about in Brazil. I'll be there for a few weeks. Meet me there, and I'll take you to Sweden."

I don't know why I said yes because I had made plans to visit Soledad's family and to take both Soles to Illapel to spend some time in the mountains with Jose's family, the same family taking care of my horse. "Great! I'll see ya there!" He then skied down to Farellones and left the same day.

People were packing and loading vans and buses leaving for Santiago when I stopped by to see the two Soledads and the other employees off. They were cracking jokes and laughing as usual when I surprised them inside the barracks. "Are you coming with us!" the older Sole asked excitedly. She had food in her mouth, so some of the bread she was eating blew out of her mouth as she spoke, causing the other Sole to double over and almost fall on the floor from laughter.

With a grin I said, "I can't. I have to work, but I'll see you in a couple of days."

Outside, the younger Sole checked to make sure I had her address and then gave me a big kiss on the cheek. "Hasta la vista, baby!" The two goofball ticket checkers then loaded up on the bus and waved to me from inside as the bus drove off.

As soon as the bus was out of sight, I caught one of the lifts still running and skied over to the cliff where I went off the edge. As I stood there on the edge looking down over the cliff, I couldn't believe how far I would have had to jump in order to clear several large boulders right below the cliff's edge. Only an angel or God would have known those boulders were there. Who else would have told me to jump? As I stood there full of wonderment, I thought about the Swede's invitation. It sounded like a good idea. After all, I always wanted to go to Europe when I was a kid. Maybe this was where God wanted to take me to next in my travels. Why not? I decided to visit the

Soledads for a few days and then catch a bus from Santiago and go meet the Swede in Brazil.

Brazil, England, Sweden, Poland, Yugoslavia, Greece, Egypt, Sudan, France . . .

Jose's family greeted us with great joy when we arrived at the doorstep of their mountain hacienda. The dad, having recently arrived from shepherding a herd of goats in the canyons for three days, quickly ran to prepare meat for an evening meal. Jose's wife and mother busied themselves with preparing a place for us to stay for the night. Meanwhile, the Soles and I decided to take a walk around the ranch.

When we walked past the corral full of goats, I heard a familiar sound. It was my horse braying behind the corral under some trees. When I pointed to the horse, the two Soles stopped to admire his looks and wished they could ride him. "Sure you can. He's calling us to come get him," I said with a grin.

"But would Don Ruben let us?" they asked.

"No, but I will."

Their facial expressions made me laugh. "You talk as if you own this horse," said the older Sole.

By now the horse had come up to check us out. It came over to me and snorted. As I rubbed his nose and patted his cheek, I said, "I do." A person could compare the expressions on their faces to two wide-eyed children caught with their mouths hanging open.

"Can we!" they blurted in unison.

"Vamanos! Let's go!" I shouted.

We spent the afternoon scanning the countryside on horseback. Don Ruben and his family had prepared a fiesta for us. It was a delightful evening because the Soledads brought in their familiar happy spirit and sense of humor into the occasion, which put everyone in a good mood. Don Ruben was very happy that he came down from the mountain in time to be with us. Before the sun went down, he took me for a walk to show me a sight where he was planning on building a new house. Then he took me to a meadow overlooking the river below his house and said, "If you ever want to get married and raise a family, I'll give you this meadow and we'll build you a house together." The first thing that came to mind was the Mapuche man who said the same thing to me back in Repocura. I thanked him for his generosity and gave him my appreciation.

The next morning after breakfast, the younger Sole and I went for a walk down to the river. We walked for a good stretch along the riverbank in silence. Her face and body language expressed a certain peace and pensiveness as I watched her moves. It was the first time I had seen her in such a quiet mood. We sat down on a sandy patch of beach and listened to the river gently flowing by. After a few minutes, she pulled out a bar of soap from her blouse pocket and said, "I stink. I need a bath."

I thought she meant to wash her face, so I responded with, "Yeah, I need to wash my face too."

Then she stood up and said in a totally innocent tone of voice, "All of me, both of us, come on."

With a surprised look on my face, I looked up at her and asked, "What, you're kidding? That river is full of recent snowmelt. It will be freezing."

She reached down, grabbed one of my arms, and pulled me to my feet. "We'll keep each other warm," she said. She proceeded to drop her clothing and stepped into the freezing water. "Come on. Don't be a chicken," she begged with that big, adorable smile on her face. Her dare was so childlike, so I did the same and got in the water. With a degree of incredulity, we rubbed the bar of soap on each other until it lathered our bodies. We stood there in the shallow, pristine water holding each other close. We both started laughing because we were shivering so much. Our body heat slowly warmed us as we stood all wet neck to neck with our heads looking down over each other's right shoulder. Then both of us lifted our heads at the same time and looked at each other face to face.

The morning sun reflected off the soft brown irises of her eyes amid her golden facial skin. Her big, bright eyes and face wore an expression rarely seen in my life. It was a look of sheer love and admiration for a man she wanted for the rest of her life. I knew for my part that if this was the woman God wanted me to marry, I had no complaints. With that lovely smile on her lips, she said, "Let's get married, and I'll give you six children."

At first, when I heard the number six, I thought she might be joking. "Why not seven or eight?" I said.

She suddenly pushed backward, and after splashing me with water, she leapt back into my arms, screaming like a girl, "As many as you want!"

We held each other tight as the thought of getting married and having six kids with this amazing Chilean woman ran through my mind. Then I remembered what Don Ruben told me the night before. Could this be the woman and the place where the Good Lord wanted me to settle down? *Why not?* I thought. "You have been born and raised in a big city, Sole. I was raised in little towns and have lived and worked in lonely places most of my life. Could you live in a place like this?"

She quickly responded back in her vibrant way, "With you, I could live anywhere."

Deeply moved at what she said, a sudden wave of sadness filled my mind and heart as I remembered the promise made to the Swede. Gently pulling her head toward me, I kissed her on the lips and said, "There is something I have to do first, Soledad." She stared back in anticipation with her eyes focused on mine. "It will take some time, but I promised to go with a man to visit the land of my ancestors."

She quickly put a finger to my lips and said, "*No importa!* It doesn't matter! I'll wait for you." We hugged each other and went back to Jose's family house.

The Swede was there, waiting for me on the island of Itacuruca. His voice blasted over the bay as he spotted me on the incoming boat. He came out to meet me on the dock. "You're a sight for sore eyes, bro!" he shouted as we hugged. "Are you ready to go find yur roots?" he asked.

"I am, let's go!" I responded.

Within an hour, we were back on the same boat and left the island to Rio de Janeiro to catch a flight to Caracas, Venezuela. There was a tone of anxiousness in the Swede's voice as he spoke to me on the boat about his stay on the island. He was anxious to go home. I couldn't help but wonder if the island spirits had bothered him like they did me. It was good to see him and anticipate a new adventure in my life. After stopping in to say hi and good-bye to Diana, who was now divorced and living alone, we caught our flight to Venezuela.

On the flight, Lars told me he needed to visit his host family in Caracas and spend a little time with them before leaving South America. "In about a week I'll meet you in London, at Heathrow Airport," he said.

"Sure, no problem," I said. James and Amanda had given me some addresses of their friends in London, so that would give me time to go visit them and see a bit of England. Before boarding my flight to London via New York, Lars gave me his anticipated flight schedule to London. We shook hands and split. "The best places to go in London are the pubs!" shouted the

Swede over the crowd as I boarded the plane. Several people laughed at his remark and responded with a loud, "Hear, hear!"

Lars was right; the best thing in that dull, foggy city was the pubs. There was not a lot to do except sit and drink and talk pipe dreams. Most of my stay in London was spent walking around in the streets to stay warm. When the day for the Swede's arrival came, I prayed that he would be there to get me off that big island they call Great Britain. What a joy it was to see his broad grin and hear his booming voice over the crowd. He arrived according to schedule and beamed with joy to see me also. We went to one of the London pubs to have some ale and discuss our next move. "We leave from Felixstowe to Goteborg by boat in two days. I've arranged everything. We'll be in Sweden in less than a week." We lifted our beer mugs in cheer, "Good to see ya, Lars."

"Hear! Hear!"

The trip by boat was fast and smooth for a large boat. It was the first time I had ever been on a cruise liner. After the second night in the Atlantic, we landed just as the sun broke the horizon over the port of Goteborg, Sweden. We stayed in a small but very modern town called Trolhatten before meeting his family and friends. Once settled in at his family's house bordering a lake, Lars and I decided to attack the slopes in the northern Italian Alps. The Alps were not as tall and rocky as the Andes Mountains, but the snow was perfect. It was easy to catch cheap flights around Europe, so we would bounce back and forth from an airport close to his home.

Behind his house was a large frozen lake where we would go speed skating on ice. The only experience I had skating on ice was in a building on a frozen, artificial rink. To be skating on top of a large lake was a little eerie. In some parts, my skates and body weight made the ice crack. I could hear a pinging sound shooting out in various directions as I passed over the lake's surface. Another first in my life was learning how to cross-country ski. It was amazing to discover how much mileage a man can cover on two long, thin, flat sticks. The Swedish forest and countryside were very clean of wood debris. The mountains were hilly and not very tall.

Our next skiing adventure outside of Sweden took us to Spain. The Pyrenees mountain range that divides Spain from France contains some of the steepest snow-covered slopes in Europe. We chose the weekdays to hit the slopes so we would not have to wait in long lines to catch a lift. As a result, we were able to ski nonstop the whole day long until we dropped from exhaustion. We would spend our nights recuperating on good, healthy meals and getting plenty of sleep.

One night while half asleep in our hotel room, a knock after midnight came on the door. Thinking it was Lars who had forgotten his keys, I opened the door in my shorts. To my surprise, a young Spanish woman greeted me with a semi-shocked look on her face. After partially closing the door, I recognized her as one of the hotel desk clerks. She introduced herself as Carmen and courteously asked if we wanted to go down to a dance nearby. Half asleep and tired from skiing all day, I responded without thinking, "Oh! Sure, wait, I'll be right out."

When I shut the door, I thought to myself, *What am I doing? I can't dance. Where's Lars?* But I couldn't leave her standing outside, so I threw some clothes on and went down with her to the dance. Lars was in the middle of the room dancing and whooping it up as usual when we walked in. Carmen and I started dancing. She noticed how bad I was and started to laugh. I told her I didn't know how to dance disco, so she held me close and said, "It's okay, we'll go slow." My dancing got a little better after a couple beers, but being so tired, I told her that I needed to get some sleep. She said, "Okay, let's go back to your room." We went back to my room, and to make a long story short, we engaged in a little more activity. This kind of activity, daytime snow skiing and nighttime sheet skiing, went on for a few more days until we went back to Sweden, dead tired and dead broke.

The money well ran dry, so Lars and I got jobs shoveling snow off rooftops in Stockholm, the capital of Sweden. The pay was good, but the work was dangerous. Part of our job was to break icicles hanging off the eaves of tall buildings. We would take turns lowering each other with a rope over the roof edges to chop off the icicles with axes. These icicles were large and heavy enough to cut right through the tops of parked cars underneath their flight path. Plus, the outside air temperature would drop to thirty degrees below zero, making it difficult to breathe. Some of the other Swedes who were accustomed to long exposure outside gave us lessons on how to breathe so as not to damage our lungs.

The Swede and I would spend the money we earned to go on more excursions throughout Sweden and other countries in Europe. On one trip, I met a man who told me about some friends of his who ran an underground auto repair shop outside a small village south of Stockholm. Something in me liked the idea, so after learning that I was a mechanic, he contacted his friends to see if they needed a mechanic. They were curious about an American living in Sweden, so they invited me over to their shop for lunch.

Two Swedes named Stan and Johnny had converted an old barn into a well-equipped garage specialized in repairing Volvos, Saabs, BMWs, and Mercedes. They were tough characters who rejected the heavy taxes imposed on them by their government. The average working Swedes had a little over 60 percent of their wages sapped by the Crown. When they learned of my experience working on American cars, they were happy to hire me. For them, American cars were the coolest and most valuable cars in Europe. I laughed to myself thinking how much an American pays for good European cars like the ones they commonly worked on.

Living the fast life with Lars was fun, but it got old and was taking a toll on my body. Besides that, something in me felt like it was dying. I told Lars about the job offer working with the two mechanics south of Stockholm. He thought that was great and was actually thinking the same thing about going back to school and getting a more serious job. He wished me well and told me to call him some time.

Working in a foreign black market auto repair shop in the woods of Sweden with a couple of crazy Swedes was most entertaining. Johnny, the younger of the two, would pull out a loaded gun and shoot holes through the ceiling if something went wrong on the job. Stan, cussing in Swedish, would yell at him because the cops might hear the gunshots. But the best part of working with these two men was that they were family men. They had wives and children, which is what I needed to be around for a while. Stan had a little summer cottage within walking distance to the shop. He let me stay in it for the duration of my stay in Sweden, which gave me time to be alone and quiet again. For three more cold winter months, I worked consistently during the day and pondered away the Swedish nights by the fireplace.

Something felt like it was choking me in the middle of the night while I was asleep in my little Swedish cottage. When I opened my eyes, they started stinging real bad. I quickly got out of bed to turn on the light. There was smoke floating everywhere in the bedroom. When I opened the door to the living room, a smoldering log had rolled out of the fireplace and had fallen on the floor. After throwing it back into the fireplace and sweeping the floor, I thanked God it hadn't burned down the place and sat up for a while. Staring at the burning embers caused me to go into a deep contemplative state of mind.

When I went back to sleep, I had a dream where I fell out of a plane. As my body plummeted to the ground, I could see a large city below me. The closer I came to the ground, the more I could see cars moving and people walking in the streets. There was a large, busy intersection right under me when my body finally slammed into the pavement. After hitting the pavement, I instinctively knew I was dead. Pushing myself up off the street felt more like peeling myself off the street.

When I got to my feet, I just stood there for a few moments looking at the ground. Then I looked at my body all broken up with bones sticking out all over my body through the clothes. My clothes were all wet with blood and body fluids. My hands and arms were all bloody. All my teeth were rattling around in my mouth. When I took a step, I could feel my broken feet squishing inside the shoes full of blood. I crossed the street, wondering if anyone was staring at me, but no one seemed to notice. All I could think about was getting off the street to go hide somewhere.

I climbed up a flight of stairs leading up to someone's front door. Nobody came to the door when I knocked, but the door was not locked, so I opened it and went inside. When I walked into the living room my shoes were squishing loudly. Then I looked down and saw a couch. I sat on the couch for a while wondering, *What am I going to do with myself?* The next thing that came to mind was to get off the couch and go look at myself in the mirror. I walked down a dim hallway and found a small bathroom to my right. I reached in to turn on the light, but my hand could not find the switch. I could see the mirror, but it was so dark in there that I could hardly make out my shape. I grew more and more angry and frustrated that I couldn't find the switch. When I finally found it, I could not flip the switch with my hand. My hand felt like it was powerless. Then I tried pushing with both hands, but by the time I got the switch to go on, I woke up.

When I sat up thinking about this dream, it seemed like it was telling me that right after physical death, the soul does not immediately leave the body. And perhaps, by some divine rule, I was not allowed to see it or my physical self after death. There also seemed to be some spiritual presence in the room that prevented me from turning on the light to see myself in the mirror.

One of my friends from Goteborg came to the shop and asked if we could paint his American Ford Mustang. Johnny gave me the job. To do a good paint job on a medium-size car takes several hours of sanding and then another few hours to prep and paint. They told me they would pay me well if I would do it right away. "It's a deal," I said.

From noontime to nearly midnight, I worked nonstop, sanding, blowing, taping, priming, and spray-painting the hours away. By the time I put the finish coat on the car, my brain was swirling from all the dust and paint thinner sucked into my lungs. Something in me said, "Go outside and breath in some fresh air now!" After stripping off the facemask, I looked up at the clear night sky and saw pairs of stars everywhere. I was seeing double, and my body weaved as I walked around in front of the shop. "My God, I'm stoned," I said to myself. My body started shaking from the cold, so I turned to open the door of the shop. It was locked and I didn't have a key. "You gotta be kiddin. I locked myself out!" Instead of panicking for being stuck outside in zero or sub-zero temperature, I started to laugh. My eyes noticed a small truck parked over by the side of the metal barn. The door was locked but the window was opened, so I climbed in through the window and rolled it up to stay warm.

Damn! What an idiot! How could I have locked myself out? I thought to myself. *This is going to be a long, cold night.* All I was wearing was some overalls with no jacket because it was warm in the paint booth. I was both cold and thirsty. *Well, Lord, the Swedes will find a freeze dried American in the morning.* My mind kept coming up with all kinds of crazy thoughts as I sat with my legs tucked under my body.

After several minutes of listening to my buzzing consciousness, I started humming a little song from childhood. The whole song came back to me to help me pass the time and stay awake. Other songs came back to me, and so did memories of sitting in my frozen barrack back in the Andean Ski Center. Something inside of me was doing all it could to prevent me from drifting off to sleep. The next thing that came to mind was, *Where do I go from here. Do I remain in Sweden repairing and painting cars, or do I go somewhere else?*

The question caused me to ponder the old *what's my life's purpose* question again. Not more than five minutes went by when suddenly I thought of the pyramids in Egypt. *I think I've had enough of Sweden and the cold. Let's go see some pyramids and bake in the Egyptian sun.* The last thing I became aware of before falling into a sub-zero sleep was that old, familiar yet strange, warm, inner presence gradually taking over my body head to toe.

Sunlight filling the truck woke me up the next morning with my body stretched out across the seats. My body was not frozen; it was not even stiff. The Swedes arrived just in time as I got out of the truck. After telling them where I spent the night, they laughed incredulously, but then Johnny noticed the mask on the floor and the lights on in the barn as he opened the door.

They both looked at each other with unbelief and told me to take the day off and go get some sleep. I said, "No, I'm fine. Let's get to work."

During our lunch break, both of the Swedes told me about a truck-driver friend of theirs who lived in Malmo, the southern tip of Sweden. "He's going to Greece next week. Do you want to go with him?" My eyes and face lit up as they watched me think about it.

"Sure!" I said.

"Okay, I already told him you would say yes, so he is going to get you papers as a co-driver to get through the communist countries," said Johnny.

"We're going to miss you, Steve," said Stan.

Johnny drove me to the trucker's office outside of Stockholm. On the way, he told me that someday he would like to go to America and become a Hell's Angel. It made me laugh when he told me that because he fit the image. I thought about his wife and kids and felt like telling him that the Hell's Angels have no life, but he was more of a dreamer than a doer. When we pulled into a truck stop area, a man with a cup of coffee in his hand came outside to greet us. His name was Jimmy, a Scotchman who spoke Swedish with a Scottish accent. We hit it off right away after a few jokes from Johnny about my stay in Sweden. Johnny was not a hugger, but he gave me one before I jumped into the truck to Greece.

While on the road to Greece, Jimmy told me that I survived one of the longest and coldest winters in years. "Sweden has not had this much snowfall since the sixties. You'll like it in Greece. It's much warmer there," he said.

When we reached the port of Malmo, I figured out that my stay in Sweden had lasted over six months. I arrived in the beginning of winter and it still was winter. No wonder Sweden has a high suicide rate; they spend so much time in the dark and cold.

Jimmy's truck rolled on to a large barge designed to transport large, diesel-powered freight vehicles. The trip to Athens, Greece, from Malmo, Sweden, took eleven days by truck. Jimmy's company shipped food and other common market supplies. He liked telling road trip stories, especially about his trips to Saudi Arabia and other Middle Eastern countries.

Whenever he mentioned the word Arab or was talking about the Arabians, he always preceded the word Arab with the f-word in front of it. For example, he would say, "If I see a f_____n' Arab driving a car, I'll stop the truck." Or, "You can't trust the f_____n' Arabians!"

His most dreaded assignments were driving shipments to Riyadh, Saudi Arabia. He explained, "You can drive mile after mile through the desert and count hundreds, maybe thousands of wrecked and abandoned BMWs, Mercedes, and other expensive vehicles littering the highway to Riyadh because when the f_____n' Arabs wreck them, they just leave 'em out there." He further explained to me that the Saudis have so much money, that if an Arabian wrecks his car, he leaves it in the desert, buys another one, and wrecks it too. He said they don't know how to drive. They just get in the car, stick it in drive, and push the pedal to the floor and off they go. "When I spot one coming toward me, I can tell way ahead if the f_____n' Arab doesn't know how to drive, so I'll stop the truck, jump out, and get under the back axle and pray."

One of Jimmy's best Saudi Arabian stories was when an Arab passed him up, and then about a mile ahead, the driver stopped the car, blocking the highway. When Jimmy came to a slow stop about fifty yards from his car, the driver pulled a rifle out of his car and ran up to Jimmy's window, wide-eyed and screaming wildly, pointing to something on top of his truck. The man then took aim and shot about six to eight rounds of bullets at whatever it was on top of his truck cab. The Arab then ran back, got into his car, and floored it down the highway as fast as the car could go. Jimmy opened the door to look up at what he was shooting at and discovered his Michelin Tire Man cab ornament was full of holes. When he got to Riyadh, some fellow truckers told him that the image of the Michelin Tire Man is the spitting image of an evil spirit in the Islamic culture.

We drove through a few communist countries like Poland, Czechoslovakia, and Yugoslavia. At every truck stop, the waiters in these countries would call European drivers George. "What would you like to drink, George?" or "What can I bring you, George?" They never greeted me with a smile or any enthusiasm. In every bar or restaurant we stopped in to eat, the workers looked bored stiff. Their personalities were all the same, like they had been cloned. Jimmy told me that Socialism took away their joy to live life. "They just exist . . . that's all." Communist restaurants possessed a very depressing atmosphere to sit in, plus the food was usually bland, and the coffee was always burnt.

Jimmy liked beer, and I was amazed at how well he could drive that big rig through small towns and villages. Most of the roads were narrow and one way. One mistake could spell disaster if he misread a turn, but the beer (no matter how much he drank) didn't even faze him. *It had to be his Scottish blood*, I thought.

But then you had the Finns. The Finnish truck drivers could sit and down a whole fifth of vodka in one truck stop, get back in their trucks, drive a few hundred miles, and do the same thing over again at every truck stop. When he pointed them out to me at the stops, these guys were huge. The average Finnish truck driver weighed anywhere from 250 pounds to 350 pounds, and they were loud and talkative. They would spend a good hour drinking, eating, and laughing at God knows what, get back in their trucks, and drive as if they were stone sober. I asked him, "Aren't these guys dangerous on the road?" Jimmy told me that he had not heard of a single accident involving a Finnish truck driver in all his twenty-five years of commercial truck driving.

The Swedish-built big rig came to a halt between the old and new city of Athens on a sunny morning. It was the first time the outside air felt warmer than the inside temperature of the truck cab. Jimmy walked around to check the tires as I grabbed my backpack and made sure everything was there.

"Well, it's the end of my road to the south. Egypt's that way," Jimmy said as he pointed in the direction to the port of Athens.

"Thanks Jimmy," I replied.

He looked at me and said, "It was a pleasure having someone to drive with. Watch out for them f_____n' Arabs, and stay out of trouble."

Athens was a busy city full of modern structures and old Greek ruins. There were tourists at every corner and shop in the streets. The noise and smog levels reminded me of Mexico City. After a few days of walking hard city streets, my legs got tired and my feet grew sore, so I decided to go visit some islands and make my way to Crete. The south side of Crete had little, quiet villages spread out along quiet beaches. They were not as pretty as the beaches around the Brazilian islands, but at least I was able to catch up on some well-needed sleep and rest. After a two-week stay on Crete, I grabbed another boat to Alexandria, Egypt.

Jimmy was right. I rode a public bus from Alexandria to Cairo, and in the two hours it took to get to Cairo, I probably aged five years. The driver weaved in and out of traffic as if his bus was the only vehicle on the road. Walking around Cairo was like walking around a huge zoo. There were people and animals from every corner of the world in this place.

Cairo, I learned, was the hub of North Africa. Most of the shipping trade from Sudan, Ethiopia, Kenya, and other neighboring North African countries would come down the Nile to Cairo to market their goods or ship them overseas, especially to Europe. The streets in Cairo were full of people and traffic twenty-four/seven. The only available cheap rooms for rent were situated on the higher floors of old, cockroach-infested, concrete buildings.

While walking the streets searching for places to stay, I ventured into ghetto areas on the outskirts of the city. In the middle of some empty lots there stood giant piles, two stories high, of trash mounds. There were people living in holes dug in and shored up inside these trash heaps. Kids were playing and digging around in the debris outside of their holes. The smell in the heat of the day was atrocious. As a matter of fact, the smells of these areas was so bad, you could get a whiff of these monstrous dung hills from just about anywhere in the city. On one of my wanderings near the ghettos, I came across dead bodies of animals next to an old, broken bridge. As I ran under the bridge to get away from the stench, my eye caught a scene I have not seen in any other country. There were a couple of badly decomposed human corpses shoved under the bridge as well.

The noise, the smell, the heat, and the cockroaches crawling over me at night made it nearly impossible to get some sleep. The only place I found some rest was around the Pyramids at the Giza Plateau. The Giza Plateau was about ten miles to the west of Cairo. It was the only place that was not swarming with two-legged creatures and motors. The Great Pyramid was an amazing structure to behold. It was also the coolest building to occupy with outside temperatures of 120 degrees Fahrenheit and above during the day. I was fascinated by the way this thing was built. In my high school and college days, I had read some books about its construction. It was the first on the Greeks' list of the Seven Wonders of the World, and it is the only one still remaining today. During my stay in Egypt, I spent a minimum of fifteen days at the Giza Plateau. There is so much mystery built into this one pyramid that it staggers the mathematical and scientific mind.

The Nile River was another place where it was peaceful and cooler too, so I decided to go for a trip up the river on a small sailboat. The owners of the boat were fishermen who would take a handful of tourists for excursions up the Nile to the Aswan Dam. They liked that I attempted speaking Arabic, so they gave me a job gathering tourists in the towns bordering the Nile. My pay was free room and board on their sailboat during the excursions up and down the Nile River. It turned out to be a good deal because I was able to see a lot more of the Egyptian countryside from the river than walking or traveling by land. It was also a lot cooler over the water.

The Egyptian nights were beautiful floating along the Nile amid immense open deserts. The captain and his assistant were the only ones awake steering the boat, but I would sit up watching and listening to the surrounding sights and sounds of the river and desert. Besides, I learned to sleep with one eye open because, like Jimmy said, I couldn't trust the Arabs. Ever since I had discovered those dead bodies stashed under the bridge in the back streets of Cairo, my guardian angel would not let me fall completely asleep.

The Aswan Dam was an architectural spectacle, but it was a boring place to be compared to the Giza Plateau and its Great Pyramid. From the dam, I decided to take a train down to Wadi Haifa, Sudan. Depending on the rainy season, Wadi Haifa was the center for catching boats further up the Nile to countries further south, but by the time I got down there, the monsoons had begun. People coming north were telling those going south that the roads were flooded, so I decided to turn around and go back to Cairo. My Arab fishermen friends were still in Aswan when I returned, so I jumped back on board with them to go back to Cairo. Two days down river, we arrived in a town called Luxor to pick up some food and water. There were about a half dozen young tourists interested in sailing to Cairo. Among the group were a couple from Australia, two women from France, one Swedish woman, and an Englishman. They were all glad to get off the hot, dusty tourist trails along the river.

Another two days downstream, the river dropped down to within two to three feet in depth. It was so shallow in some spots that the assistant had to get out and pull the sailboat with a fifty-foot piece of rope while the captain pushed off the bottom of the river from the stern with a long wooden pole. The assistant was only a boy, about sixteen years old. After a while, he could hardly go any further, so I jumped in the river to give him a hand. Pulling that boat in shin-deep mud was not easy.

We had gone about a hundred yards when I stepped on something that went through the bottom of my sandals and into the bottom of my foot. Whatever it was, it went to the bone, and blood was spurting out of a good-sized gash. I hobbled over to the riverbank and sat down on the mud-covered beach. *Damn! This river is full of diseases!* I thought. The first thing I did was let the wound bleed for a good five minutes. Then I took some old dried rags I found lying in the grass, wrapped my foot in them, and waded back to the boat.

Memories of people lying sick in cheap hotel beds all over Cairo from blood poisoning haunted me. Most of them were foreigners down with dysentery and other food—and water-related illnesses. My mind recalled other harrowing stories about the Nile River water possessing the worst infectious bugs in the world. Just then the captain called out to the boy to get back in the boat because the water was rising again. The smiles on their faces put hope in my heart, so I sat there calmly praying like I did in the Argentinean fort for the good Lord to heal my foot and take care of the sick people back in Cairo.

Two days later, I was walking on my foot like nothing had happened, without any fever whatsoever. One evening after eating fresh fish caught by our hosts, I went to sit on some boulders overlooking the river. A few minutes later, the two young French women came up to sit down next to me. They shyly greeted me and asked where I was from and how long I had been traveling. After answering a few more personal questions, one of the girls finally came out with it to ask me if I would do them a favor.

"Sure, what do you need?" I asked.

"For the last two nights, the captain and his son or assistant have been trying to get into our sleeping bags. We still have four more days till we reach Cairo. Could you protect us?"

By the looks on their faces, I could tell they had not slept in the last couple of days. Their hair was a mess, and there were rings under their eyes. They looked to be about nineteen or twenty years old.

"What do you want me to do?" I asked.

"Would you sleep next to us? Maybe if they see you so close to us, they will leave us alone."

Judging by the look on their faces, they were genuinely scared and serious. "Sure, I'll do it."

They thanked me and returned to the boat. For the next couple of nights, I hardly slept because the girls were right. Out of the corner of my eye, the two Arabs made subtle moves toward the sleeping girls, so I would sit up and stare at the horny captain and his young playboy.

The next day we ran out of water and still had a good day's journey to reach the next fishing village with available water. That night while sitting up and watching over the two French girls, I noticed the two Arabs bending over the side of the boat to scoop water into their tea glasses. They would then drink them down without boiling the water. My throat was parched and my body thirsted something bad, so I prayed to God to let me drink some of the water.

In my broken Arabic, I asked the captain why he was not afraid to drink the water. Using sign language and speaking Arabic, I understood that we were over a deep part of the river where clean water wells up from way under the surface and comes to the top. *Well, Lord, into Your hands I trust my life,* I thought as I reached over the bow and scooped up a couple of glasses of Nile River water and drank it down. The night passed by tranquilly as I sat up thinking about the river, the earth, the moon, and the stars. Something in me told me the river was not going to harm me.

When we arrived in Cairo, the Australian couple was grateful for the ride, and the others thanked me for all my help. The Swedish woman showed me the way to the American Consulate because I needed an extension on my visa to stay in Egypt. Inside the consulate, I recognized two men from the same hotel flat I had stayed in. They were from Haiti and about my age. They too needed visas to stay longer in Cairo because they were waiting for some business transaction to take place before leaving Egypt. One of the Haitians told me the consulate told him he had to wait a minimum of two weeks to get his visa. They were planning on going down to Nigeria to visit relatives of theirs, but they needed entrance visas. The more they described Nigeria to me, the more interested I became in going with them. "We will take you der, mahn. You will have a guud time, mahn."

As time dragged on in Cairo waiting for visas, I went back to the Giza Plateau. This time I went inside and climbed up into the King's Chamber. Even with a few babbling tourists, it was profoundly quiet inside the chamber. I sat down on one end of the room facing the open coffin. After careful consideration of the inner passageways and room sizes in proportion to the overall size of this pyramid, something in me knew that the architects of this structure had something else in mind other than its use as a monument for burying some dead king's body.

There came a moment when the room emptied out and I was alone by myself. This gave me the opportunity to revel in the awesome silence. As a matter of fact, after a few minutes of purposely breathing slowly and quietly, I could hear not only my loud heartbeat but also the blood rhythmically pulsing through certain arteries from the heart on up through my brain. My self-consciousness seemed to drift from the area of my brain to other parts throughout my body, focusing on specific areas of my anatomy.

For example, I saw how the electric synapses fired when transferring a message from one brain cell to another. Then in another instant, I could see clearly what the inside of one of my lungs looked like and how oxygen atoms passed through the membrane of their air sacks to be absorbed by blood cells passing through a fine network of capillaries within the transparent sacks. Next, it would wander down to one of my feet, and I could see not only the incredible amount of bones in my foot but also how the muscles and ligaments were designed to aid the heart by pushing blood back up the long limbs of my legs when I walk on them. These and other conscious visions of the interior of my body took place until they were interrupted by tourists crawling into the chamber.

Upon exiting the Great Pyramid, I walked over to the pyramid about half as big and climbed to the top of it. As I gazed at the Great Pyramid, my mind ruminated over the colossal stones in the king's chamber and how precisely each stone was cut and placed with a thumbnail thickness of mortar all the way around it. My mind refused to believe that ordinary men built this thing, so who built it? Whoever built it had to be an extraordinary being. The builder would have had to possess supreme knowledge of math, geometry, and the physical sciences, especially astronomy. Why was it built? After that intense personal experience inside the king's chamber, I was convinced it was built to enlighten the human soul on the mysteries of natural life, and perhaps even supernatural life.

Two mathematicians named John Taylor and Sir John Herschel discovered that the number of perimeter units (based on the cubit) of the Great Pyramid coincided with 366, the number of days in the solar year. Their deductions and conclusions came very close to the modern measurement of the earth's circumference. There are other mathematical discoveries of secrets hidden in the Great Pyramid using the number 366. "Taylor concluded that the proportions of the Pyramid had definitely been intended to incorporate geometric and astronomical laws simply and easily expressed, and that its purpose had been to preserve and pass on this knowledge to future generations."[23]

After nearly thirty years since that experience in the king's chamber, first, I would venture to say the man named Enoch who lived 365 years before "God took him" (Ge 5:24), built the Great Pyramid before Noah's

---

[23]   Tompkins, Peter. *The Secrets of the Great Pyramid*. Harper & Row Pub.: New York (1971) 75.

ark and the great flood. Second, if I may be so bold, Enoch, who "walked with God" (5:24), must have had a very close relationship with God. God, therefore, as He did for Noah to build an ark, gave the instructions and the power to Enoch to not only build an eternal monument but also a place, if used wisely, to assist a person in discovering his or her eternal self. After all, Enoch did not die like the rest of his ancestors; he simply "was no longer here" (5:24). Perhaps, by the grace of God, Enoch discovered his eternal self and learned how to transcend body and soul into the next life. Third, I would even like to humbly speculate that the reason the Great Pyramid was built was to aid a God-fearing, Christ loving human being to discover and learn to imitate Jesus' transfiguration of the body.

My two Haitian friends were running out of time and money. The Egyptian Consulate refused to give them extensions on their visas, so one of them asked me if I would lend him some money to go finish business with someone in Alexandria. "You lend me five hundred dollars and I will pay you back double in three days, mahn." Like a fool, I gave him the money.

The other Haitian and I waited three days, four days, five, six, and by the end of ten days with no sight of his friend, I said, "I'm outta here, man. I can't take sleeping with cockroaches and dealing with annoying Arabs anymore. I'm going to France." He practically started crying and told me not to leave him alone in this God-forsaken hellhole of a country.

"Well, what do you want me to do, man?" I asked him.

"Give me money to buy a ticket to France, and I will meet you in a place called Taize." I had already bought my ticket on a flight scheduled to leave in two days.

"Look," I said, "how can I trust you after your friend took off with my money?"

He put his head down and said, "You can trust me, muhn. He betrayed me too. I will be there, and I will pay you back everything we owe you." So, like a bigger fool, I gave him five hundred dollars too. He came with me to the airport and saw me off to France. When I shook his hand good-bye, somehow I knew that would be the last time we would see each other.

The plane touched down in Charles DeGaulle International Airport outside Paris, France. My only desire was to catch a train to Taize and get out of that huge city as soon as possible. The hustle and bustle of large cities always made me nervous. Paris, for all its glitz and glamour, was just another big, traffic-congested noise trap. The only thing I knew about Taize was that it was south of Paris. It took a good hour on foot to reach a sub-station to the main train station. When I got there, the ticket clerk told me there were no trains available until tomorrow.

That did it. "I'm hitchhiking," I said to myself as I picked up my pack. Within a half hour's walk from the train station there was an on ramp to a major highway. A blue sign read "Toulouse sur" on it, so I stood next to it with my thumb up. Fifteen minutes went by when suddenly a little car pulled over and a young woman said something in French. She immediately understood I couldn't speak French, so she asked in broken English, "Where are you going?"

I responded, "Oh, I am going to Taize."

She pushed the door open and motioned me to get in. God is amazing. It turned out that this girl not only knew where Taize was, but she lived in a town close by the place.

The French girl drove for several hours in silence. Long days without much sleep in Egypt caught up to me as I dozed off in the passenger seat. It was late in the evening when we finally stopped. She got out of the car in someone's driveway and told me to come inside. An older woman, probably her mom, greeted us at the door. They took me into the kitchen for something to eat, but the expression on my face was not one of hunger, so the girl showed me to a guest room and said, "See you tomorrow." When she shut the door, all I can remember was closing my eyes and opening them in the morning.

After a good night's sleep and a quick breakfast, the French girl drove me to a fork in the road where I could catch a ride to Taize. *"Ale, bon voyage,"* she said as she drove off. Taize was only twenty minutes away by car, and someone else dropped me off in front of a monastery. There were hundreds of people milling around a wooden church building about fifty yards from the road. Many of them were standing in food lines serving themselves outdoor breakfast, so I joined in to mingle a little. After breakfast, I went over to what looked like an office. There were some people inside who spoke English, so I asked them if I could stay for a while to wait for a friend coming from Africa. They said yes and showed me where to camp out.

For the first week, I walked around, observed the action, and learned what the different groups of people from all over the world engaged in. In the second week, I met a young man from Uganda who was deciding whether or not to become a priest. He told me Taize was formed by an ecumenical religious group of men to provide a place where people could come and make a spiritual retreat. The chapel held daily masses and confessions every day.

In the evenings, the people would gather to participate in meditations or chants during certain hours. On some days the chapel was full and other days it was nearly empty. It had been years since my last confession or mass attendance, and I was not interested in going back to church. Instead, I spent two more weeks walking around the countryside and waiting for the Haitian to show up from Africa. Toward the end of my fourth week in Taize, this gullible American knew he had been fooled and taken.

Having carefully studied a map of Europe in the Taize reception office, I decided to head south to the Pyrenees Mountains. Mountains had proved to be good places of refuge in my life so far, and perhaps I would find some more answers to the reason of my existence between France and Spain.

A Stone Mason's Challenge

By a road in the middle of France stood a wayfaring American thumbing in the southerly direction when a car pulled over to give him a ride. This time a Frenchman about my age opened the door and asked me where I was going.

"To the Pyrenees Mountains," I said.

"Get in," he said, "I am going there too!"

The man, whose name was Giles, had a small chateau house in the French Pyrenees, and he enjoyed going there on his days off. He was close in age to me, and he dreamed of adventures in America, so he was curious as to why I was hitchhiking in France. For him America was where a young person should be traveling, not France. After hearing some of my stories and experiences in South America, he saw that I was actually living out what he dreamed of. We spent a few days walking in the mountains around his house and visiting a few small villages in the area. They were mostly farming towns whose occupants participated in some form of generational related business. There were a mixture of French, Spanish, Catalan, and Basque languages spoken throughout the region.

One afternoon, we sat down to have a beer in the plaza located in the middle of a little medieval village called Eus. Eus was a village full of old stone houses built on a hillside with a splendid view of the Pyrenees mountain range to the southwest. Giles and I were sipping on our beers when he casually asked if I was interested in finding work. "We are in the middle of grape season. Maybe someone is looking for a grape picker. Do you want me to ask around?"

The thought of working in a vineyard in France sounded good. "Sure, why not?" I responded.

Giles got up and said, "Stay here while I inquire in the local shops."

About twenty minutes later, he came back to tell me that no one was looking for a farm worker, but he had talked at length with a man in the bakery who needed a hod-carrier. When he mentioned the word hod-carrier, I immediately reflected back on my high school days working as a hod-carrier on the weekends. My friend's dad worked in construction, and every once in a while he needed someone to help carry bricks and mortar on the job. It was hard work, but the pay was good.

"Do you have any experience in construction?" asked Giles.

"A little," I said.

"He can't speak English, but he can speak some Spanish. Are you interested?" he asked.

After downing my beer, I said, "Let's go meet him."

A tall, lanky, middle-aged man with a hunched back greeted me with a smile and a strong handshake. "Hello, my name is Guy Galear. Can you speak Spanish?" he asked, almost yelling.

"Si, senor!" I yelled back.

He laughed and was relieved to hear that I did because he could not speak any English beyond the word hello. We spoke in broken Spanish, and he seemed to enjoy expressing himself in a different language. There was something about this man's spirited character that made me want to work with him. We walked over to one of his job sites near the plaza. He and a couple of men were in the process of pouring concrete on the cellar floor of an old house. When he finished giving his men some instructions, he turned toward me and asked, "*Hombre! Quieres trabajar?* Man! You want to work?" I said, "Si." Then he asked if I was willing to earn a little less but learn the trade of stone masonry. I said, "Si, hombre!" He nodded his head and told me to come to the plaza in two weeks and that he would put me to work.

With two weeks to kill, I decided to go over the Pyrenees Mountains and into Spain. This gave me the opportunity to do some hiking in the Aguas Tortas mountain range near Andorra, one of the smallest countries in the world. One thing I learned about Europe is that people like to hike. There were mountain trails all over the place equipped with little bunkhouses for long-distance backpackers going over high passes. I didn't like the beaten trails, so I would sleep out in desolate places. One morning, right after sunrise, I caught a glimpse of a herd of wild, high mountain goats grazing at a ten thousand—foot pass. The wind was blowing the opposite direction, so I was able to watch them for a long time. It was a beautiful scene.

My travels in Spain went no further south than Madrid. Carmen had given me her phone number before the Swede and I left the ski resort, so when I arrived in Madrid, she immediately arranged to see me when she got my call. We met somewhere in what looked like a business district. She was very excited to see me, and after wandering around in another big city, I was glad to see her too. We wined and dined and enjoyed each other's company for three days before I had to return to France. She was surprised to know that I had been employed in France. "*Vas a vivir en Francia?* Are you going to live in France?" she asked.

"*Quizas.* Maybe," I responded.

"*Llamame.* Call me!" she yelled out as the train pulled away.

The train went as far as Zaragoza, so from there I had to hitchhike my way back into France. A young couple picked me up at the base of the Spanish Pyrenees on their way to Andorra. In some places, the road over the mountain range was steep and slippery due to melting snow. At around eight thousand feet we came to a bridge crossing a small river on the outside of a high mountain town called Seo de Urgel.

The woman driving the car was engaged in a very animated discussion with her boyfriend as we approached the bridge. Looking ahead from the backseat, I could see ice on the bridge and instinctively knew that if she doesn't slow down a bit, she was about to take a left hand turn on to a slippery bridge with way too much speed. It was too late to say anything. As soon as she turned on to the bridge, the car slid way to the right while she attempted to straighten it out. Then, because she overcorrected her turn, the car went into a spin, and somewhere over the middle of the bridge, the car went up the left curb, smashed into a two-foot stone barrier, and flipped over to fall into the canyon below upside down.

The same out-of-control falling sensation happened again. Everything went into slow motion, and my body felt like it was suspended in time and space, only this time the impact was noticeable. The car landed smack dab in the middle of the river. Instinctively, I braced myself for impact by pushing against the ceiling of the car. The water absorbed most of the shock upon touchdown. For a few moments there was dead silence in the car, and then I pushed open the door before it sank to the bottom. When I got out of the car, the other two were still in it, so I pulled open the driver's door and helped the woman out while the boyfriend managed his way out by himself.

As we stood on the bank of the river, dripping wet, we all stared at the position of the car. It had fallen in the only section of the river below the bridge where there was a pool of water deep enough to take the shock out of the crushing fall. If we had fallen five to ten feet away from anywhere around its position in the pool, we would either be dead or badly injured. We all walked away wet, alive, and smiling.

After drying out and wandering in the mountains until the two weeks were up, I returned to Eus. Guy the stonemason was working on a house a few blocks from the plaza. One of his workers, a man from Algeria, told me Guy had gone to get some supplies and would be back soon. While waiting for his return, I took a little tour around the village. Everything in the village was made of stone. It had cobblestone streets, stone fences, an old Gothic Catholic church made in stone, stone stairways, public baths made in stone, and stone fountains. The view from the steps of the church was the best view in town, since it was located at the highest point above Eus. There was only one road in and out of the town; it had no thoroughfare. As I stood staring out at the view, a little two-cylinder Citroen car came around the bend and putted up the hill toward Eus. It was Guy. I could recognize his profile hunched over the steering wheel.

The little car pulled up by the edge of the plaza just as I came down from above the town. Guy smiled to himself when he turned and saw me walking across the plaza.

"*Hombre! Como estas!* Man! How are you!" he yelled out.

"*Estoy bien, gracias*! I'm fine, thanks!"

It was funny to see such a tall man get out of a tiny car. He came over and shook my hand with a big smile, "Are you ready to start work?" he asked.

"I am ready," I replied.

He turned and motioned me to follow him to a house adjacent the plaza. He opened the front door and walked in with a hammer and chisel in his hands. We went straight through the living room to the back wall. Drawn in pencil on the wall looked like the dimensions for a three-foot by five-foot window. He put the chisel with his left hand against the wall, and with a few steady, swift hammer blows, he dug out a stone from the wall. He knocked out a few more before he stopped, turned toward me, handed me the tools, and said, "*A ti te toca*, it's your turn."

I took the tools in my hands and chiseled out a stone, and another, and another. He stopped me and said, "*Eres bueno con las manos, hombre!* You are good with your hands man!" He then told me to keep taking stones out but not to go past the pencil drawing on the wall. "I'll be back to check on you later," he said and then left the house.

It felt good to be doing something with my hands again. As I pounded away on the wall, there was a sense of well-being flowing through my veins. It was like I was meant to be there in this house working for this stonemason at this very moment in my life. I did not even know this man—his culture, his language, his history—and yet I inwardly knew he was a dependable man who made me feel safe, secure, and wanted. There was something in his actions and facial expressions that spoke louder than words. The man was easy to read. He had a simple, transparent soul that lit the room up no matter who was in it. People talked to him as if he were their brother or best friend. My inner instincts told me it would be a joy to learn a new trade from this tall, thin, funny-looking Frenchman.

By the time Guy came back to inspect my work, the wall had a good-size hole in it, with a view of the mountains behind it. *"Ay, hombre! Vamonos!"* he shouted after looking over the hole with a smile on his deeply lined face. We walked together down a few stone-covered streets and stopped in front of a little, single-story stone cottage. He pulled out a key from his pocket and unlocked the door.

"Pase adentro a tu casa. Come into your house," he said while telling me that this would be my living quarters in Eus while working for him. My eyes scanned the joint with delight, especially when they came upon a large window with a magnificent view of the valley, river, and mountains. Guy then took me upstairs to a little flat rooftop that had a couple of lounge chairs and table overlooking the whole town of Eus and the region of Catalonia. It was a beautiful afternoon, and the breeze felt good since it was a hot summer day. Guy told me to sit down and enjoy the view as he descended to the kitchen to climb back up with two French beers in his hands. The expression on his face told me that he was not only satisfied with my work but that he was also happy about having an American interested in working for him. We conversed for a good half hour about our likes and dislikes and things in general. He then gave me the rest of the day off to move in and enjoy the town.

For the rest of the afternoon and well into the night, I reflected on the providential care God had shown me throughout my travels. The good Lord always made sure that no matter where I went, He would put a roof over my head, food on a table, and clothes on my back. In other words, no matter how many struggles came my way, as long as I hung in there and put my trust in Him, all my physical needs would be met. This reflection caused me to realize that nothing really happens by chance. I recognized that as difficult and mysterious life is, as long as I continued to make room for God in my day, God would make available a new piece of the puzzle of life to me. From that day on, I decided to make sure a day would not go by without spending at least a few moments of it devoted only to the contemplation of God.

Guy was of the old school of stonemasonry because he believed in restoring old stone houses by hand and not by machine. This was truly a delight because we would go into the mountain forests with hand saws and axes to cut down timber to make wooden beams; we would go down to the river to shovel sand from its banks to make mortar; we would quarry and load our own stone to build walls. Most of the labor was done by hand tools like shovels, hammers, and chisels instead of electric or gas-powered tools. Laying stones in a wall is not like laying bricks or blocks. Bricks and blocks have uniform dimensions that allow the bricklayer to move along course after course with ease. A stonemason needs to develop an eye for spotting stones that will interlock with each other in a somewhat jigsaw puzzle like manner. Since stones vary in size, there are no uniform courses. Last but not least, a good stonemason needs to know how to cut stones with a hammer.

For the first few months of work, I learned how to quarry stones, collect sand, and mix mortar. Outside the village, down in a dry part of the riverbed, I learned how to crack open large granite rocks with a sledgehammer. Then I would take a smaller hammer to chip away at the round edges to give it more of a rectangular shape. I used a chisel when I needed to make a more precise cut. When Guy noticed that I was capable of producing a significant number of hand-cut stones per day, he gave me a chance to lay some stones in a wall. At first it was a struggle, but once I got a stone set in place that fit snug without rocking or slipping out of place, I felt a sense of accomplishment. As the work grew substantially larger, I was able to step back and say, "This is going to be here for a long time." Some of the houses that I worked on were ten or more centuries old!

At the end of a workday, I would wander up into the hills above the village of Eus to bask in the silence and contemplate the mysteries of God and life in general. About an hour's hike away, I happened upon an old, abandoned village where only a couple of shepherds lived. During the two world wars, the people who lived in the valley retreated to the hills, where they hid out and then went back to Eus and their villages in the valley below after the great wars were over. One thing I noticed in other abandoned villages similar to the one above Eus is that they all had a little Catholic chapel located near the center of the village. Guy told me that he worked in some of the old Catholic churches and that one day he would take me to visit some of the more famous castles and cathedrals in the southern region of France. Guy loved history, especially history of Catholic art and cathedrals.

One day on one of my afternoon hikes into the high country, I decided to visit one of the ancient Catholic churches and just sit in one of them and pray. My daily hikes, meditations, and silent retreats into sacred places of past generations slowly shook the tree and irritated another old entity—my age-old enemy who comes from a dark and deadly world. Mentally tired and physically exhausted from banging on rocks all day long and struggling to make them fit into a wall left me with only enough time to eat and sleep after my daily hikes. Before falling asleep, I would sit on the windowsill and stare out into the countryside in silence. Sometimes I would hum a song or utter a few prayers the nuns had taught me in school. These were the same prayers I recollected during my imprisonment in the Argentinean fort.

One night at around 3:00 in the morning, a dark visitor came into my room. My ears perked up at some strange noise that sounded like it came through the window with the view. I would leave the window open at night to let in fresh air, especially during the summer months. Whatever it was, I heard it pass through the room and go downstairs to where the kitchen was. It then returned to the living room floor where my mattress was situated and came toward me. My whole body fixed on it, as if I had eyeballs in my hands, feet, chest, legs, arms, and all the rest of me. I remember going into the typical paralyzed state, but my mind reminded me to take a deep breath before it got any closer. As soon as I sucked in a lung full of air, the dark visitor retreated back toward the open window, and I woke up. I got up and ran over to the window to take a quick glance outside to see if anyone was on the roof. There was no object in sight or anything to be heard, only darkness and the silent, nighttime stillness.

As I climbed up on the windowsill, I decided to sit down and hang my feet outside to think about what just happened and why these evil spirits kept coming after me. It had been a hot day, so the cool summer's night air helped me reflect on my most recent vision and recall past terrifying incidents.

It slowly dawned on me that this current dream, this current spirit, was connected and followed similar patterns to the other past dark incidents and past evil spirits searching to destroy a possible threat: me. For some reason, the dark powers wanted me dead. Not only did they want to choke the life out of me by night, but they also attempted to kill me by day. In two incidents, they tried to kill me by leading me off a cliff and pushing me off a bridge in broad daylight. But why me? I was a nobody—a little man lost in time and space wandering around the earth looking for his place in it. *Maybe that's why these things are coming after me*, I thought to myself, *because I am making an all-out effort to try and discover the truth of who I really am!*

Another connection came to mind. Every time I made a serious attempt to pray, meditate, or contemplate on the mysterious things in life, especially on God, these evil incidents would occur. When I was busy traveling, skiing down mountains, doing immoral acts, or getting angry or frustrated at work, I posed no threat to evil powers and their designs. It was only when I would settle down in a place for a while and try to venture into God's realm, searching into His plan for me, that evil visitors tried to thrash me. I was damned if I did, and I was damned if I didn't. In other words, I would be attacked by devils and demons if I prayed, and I would be condemned to spend an eternity with evil spirits if I didn't pray for God's protection.

The lyrics from a stupid old song, "We Can Be Together" by Jefferson Airplane plagued my mind as I meditated on my predicament. As the dawn approached, there was only one way to deal with this predicament: keep praying no matter how much torture the evil spirits put me through. I was tired of being cornered against a wall, afraid and harassed by these ugly things from hell. *It's either I kill them or they kill me*, I said to myself. *It's time for war. I must face these things with courage, and may God help me.*

Spiritual Agony and Ecstasy

The hot summer months passed into the warm months of autumn, and before long the first winds of winter blew into Eus. My skills in stonemasonry were moving along in time also. Building walls in stone picked up speed the more my senses grew accustomed to certain suitable shapes. My eyes and hands developed a keen sense of selection for the right stone when browsing among the rocks in the riverbeds. Also, the more I worked with stone, the more I appreciated the lives of the men who built such magnificent churches and cathedrals in Europe. There was something very satisfying about building in stone.

Guy took me around to various old forts and castles throughout the region to show me a few details found in ancient stone works. Some of the most extraordinary stonework was found in old monasteries. The walls in these old buildings were three feet thick or more at the base. The towers could stretch up to a height of a ten-story building and still measure eighteen inches thick. The ornate, hand-chiseled artwork found inside and around the outside of the old stone churches was impressive and attracted me all the more to learn the trade.

Day after day, I enjoyed the challenge of learning on all three fronts: physical, mental, and spiritual. As my trade skills increased, Guy gave me more access to actually cut and lay finished stone on my own. From sunup to sundown, I buried myself in work, learning and developing stonemasonry skills, exploring the terrain on foot, and practicing silent prayer, especially at night. Without the heat and humidity of long summer days to make me groggy, I was able to do some reading in the evenings. The only book I could find in English was the Bible, but it helped to train my thought. Of the three fronts, the spiritual one was the most difficult to tame and control.

One night, after reading the Bible and sitting up for a long meditation and silent reflection, I lay down on the mattress and closed my eyes. Not quite fully asleep, I heard something land on the sill of my favorite window that I kept open during the night. Immediately, an alarm went off inside me, and my eyes snapped open to see what it was as my body went into high alert. My involuntary reaction to this thing told me that whatever it was standing on the windowsill was not an owl or anything natural to the area. My eyes zoomed in and focused on what looked like a fat, ugly, bird-like creature. It then jumped down from the sill and landed with a plop on my floor.

Without blinking an eye, I quickly sat up to watch its moves. Next, it turned and came toward me while expanding itself into a large, bat-like creature readying itself to jump on me. Only this time, I looked directly at it and said something like, "Oh no you don't." Then suddenly these laser-like beams of light shot out of my eyes right back at this dark, life-threatening thing. It began to shrink down to a tiny, weird, rat-like thing that ran from one corner of the room to the other, trying to avoid my gaze until it shrunk down so small that it ended up exploding into thin air.

I remember throwing my arms up in the air and yelling, "Yeah! I got ya!" Then I noticed my arms were glowing like the color of the moon. I thought, *That's strange, the moon is not shining through the window.* I didn't care. I felt good and happy for the first time in a long time. I got up and started putting my pants on. That's when I noticed my legs were glowing also. When I straightened up and stood next to my mattress, my body felt like it had the strength of ten men. *How strange. Oh well,* I thought, and then I had a deep urge to go outside for a walk.

When I took a step toward the front door, it was as if my body glided over the floor with no effort at all. When I stopped in front of the door, my mind tried to make sense of what had just happened because things were moving so wonderfully swift that it didn't have time to think. I could hardly wait to open the door because something in me wanted to go to the moon! As my glowing hand reached for the door, my vision seized upon a warm and beautiful light coming down from above my head. When I looked up at it, my body stood still, as if it were caught by a parent stopping a child from doing something dangerous.

This nonthreatening, beautiful form of light came down from above the ceiling, descended to the floor, and stood right next to me. Whatever it was, it had a very tender but powerful presence. When I looked at it, it reached out its glowing but much brighter hand and took my arm. Without saying a word, I obediently let it gently pull me by my arm back to the foot of my mattress. It stopped next to my bed, turned, and looked down. When I looked down, I saw someone lying there asleep. Then I took a step closer and thought, *It's my brother Dave.* Dave is one year younger than I am.

With a tone of surprise in my voice, I called out to him and asked, "Dave! What are you doing here?" My brother opened his eyes and cringed at me with an expression of fear on his face. Then I remember saying to him, "Dave, it's me, your brother," but he got even more frightened, so I reached down to grab his hand. He then hesitantly reached up to shake my hand. In a split second before our two hands met, a lightning rod-like spark jumped between our hands. In another split second, I felt a sensation comparable to an electrical surge draining out of me and rushing into my brother. The next thing I knew, it was dark and I was lying in my bed, back to normal again. I sat up and noticed that my arms and legs were no longer glowing. In amazement, I reached over and turned on the light, got up out of bed, and walked around the room, trying to figure out what had just happened.

This was the first time in my life that I woke up after going through one of these types of dreams with a smile on my face. Immediately after having a dream like this, I would usually be filled with anxiety and paranoia, but not this time. This time I spent a good couple of hours joyfully reflecting back on that victorious, extraordinary event. It slowly dawned on me that the person lying in the bed was not my brother but my own sleeping body. The person who floated to the door feeling like ten men wrapped into one was my supernatural self. The evil spirit that disintegrated in a puff of smoke could have been inside of me and wanted to get back in, or it could have been another one trying to get into me for the first time. Either way, God allowed me to see what it was and trash it.

Then God gave me a taste of being in heaven. Words can only attempt to describe what I experienced next, because they fail to convey anything near the reality of it. The whole atmosphere in that room was very different and super-alive while I was in my supernatural state. It was the most amazing and powerfully beautiful moment I have ever experienced in my life. As I remember back, the air was like some kind of vibrant, roseate liquid that surrounded my body with a warm, living love sensation all over me. Every one of my senses was at peak performance. My hearing was as good as new and even better because I had lost some hearing in my left ear years before due to excessive shop noise and ear infections. In some surround sound distant background, I could actually hear many faint melodic voices coming in layers stretching way beyond the room.

The room smelled like my favorite foods that seemed to quench both my thirst and satisfy my hunger. My vision has never been so clear and perceptive as it was at that moment. A light that made every object come alive and emit a particular living color during the whole event lighted up the room. I didn't care where such a beautiful light came from in the middle of a pitch-black night. All I knew at the time was that it did not come from the moon or a lamp. The question on the origin of this light came later, and it took years of a type of mystagogic (an unfolding of the mysterious event) reflection to discover the answer.

Since this extraordinary night, the demons have not been able to come very close to me. There have been several attempts since then, but each time one tries to invade my body, my soul chases it off. What made this night such a victorious event was that I knew in my heart—a heart so full of joy at this precious moment in my life—that this was real. I did not know what reality was until that night. The world and the flesh are only a shadow of what is real. That night, God confirmed, or better yet, He let me confirm for myself, that the Devil and evil spirits are real and must be defeated. Until that night, I thought demons and evil spirits were just dreams or imaginations that really did not need to be taken seriously. After all the attacks I had suffered in the past, I could not bring myself to fully accept the fact that they could be real. When a person *sees* the truth or reality of something so mysterious and yet known to exist, that person must believe it, or so help him or her God! I would be a fool not to believe in what happened that night after personally experiencing simultaneous life in both my natural and supernatural bodies. After that experience, to deny the existence of my divinized self would mean to deny the existence of my human self and vice versa.

"May the eyes of your hearts [your innermost vision] be enlightened that you may know . . . the immeasurable scope of His power in us who believe" (Eph 1:18-19).

The Devil or evil spirit up to this point in my life was always elusive, but now it could not get away. Something in me had developed more power over the elusive dark enemy. For the first time, the Devil was caught and held by a beam of light under whose power it could not break loose. The more I kept my eyes fixed on it, the more it shrank down to utter disintegration. What I did not know then was that I was dealing with a real demon, not just an imaginary evil spirit. There is a difference between the two groups of evil spirits, and there seems to be many more imaginary evil spirits than demons.

Evil spirits, on one hand, are more like psychological thoughts that swarm the mind like clouds of annoying insects in order to be effective. Demons, on the other hand, consist of a hierarchical power according to their rank. Demons are more versatile and can take on a natural life form. They can take on a bodily form and can even touch human beings. Evil thoughts cannot touch people's bodies. Evil thoughts can conjure up spiritual images that affect people's minds and moods if a person allows them into their interior. This is what brings on temptation to sin. When we commit ourselves to unjust temptations, we become vulnerable. Committing to sin opens up holes to our inner sanctuary and eventually to our souls. Demons take full advantage to enter into an undisciplined person's interior realm and are capable of causing physical harm and even immediate death. As a matter of personal fact, that is what they wanted to achieve with me and still try to do. When demons come after you, it is because you threaten them. They will do everything in their power to kill your body before your soul gains enough power to expose them and cast them into hell. The remedy is power from God, which is what I was personally discovering through prayer and moral self-control.

Ever since that night in Eus, France, in 1982, I have come to the understanding that demons have been desperately trying to kill my body and steal my soul. Once a person's soul is outside of his or her dead body, without God's help, the person cannot go back inside the body. The body remains dead. That night, God empowered my body and soul to defend itself from another demonic attack. The demon again tried to steal my soul, but it failed. Then God preserved my mortal body after the confrontation to allow my soul to experience its immortal body. But! If the demon had succeeded in chasing my soul away from my mortal body before I was given the power to ward it off, I would not have been able to destroy it, disintegrate it, cast it into hell, or whatever I did to the infernal thing. I would have been powerless and at the mercy of the demon to do whatever it wanted with my soul because I would have had no power to fight it off. This is why it is so important to learn who God is and to at least have some access to His divine power while we are still alive. Divine power comes from certain types of grace provided to us through faith and trust in God, even blind faith.

It is horrifying to imagine what happens to a poor soul at death who cannot return to its dead body and is stuck outside of it, powerless to defend itself. From my experiences with demons or evil spirits, they are not always alone. There can be others that could swarm around a soul like sharks to a wounded fish, vultures to a dying animal, or flies to a festering wound. Perhaps a soul that rejected God could easily be stolen away from its body at death and drug into hell by evil spirits. One could speculate to say that purgatory could involve a defenseless soul stalked by coyote-like demons chasing its prey from one end of the universe to the other until it is rescued by God's angels. Demons or evil spirits show no mercy because they have no mercy, only hatred of God and His creatures. The Catholic Church teaches that souls who die in the state of mortal sin will end up in hell, whereas souls not completely in the state of grace must undergo a time of purification.

"Go Home to Your Roots"

Guy picked up a house renovation project across the river in the valley below Eus. A young family from Paris moved into the region and was fortunate enough to meet Guy Galear while they were touring Eus one day. The new landowners had two old houses that needed major repairs. The husband and wife were both involved in the theatre, so they had a very different lifestyle compared to the Catalonian country folk. These people were city slickers, not the farming type. The country people were very plain and simple. The city people were very elegant and sophisticated. The only ones they considered their friends for the first year in the region were Guy, his workers, and me.

Their houses needed wall restoration, a new roof that included hand-hewn wooden crossbeams, and old, classic roofing tiles. The amount of work needed on their property was ongoing and lasted the whole time I was in France. The job was only a pleasant half-hour walk from my house, plus it gave me an opportunity to go down to the river after work to enjoy the peaceful brook. On the weekends, I would go swimming in an area where there was a fairly deep pool by the bridge. The river inspired me to pray and helped me empty my head full of mental frustration from daily work-related challenges. It also helped me to concentrate and stay focused on certain peaceful sights and sounds in the area. Every day, I religiously followed a routine of prayer, work, relaxation, and more prayer before retiring for the night in my stone house in Eus.

As the winter grew colder and wetter, outside work slowed down to almost a stand still. The new French family took a liking to me since they could speak some English and a little Spanish. The woman, Florina would teach me some French during lunch breaks, and the man, Jacque, would discuss French culture and other topics after work. Guy put me in charge of doing the finish work and other indoor jobs, like tiling and plastering, during the long winter months. Both Jacque and Florina enjoyed discussing various topics covering religion, science, politics, and history with me. They even took me to French cinema, foreign movies, local theatrical plays, and musical concerts put on by folkloric artists in the region.

After the winter solstice, the snows began to fall in the hills above Eus. The Pyrenees Mountains were covered with a white blanket, and my stone house turned into an icebox at night. The cold, damp weather, the strenuous work schedule, and malnourishment caught up to me. One day while working outside on the family's chicken coop, I noticed a deep red streak climbing up my left arm from my hand. When I showed it to Guy, he immediately took me to see a doctor. The doctor said I had blood poisoning, so he put me on some antibiotics and told me not to work for ten days. When Florina found out about my health condition, she gave me some homegrown medicine and offered to wrap clay over a large boil in the middle of my left palm every evening before I returned to Eus. In a week, the blood poison was gone and the clay pack had cleared up the boil in my left hand. My body felt better, so I went back to work.

That was a mistake because apparently my immune system was weak and not up to par. Within two weeks, I developed several canker sores inside my mouth that brought on a bad sinus infection and cold. Jacques and Florina caught colds also from their little boy, who brought it home from school. Next the little boy developed the flu, and since he liked playing with me, I got the flu too. The infection then turned into a long-lasting flu that eventually led to an ear infection. The ear infection started affecting my equilibrium, so once again, Guy took me to another doctor. My health got so bad that I had to stay in bed for several days. Guy would come by once in a while to bring me something warm to drink. Each day I would force myself to walk over to the family's house, where Florina would serve me a healthy noontime meal.

The cold, wintry days seemed like they would never end. Every morning I woke up to a grey sky that chiseled away at my spirits. The cold rain and dampness felt like it went to the bone. When I tried going for a walk, chills would run all over my body and drive me back inside the cold house. The only thing I could do was wrap myself in blankets to keep warm and wait for spring. I had been in the snow and colder climates before but never so sick and physically rundown. My mind started in on me also. It conjured up lonely thoughts, thoughts of being forever a loner and dying alone in some desolate, faraway place with no one around who cared or even noticed I was gone. Depression is like a stagnant pond filled with detestable creatures that slowly suffocate you to death. It has a way of gnawing at your person, your beliefs, and the image of yourself, thus making you feel like nothing and that life is empty and meaningless.

Then I remembered the man Jesus of Nazareth who, after spending several hours in deep depression the night before He died. As lonely and empty as that moment was, He freely went and died on a cross with conviction and without fear. What made Him do that? How could He be so sure that that was the right thing to do? Then something in me said, "He did the right thing, and He did it for you." That's when I got up and reached for that Book and opened it up to the New Testament. Only this time, I didn't just read the words on the life of Jesus; I ate them, chewed on them, and let them pass all the way through me, whoever me was. My meditations and prayers lasted hours and went on for days. I lost track of time, but I didn't care because somehow time didn't matter; only knowing God mattered, nothing else.

Yielding to rest and less stress, my health gradually took a turn for the better. The first thing I did when my body could walk again was to go see the mayor of Eus. When he came to the door, I asked him if it were possible for me to visit the Old Catholic church. He smiled because he knew I worked for

Guy Galear. After disappearing for a minute, he came back with the key and walked with me to the church. While opening the church door, he told me to stay as long as I wanted and that he would return later in the evening to lock it. After thanking him, I went in and sat down in one of the old wooden pews. It had been so long since I sat in a church. All I could do was sit and stare. It took a long time for my eyes to get used to the dark. As my eyes adjusted to the dim light, my first impression was that it looked dark and ugly inside. At least the stillness was calming, and the stained glass was both inviting and revealing. The more I could observe the art, the more it invited me to recall the life of Christ and what He died for.

Ever since that amazing night when I blew the Devil away, my curiosity about the Catholic Church started to bud like a dormant tree after a long, difficult winter. Every time I heard the bells toll on the hour, my mind would reflect back on my Catholic roots. These roots were all that was left of a sorely pruned tree trunk. The last time I went to attend a mass and received communion seemed like ages gone by.

As I gazed on the old statues in the building, their facial expressions looked like they were in so much pain. The body of Christ hanging on the cross above the altar on the back wall looked so painful and sorrowful. When I went up to take a closer look, I stood there looking up at the expression on His face. For some reason or another, His expression told me that He didn't mind going through this horrible death and that it was worth it. I sat back down in the front pew and continued staring at His face.

The words, "He did the right thing, and He did it for you" came back to me. The "right thing" was to suffer. This hit me like a ton of bricks. All these years, I had been running away from home, away from family, away from my country, and especially running away from pain and suffering. This Jesus could not do this. He did not go far from home; He did not run away from family; He did not abandon His countrymen; and He was not afraid to suffer and die a very painful death. Why? Because He had God in His heart, and God had Him in His heart too. In other words, He knew His eternal self and what He was doing to secure eternal life, not only for Himself but also for all who follow His example.

Due to evil influences, sin, pain, suffering, and death came into the world and have remained. But because of Jesus Christ, sin, pain, suffering, and death cannot last forever. His resurrection from the dead put an end to the reign of evil. My experiences with death in so many dreams, with diabolic attacks, deep fears, loneliness, mental depression, and stress-related illnesses were coming to an end because I did not give up believing in and following this resurrected Jesus. Before I left that dark, ugly old church, it looked rather beautiful and majestic.

The grass in the valley was sprouting, the fruit trees were flowering, the vineyards were budding, and I was beginning to feel my oats again. The French family asked Guy if the American could work for them, Guy agreed and gave me little jobs to do around their houses. It felt good to be back to work, but my body was sorely out of shape to do much lifting. Laying stone was an interesting challenge, but the materials (stone, sand, gravel, clay, cement) are also heavy. The temptation to do strenuous lifting was there, but I forced myself to keep it to a minimum. Florina made sure I was well fed and monitored my actions. She was very perceptive and became familiar with my impatient ways of doing things. Her husband would make subtle suggestions to keep the workload lighter than what I was accustomed to do.

As the climate got warmer and the daylight got longer, I was able to spend more time after work walking in the hills again. There was a little dirt path on the eastern side of town that passed by the church. Every time I walked past the old church, my eyes would gaze on the amazing stonework. Whoever built it did so with patience, precision, and devotion. There was something that attracted me to this building. Sometimes I would spend a good deal of time after work sitting outside the church facing the Pyrenees Mountains. One day while sitting there quietly, my eyes focused on a cloud formation in the sky just above the western horizon. There it hung, about an hour before sunset, a perfectly formed cloud shaped like the United States of America. The light coming from the setting sun filtered through, giving it a golden glow.

It had been so long since I thought about my country of birth. Thoughts ran through my mind of home back in California. A whole bunch of memories came flooding into my mind's eye. I saw the faces of my mom, my brothers, my cousins, my uncles and aunts, the nuns and friends from my school days, people who I worked with, and many more familiar faces. It was a nostalgic moment that made me yearn for a way back home, but I didn't know where my home was. After five years on the road, I had lost all contact with my mother or anyone else in the United States. I felt like Dorothy in *The Wizard of Oz* when she wanted to go home to Kansas but didn't know how.

The cloud kept its shape in that beautiful evening-colored light as I gazed on it in silent admiration. After her only chance to get home took off in a balloon, a homesick Dorothy asked the Good Witch who descended on the city of Oz if there was any way she could go home. The Good Witch told her that she always had the way home on her person. All she had to do was tap the heels of the ruby glass slippers she wore together three times and make a wish. "There's no place like home," repeated Dorothy as she tapped her heels three times, and then she woke from a dream to find herself back home in Kansas surrounded by relatives and friends.

In my mind the phrase, "There's no place like home" kept repeating itself as I watched the cloud slowly expand and dissipate into the sunset. When I returned to my house in Eus, the image of the cloud was still in my head as I sat on my favorite windowsill staring into the western horizon twilight. Submerged in contemplation, the most impressive scenes and images of events played themselves back like a well-edited video of my five-year journey away from my home and country. Moments after the replay ended, a calm and gentle voice deep within me said, "It's time to go home to your roots." The next day when I told my boss that I was thinking of returning to the United States, he said, "Hombre, it's about time. Let me buy you a ticket. You deserve it."

Part III

THE RETURN

Back Home in Two Mothers' Hearts

It was dawn when the flight from Paris touched down in San Francisco International Airport, and it also dawned on me that I had no idea where to go. The last I had heard from my mother was that she moved out of Santa Cruz, but I had neither idea nor address of her whereabouts. My brothers had also moved away from our old home in Aptos, California. The only person who came to mind was my uncle. He was the only relative who would most likely be in the same place.

The thought of going to the high desert of Nevada sent a chill up my spine, because it was there, alone in the canyons above the desert floor, where I received the call to go to South America. *What better place to go to find out what God wants me to do next in this life than the desert?* I thought. Immediately, I headed for the Greyhound bus line to purchase a ticket to Reno, Nevada. From Reno I hitchhiked to Eureka, Nevada, a tiny mining town about twenty-two miles from my uncle's ranch. There was a rancher in town who gave me a ride out to my uncle's ranch.

Halfway to the ranch, I recognized one of my uncle's trucks coming toward us. When I waved at the driver, my aunt, who was driving the truck, stopped and rolled down the window. Leaning against the door, I could see my uncle in the passenger seat.

"Hi, Steve," my uncle said in a weak voice.

"We'll be back in a bit. The house is open. Go have something to eat. Ron's having a heart attack!" yelled my aunt.

Surprised by the look on my uncle's face, I yelled back, "Okay, see you in a bit!"

My uncle and aunt returned to the ranch in the late evening about two hours after sunset. They were both glad to see me. My uncle couldn't talk much, but he told me he couldn't drink and smoke anymore. Then he said, "Stay as long as you want" before he went to bed. My aunt talked about ranch life and things for a while before she informed me that my uncle had cancer. "He's lucky to be alive!" she said as she listed one thing after another about his health. "Hell, he can't drink, he can't smoke, and he can't f__k anymore. What's the poor man to do?" She laughed as she sipped on her drink.

"I'm going to go up into the canyons tomorrow morning," I told my aunt.

"Be careful, there's snakes up there," she said.

I smiled and said, "Good, they'll keep me company."

After a two-hour hike deep into the canyons east of the ranch, I dug in and built a stone shelter. For eleven days, I gathered stones from the mountainside and constructed a circular stone house about eight feet in diameter by five feet tall. Using old mining camp timber, I was able to put a roof over the building. The nights were silent and still, with stars shining so bright that they seemed happy to see me again. The old fears of the desert were nonexistent. Instead, I felt as if I were right at home with old friends and relatives.

My food supply ran out after the first day, but I didn't feel any hunger after the third day. It was as if my body shifted into another gear. My body didn't mind not eating, and I discovered that we really were not meant to eat a lot of food. I had more strength and alertness take place within my body during those ten days without food than I ever had any day with food. Since I could not sleep at night, I would sit up and listen to the noises of the desert night. My ears picked up on coyotes calling to each other all over Diamond Valley that covers an area of over six hundred square miles. During the day, high up in the eastern canyons, my eyes were clearly able to spot things ten to fifteen miles away moving opposite the valley below on the desert floor. All my senses seemed heightened to a degree of rare acuteness.

It was sunset of the eleventh day while immersed in the wonderful embrace of my Lady of the Desert when I heard her voice tell me to go look for my mother and brothers. Somehow I knew without a doubt that that was my next move, so I picked up my gear and went back down the canyons to my uncle's ranch. When I arrived early the next morning, my aunt gladly fixed me breakfast. "You were gone so long, we thought you got lost!" exclaimed my aunt. "Your uncle almost went looking for you."

I looked at her and said with a smile, "Time flies when you're having fun."

She looked at me and shook her head, but before she could say another word, I asked her if she knew where my mom lived. She had only heard that she lived in Sacramento. "I have her older sister's phone number. Maybe she can tell you where your mom is."

When I called my aunt, she gladly told me, "Your mom will be so happy to hear your voice." When I called my mom, I could sense her rising heartbeat by the way she spoke, and while she was holding back her emotions, I could also sense in her words her excitement that her son was coming home to see her. My mom picked me up at the Sacramento Greyhound bus station. Words cannot describe the looks on her face. They were priceless. One thing

I learned by those looks on her face was that I would never go that long again without keeping in better touch with her. With my mother in my arms, I knew I was home.

After a period of acclimatization, life back in California took on a new meaning as I focused on reclaiming my place in American society. My family, especially two of my cousins, helped me get back to work. One had a pool-cleaning business, and the other worked in construction. Between the two of them, I was able to save enough money to buy some land in Durango, Colorado. After spending a couple of years working for my cousins, I moved to Colorado to dig a well and build two small dwellings on forty acres of land surrounded by a Hopi Indian reservation. A local contractor hired me for part-time construction work. The town of Durango and many other towns in Colorado, however, fell into hard economic times. Jobs in and around Durango were scarce, especially in construction; therefore, my land went into bankruptcy because I was unable to make the mortgage payments. To make a long story short, I moved back to Aptos, California.

Fortunately, my mother had hung on to our old home on the California coastline. It was the last house we all lived in before I left the United States to go to South America. It was fun restoring the old house now that I had acquired various construction skills. The house was built of cinder blocks, so my masonry skills came in very handy. My handyman skills kept me busy both on the house and around the town. Eventually, I got a masonry contractor's license and enjoyed being self-employed.

One day while picking up some building supplies in Santa Cruz, I passed by Holy Cross. Holy Cross is the oldest Catholic church in town, built right next to the old Spanish mission site. While walking around admiring the old building and thinking of the church in Eus, I noticed a Catholic nun walking across the street and going into a school building. I thought, *What the heck, I'm going to introduce myself to her.*

After exchanging our names, I told her about my Catholic background and a brief synopsis of my journeys in foreign countries. She seemed very attentive as she listened to me divulge my history. When I finished my story, she asked if I could volunteer to help the church. Thinking that the school might need some construction work, I said, "Sure."

She then came back with, "How would you like to teach children Catechism classes?"

Thrown for a loop, I said, "Sister, I left the Catholic church over twenty years ago. How can I teach kids Catholic doctrine without knowing my own faith?"

She looked me straight in the eye and said, "You would make a good teacher. The kids would listen to a man like yourself because you have experience. Besides, I'll refresh your memory on the church's teachings."

Sister Mary Kelly and I taught seventh—and eighth-grade students catechism classes on Sunday evenings for two school years. Toward the end of the second year, she let me solo the last few classes. There was something about teaching youth about their faith that made me dig deeper into church documents and other Catholic related rites and devotions. Every Sunday the kids would meet me for the 9:00 a.m. mass inside Holy Cross church, and afterward I would take them over to the classroom for their lessons. During the liturgy of the mass, I enjoyed listening to the readings, but I would not go up to receive Holy Communion. For some reason or another, I thought receiving the sacraments was not that important, especially the Sacrament of Penance. I also thought telling your sins to another man was ridiculous. I thought all I needed to do was pray and read the Bible.

My business picked up in the area, and I made enough money to pay bills and get more involved in the church. A man who worked in the Holy Cross Soup Kitchen asked me if I could go to the juvenile hall with him some evening. I said, "Yeah," more out of curiosity than anything. After an hour and a half of visiting delinquent youth behind bars, the man turned and asked if I would be willing to continue visiting the little jailbirds on my own. The man was leaving the area to go to a seminary and study to become a priest. "I've been looking for someone to take my place, and you seem to fit right in. Can you do it?"

At first, I thought, *No way, it's too depressing*, but suddenly the word yes leaped out of my mouth. The man gave me a hug and thanked God for finding someone to replace him. "I prayed to God to find me a replacement so that I would not have to abandon the kids."

For nearly four years, I would make a visit one to two times a month. As nasty as it was to be inside a jail facility, their lonely hearts grew on me, so I went more often to see them and listen to their problems. Because of my own troubled youth and my difficult experiences in foreign countries, I could relate to their rebellious and agitated lives. Every once in a while, a teen would come up to me and wanted to know if I could hear his or her confession. Some would ask if I could give them Holy Communion. They thought I was a priest in disguise. All I could say was, "I'm sorry, but I am not a priest."

One springtime evening, I received a phone call from my mother asking me if I wanted to go to a place called Medjugorje in what used to be Yugoslavia. "Why there? That's a Communist country," I told my mom.

"Mary, the mother of God, is appearing to six teenagers," she answered. She went on to tell me that since 1981, the mother of Jesus was appearing to four girls and two boys who live in a small village called Medjugorje. "Thousands of people from all over the world have been going there to hear her messages coming from the children who see her. Do you want to go?"

My first response was, "No, Mom, I don't need to go there." She then told me that some of the kids had received ten secrets concerning final chastisements that would happen to the world before Jesus returns. After a few moments, I told her in a sarcastic way, "Mary is a nice lady, but I doubt it if she would want to see me." To tell the truth, I didn't really want to go on a tour bus with church tourists and get involved in churchy stuff. Plus, I was more interested in working and studying for my contractor's license than traveling to a communist country, so she made the trip with my stepfather and one of my aunts.

About a year later, my mother called me again to see if I would accompany her, one of her sisters, two of my brothers, and one of my cousins to Medjugorje. My daily schedule included eight to ten hours of work, evening classes in business law, catechism class preparation, and walks and hikes in the Santa Cruz Mountains in my spare time. When my mother invited me to go to Medjugorje this time, I thought, *Why not? I could use a vacation.*

We all flew to Belgrade, Yugoslavia, and joined a busload of pilgrims to Medjugorje. The people in the village had opened their homes to house all the pilgrims coming to see the visionaries. It was very impressive to be around so many people walking the streets with rosaries in their hands and filling the one large Catholic church in town. It seemed like there was a Mass being said every other hour in a different language.

My family and I walked around the area visiting the homes of the visionaries to hear them speak. The young visionaries would describe their encounters with the Virgin Mary and then they would offer answers to questions from the crowd. Many people wanted to know what the ten secrets were about, but the visionaries would tell them that the Blessed Mother told them not to disclose the secrets until she said so. My family spent a good week in Medjugorje before visiting other sights in Yugoslavia. When we boarded the plane to make our return trip to the United States, the chain links of several members of my families' rosaries turned to gold, including mine.

When I returned to my house in Aptos, I got into the habit of praying a rosary each day. There was something soothing about praying and meditating on the mysteries of Christ's life. Before the trip to Medjugorje, I used to think praying the rosary was something little old church ladies would do because they didn't have anything else better to do. Well, here I was doing something that I always considered a waste of time. In two months' time while still praying the rosary, I joined the RCIA program at Holy Cross parish to sponsor a young man into the Catholic Church. By sponsoring him, I received a refreshing history and re-indoctrination of the church's teachings. Praying the rosary gave me an insatiable appetite to read many books on the saints, including books and documents written by popes and famous theologians throughout church history. Sometimes, when I was sitting at Mass on Sundays, I yearned to go receive communion, but something in me knew that would be wrong. Meanwhile, I kept coming up with all kinds of excuses, telling myself it was not necessary to take the Sacraments of Penance and Eucharist.

After another year back home and immersed in work, I got another call from my dear mother, who once again invited me to go to Medjugorje with her, only this time just the two of us. *Why not?* I thought. There was something going on there that attracted me, and I wanted to know more about why the Mother of God was appearing to these young people. From what I recalled from the visits I made to their homes, they seemed like ordinary, sincere, and smart kids. They didn't strike me as a group of pranksters trying to pull the wool over everybody's eyes to gain some international fame. They were all basically simple and shy teens raised on strict, Catholic family values. Medjugorje almost seemed like a hidden village out of the past where the modern world passed over it without spoiling its Christian spirit. What impressed me the most was to see that the main form of community entertainment was for the town folk to go to church on Sundays and share common religious festivities together. My mother made the arrangements, and away we went, with our rosaries in our pockets.

It was a beautiful time of the year to go to Medjugore because the summer rush was slowing down and the weather was cooler. The town was growing rapidly from the flood of pilgrims pouring into this tiny village looking for consolation from heaven. The Croatian people were building little apartments all around town. My mother and I stayed at the house of a young Croatian couple with a little boy and a newborn infant. They were both very hospitable and kind to us. My mother told me this was the family she and my stepfather stayed with when they first came to Medjugorje. This time, my mom and I spent a good portion of our stay taking long walks, praying the rosary together, reading, and meditating on some of the Virgin's messages to the visionaries. Without large crowds and with less traffic, we were able to spend some time in the central plaza area near the church in peaceful contemplation. In the evenings we would look for restaurants in or around Medjugorje where we could enjoy Slavic meals together and discuss spiritual things taking place in our lives.

The nights in Medjugorje were very quiet and still, which made it very easy for me to fall asleep early. One night I woke up between 2:00 and 3:00 a.m. feeling totally rested. As I lay in bed, I started feeling a little agitated because I could not get back to sleep. The image of Mount Krizevac came to mind as I lay there remembering a hike my mother and I went on with a large group of pilgrims being led up the mountain by a priest. The priest led us up a steep, rocky path to the top of Krizevac while stopping to say prayers at each Station of the Cross along the way.

After a few moments of silent reflection, I suddenly felt a powerful urge to get up and go for a hike back up that mountain by myself. There was no way I was going to fall back to sleep, so I got up, put my clothes on, and snuck out of the house. The walk through the village only took me ten minutes before I reached the rocky path at the base of the mountain. When I reached the top of Krizevac, I walked over and stood behind a large cement cross. While gazing out over toward the western horizon, I reached in my pocket and felt my rosary. My thoughts then turned to Mary as I began to wonder why she was appearing to these young people. When I pulled the rosary out of my pocket, I decided to find a quiet spot a little ways down the western side of the mountain and pray it alone.

Sitting straight up with my eyes closed and halfway through the rosary, I suddenly heard a strange but familiar sound fly directly over my head and crash into a bush about ten yards below me. It was strange because this particular noise could only come from a certain creature that I have never heard of flying around in the middle of the night. These creatures only sing in the middle of a hot summer's day. Their buzzing noise is very distinct and unmistakably belongs to one type of bug called the cicada. As a kid, when they sang their song, I could follow the noise and then sneak up and catch them for my junior high school insect collection.

What the heck is this bug doing flying in the middle of the night? I thought as I stood up with a smile on my face. This night-flying cicada made such a comical, broken buzzing sound before it crashed into the bush that it made me laugh. *I've got to see this thing,* I thought, so I took a couple of steps towards the bush. When I looked down to see where I was stepping, a long shadow of myself appeared on the ground, as if the sun was barely rising. *Wow!* I thought. *It's already dawn?*

I didn't take much more notice of my shadow, so I took a couple more steps forward. Then while looking down again, I noticed my shadow was shorter and a lot darker, as if the sun was at nine o'clock in the morning sky. *That's strange,* I thought, but for some reason I didn't care about the shadow. I really wanted to find the cicada, so I took a couple more steps in the direction of the bush when suddenly I noticed my shadow again. This time I stood still with my head hanging directly down with my mouth open. My shadow was as dark as night, and it was so close to my body that only a sun directly above me could make it appear like that. The brightness of the light around me made me think it had to be around noontime!

When I lifted my head to look at the bush, the whole area was lit up as if it were midday. The bushes in the area for as far as I could see were all glowing with beautiful soft pastel colors. Every bush gave off a soft light that radiated the colors of the rainbow. Their leaves and branches seemed to be undulating, as if they were on the surface of a lake or calm stream. There was a sweet fragrance coming from all around me.

Forget the bug, I thought. *What is going on here? It's night time, so how could this be happening?* It was absolutely amazing. My mind and my attention were totally captivated for a few moments when suddenly my heart started beating rapidly as the thought entered my mind, *It's Mary. She's standing right behind me!*

My instant reaction was to turn around to see her, but my body felt like it was locked in place. There I stood frozen to the ground. My neck would not respond when I tried to turn it to the right or to the left. My eyes gazed forward looking at the lit-up bushes, but my heart was full of anguish. An intense shame came over me as I tried to reason why I could not turn around to see her.

Then once again, I started seeing all the evilness inside of me. When I looked down, my shadow was darker than I have ever seen it before. Somehow

I understood why I could not turn to see her. I was full of corruption. My soul was a mess. Sin prevented me from gazing on such a beautifully immaculate creature of God. The last time I felt so ashamed of myself was when I skied off the cliff in Chile. My eyes slowly drifted down to the ground in shame while I watched my shadow slowly dim and recede into the bush. The brilliant noontime light also receded back into the eastern horizon, as if the sun was put into reverse. The bushes regained their natural dull colors, and my body was free to move again. I remember turning to my right to look up and behind me just in time to spot a woman's silhouette standing on top of the mountain. The sun was barely breaking dawn behind her. When she spotted me looking at her, she turned and walked away. She was a young pilgrim who apparently climbed to the top of Krizevac to watch the sunrise; she was not the Virgin Mary.

My mind was clear. No thoughts entered in, only a serene awareness of a peaceful dawn taking its natural course over Medjugorje. The bush where the cicada landed was about twenty feet away. The whole landscape was rough and cold looking. It all looked so boring compared to what it looked like a few moments or hours before. My reasoning process could not figure out how much time elapsed for the duration of that incredible vision. When I looked to my right, there was a path going down the backside of the mountain to the valley floor. As soon as I went about ten yards down the path, my nose simultaneously became aware of leaving a sweet-smelling atmosphere while entering into a natural brush-scented atmosphere. The transition between the two fragrances was so obvious and strong that I turned around and ran back up the hill to try to get back into the sweet-smelling zone again, but to my disappointment, it was gone.

My whole body felt completely rested and strong as I descended Mount Krizevac to the village of Medjugorje. The thought crossed my mind that maybe it was not the Blessed Mother of God that came to see me. It didn't matter to me if it was Mary or Jesus or some other celestial being; it was wonderful, and it was real. What I liked about this event was that it took place when I was wide-awake and away from any familiar room. Then I remembered that I was praying the rosary when it happened, so it could not have been something diabolical or some evil illusion.

When I got down to the bottom of the mountain, the sun was above the horizon, and it was going to be a warm and beautiful day. As I stood looking down over the town from the base of the mountain, I reflected back on how I missed my chance to see Mary. Why couldn't I turn to see her? She was so close. Why didn't I call out to her to help me turn to see her? Then it came back to me. I was frozen in my sinfulness and ashamed of it. It would have been too disgusting to let her see my ugly soul. Maybe I would not have been able to survive her impeccable beauty and I would have died from sorrow on the spot. As I stood there remembering and thinking about that incredible encounter, my stomach told me to go get some breakfast. When I got back to our Croatian family's house, the woman host had breakfast prepared and ready for both my mother and me.

The day passed swiftly as we went to visit some of the visionaries' houses. This time around we were able to listen to the oldest and to the youngest recount their stories of meeting the Blessed Mother for the first time. After they finished talking to the gathered pilgrims, my mother and I went for a walk around the village. We climbed up to the base of Krizevac and sat down on the side of the road. We both looked over the town for a little while and admired the view. We sat in silence for a few moments until my mother broke the silence with an expression of peaceful joy on her face, saying, "I'm so happy to be here." Then she added, "I think the Blessed Mother is really glad we are here too."

After glancing over at her, I put my head down and smiled to myself, wondering if I should tell her what happened last night. "Did you hear me get up last night mom?" I asked. She said no as she shook her head. "Well, I'm not totally sure of it, but I think Mary came to me last night," I said.

"Did you have a dream about her?" she asked with curiosity in her voice.

"No, not exactly." She looked at me in an inquisitive way that spurred me to recount the whole event to her from the moment I got up in the dead of the night to the moment I returned to the house after dawn.

Right as I finished telling her the vision, the bells started to ring down below in the church's tower. We both stood up to stretch and listened to the bells. It was at that moment I had an overwhelming desire to go to confession. When I looked down at the church, I could see lines of people standing outside the church waiting to go to confession.

"Mom," I said in a sudden but low voice. "I want to go to confession."

She looked at me and said, "Yeah, me too."

We walked back down to the church plaza and stood in line for confession. There were several little makeshift booths built along one side of the church. Each little confessional had a sign on the door that read which language the priest spoke and understood. The booth in English had a long line of people waiting outside of it, and then I spotted one of the booths with a sign that read, "Deutzch, German." Germans can usually speak some English, and there was no one standing in line. Plus, he might not understand what I said, so I walked over and opened the door.

"Uhh, Father, is English okay?" I asked.

"Yah! Come in, just go slow," came back the priest's response.

Well, here goes, I thought to myself. "Father . . . it's been over twenty years since my last confession and these are my sins . . ."

I was amazed at what came out of my mouth. It actually scared me, but it was all the truth. It was a load that I really wanted to dump. My confession probably lasted a good twenty minutes or more. By the time I finished telling that poor priest my last sin, I felt sorry for him and thought, *Poor guy, he'll probably need a tall glass of Schnapps after this one.*

When I told him I was done, he opened a little window between us and said, "That was a very good and very real, heartfelt confession. Have you ever thought of becoming a priest?"

First, I was shocked that he could speak English so well because that meant he understood everything I told him. Second, I felt like the lowest scum of the earth. Third, I thought, *You gotta be kidding! Me . . . become a priest? That is the last thing I would ever consider in my life.* "No Father, I have not."

He looked at me with a very warm expression on his face and then said, "You should consider it. With your experience and fearless spirit, you could be a good disciple of Christ."

I didn't know what to say except, "Thanks Father."

When I got up to leave the confessional, he said, "Wait a minute, I need to give you penance and absolve you from your sins." He told me to say some prayers and then prayed over me. When he finished he said, "Go in peace, and may God be with you." When I left the confessional and walked back toward the church, I felt as light as a feather.

It was the strangest thing—my body actually felt young again, like I was ten years old. Everything seemed so bright and clear, as if I had just waked up after a long, refreshing sleep, the way I used to sleep when I was a kid. My face could not help but smile. If someone looked at me, I would smile at him or her. In this happy, almost childlike state of being, I passed in front of the church steps. The sound of music and singing flowed down the steps into my ears coming from inside. After pausing for a minute, I thought, *Hmm . . . sounds good. Wonder what's going on?*

At the top of the steps I peeked in through the open doors and spotted several priests standing near the altar in the middle of the building. From the back of the church, I stood watching and listening. It was the time of communion, and the last of the communicants were receiving Holy Communion. *Darn, I missed the Mass. I'll come back tomorrow,* I thought.

Then one of the priests standing in front of the altar looked up at me. He pointed his right hand toward the back of the church and waved someone to come up for communion. I turned around to see who it was. No one was there. When I turned to look toward the altar, he pointed again at me and nodded his head as if he were saying, "Yes, you." I pointed to myself and said, "Me?" The priest reaffirmed with another nod of his head, so I started toward him to go receive Holy Communion.

As I got closer to the altar, I noticed I did not feel my usual arrogant and prideful self. It was as if something in me really wanted to take in the body and blood of Jesus. I felt a little uneasy as I got up close to the priest, but my heart wanted it, so I opened my mouth and the priest laid the host on top of my tongue. The next thing I knew my knees were on the marble floor. I don't even remember going down on my knees, it happened so quickly. Then I heard a voice, a voice that came from some inexplicable origin but was not mine that said, "Welcome home, my son." Uncontrollable tears started streaming down my face, not out of sorrow but out of indescribable joy.

For all these years living outside of communion with God's Son, I realized at that moment that my being, my person, my soul had been neglected the very food and spiritual nourishment it needed to grow on to sustain itself in the midst of a hostile mind and heart. My stubborn, intellectual pride melted in tears thanks to Mary's heart. My heavenly mother came to bring a wayward son home to her Son's church, where both Jesus and my spiritual mother, Mary, embraced me.

What happened in Medjugorje was a pivotal event that allowed my soul to be plugged back into the greatest source of divine food available on earth. The body and blood of Jesus were and are transforming my sinful, ordinary human nature into a holy, extraordinary human nature. It would take several years later to learn through contemplation that it probably was the Mother of Jesus, the Mother of God, who gently pushed me down Krizevac Mountain to go to confession so that I could worthily receive her divine Son and hear His beautiful voice welcome me back home to my spiritual roots. These roots spread from a seed planted long ago by my earthly mother and I thank

God they were never totally uprooted by all kinds of worldly ideas, immoral allurements and acts, and evil spiritual powers.

The voice back in Eus, France, that said, "Go back home to your roots," after watching the cloud shaped like the United States of America disappear in the sunset was the same voice I heard say, "Welcome home, my son," inside the church in Medjugorje after I received Holy Communion. This had to be the voice of the Holy Spirit. No other spirit has spoken to me with such compassion and care.

I had reached another level upstream in the river to eternal life. From this point on in my personal history, I have never left the Catholic Church again. To do so would be the equivalent of being a fool. How can anyone go back to living in struggle-free mediocrity after tasting the fine wine of victory? To actually taste the true sweetness and reality of Christ's blood can only occur when a person has learned to appreciate and accept his or her struggles in life. Jesus is waiting for us at each level with a cup of pure grace in His hands, cheering us onward and upward. He knows that what is in that chalice is the essence of life itself. It is the reason for being. It is the very lifeblood of God His Father.

Jesus did not refuse that cup when He finally reached the second-to-the last level in the stream of His earthly struggles. Before He jumped up into the final level of a painful death, He took one last sip of His Father's grace. "My Father, if it is not possible that this cup pass without my drinking it, your will be done" (Mt 26:42). The last thing Jesus said to His followers before He jumped to His death was, "Get up, let us go" (26:46). But the disciples could go no further because they were still in the lower levels of the stream. Being spiritually "weak" (26:41), they "left him and fled" (26:56) to hide from death in their deep pools of fear.

The Treasure and the Pearl in Me (Mt 13:44-45)

When I left the United States for Chile, I desired to know God and His will for me, but my understanding of doing His will was very basic. My perception of doing God's will was to throw myself into any given situation and just trust in God to make things good and right happen. Just "let it be" was my idea of doing God's will. Why did I want to do God's will? The simple answer was and still is: because I want to go to heaven. For nearly five and half years, I blew around the world looking for *my way* to get into heaven. God was with me, but I would listen to the voices of the world, get caught in the desires of the flesh, and get raked over the coals by the Devil instead of listening for the voice of God's Holy Spirit, the Treasure and the Pearl. That is why I always felt alone, lost, empty, or outside of heaven (peace, truth, beauty, virtue, joy). It was not until I stopped doing what *I* thought was a better way to get to heaven did I begin to listen for and hear the voice of God. It took many years of experiences for me to get familiar with God's voice and eventually see the true way into heaven.

Going back to my teenage, pre-journey days, there was something inside me that wanted me to wise up and get a new life. My first experience of becoming aware of *something in me* occurred in the high desert of Nevada while working for my uncle on his ranch. My spirit was high in the Nevada desert, but my life back in California would always descend into a miserable condition. Full of vanity, I knew something was missing because I was never satisfied with myself.

It was not until my body started breaking down from all kinds of substance abuse and mental stress that I realized something was interiorly wrong with me. Emptiness, boredom, loneliness, and physical abuse put me in a depressed state of mind. My mother gave me a little book called *The Christ in You*, which sparked an interest in me to rekindle my faith in God and to read the Bible. Then strange and very self-revealing dreams started coming to me that made me aware that this *something in me* was trying to communicate itself to me. In time, I discovered that this "me" was a false personality made up of a combination of good and bad impressions since birth. My false *me* identified itself with worldly things and allurements, other people's perceptions and concepts about life derived from modern philosophical sources, and unhealthy physical cravings, appetites, and harmful indulgences.

Thank God this *something in me* refused to abandon the guy I thought I was. This *thing* was God's voice deep down in the recesses of my heart calling to me through my conscience. Like a child's little annoying voice, even yelling at me at times, this *thing* kept at me—my real me, my true self, my soul—trying to break my soul loose from all the unreal, sinful things of earthly life so I could make contact with the only real thing in life—the origin and Creator of the soul: God and His kingdom of heaven. Now, after many years of experiences, especially looking back at my journeys to foreign countries, this *Something in me* is, was, and will be the Holy Spirit of God telling me, warning me, or guiding me to do His will. God is in us. Aided by the Holy Spirit, our consciences become aware of the treasure and the pearl of God's voice leading us into heaven!

It was God's voice that nudged me out of my teenage party house in California to go out into the unknown deserts of Nevada. It was God's voice that prevented me from being lazy, that motivated me to work hard on the ranch, and that kept me from giving into fear of wandering out into the unknown, open desert all alone. It was God's voice that spoke to my soul and made it fall in love with the mysterious, beautiful, natural powers within the desert. That is why I became obsessed with a desire to know its mystery and called her Lady.

It was God's voice that told me to take the opportunity to learn from the Chilean basket weaver how to make baskets. This work gave me inner stability and a sense of purpose. Plus, without this knowledge, I would not have been able to establish a foothold and the means of making a living in Repocura among the Mapuche Indians. It was God's voice that told me to detach myself from modern civilized life in Nueva Imperial and to immerse myself into an ancient way of life in Repocura. It was God's voice that thundered through me when evil spirits threatened to attack my body and soul during the night. It was God's voice that told me to be truthful to myself when I was confronted with the Mapuche Indian's offering. I heard and understood God's voice telling me that even if I married the Mapuche girl, built a Mapuche hut, and lived on Mapuche land, I would always be a US American at heart.

It was the voice of God that also told me it was time to leave Repocura and the Indian way of life and to move on to the next level of self-discovery. It was God's voice that told me where He wanted me to stay for a while high up in the Andes Mountains. It was in Farellones where God allowed me to see evil spiritual beings and to become familiar with their demonic nature. It was God's voice that let me know that demons exist and that I must learn to believe that they are real and dangerous to both body and soul. It was God's voice that let me know that His Holy Spirit protected me through the image and form of a comical character I loved as a child. It was God's voice that told me to be patient and not to worry about being stuck in the Andes Mountains. God basically told me to watch and wait, for help was on the way. It was God's voice that told me to jump off the edge of the cliff with all my strength and trust that He would somehow catch me.

It was God's voice that helped me acquire a job in Sweden. It was God's voice telling me to slow down and to reflect on the direction of my life. The long Swedish winter nights alone in the cottage gave me a chance to reflect and re-focus on God and His will for me. I saw and understood how the fast life was endangering both my body and my soul. It was God's voice that told me to get out of a highly toxic environment before I passed out on the floor of an unventilated paint booth. It was God's voice talking to me all night long that kept me from falling asleep in sub-zero temperatures after locking myself outside the warm paint booth.

It was God's voice that told me to leave Sweden and go to Egypt. It was God's voice that told me to drink from the Nile without fear of catching any disease. It was God's voice telling me that the Great Pyramid outside Cairo has far more significance built into it than what the human eye and mind can see and understand. It was God who gave me the power and the honor to defeat my elusive adversary the demon and death. It was God that empowered my soul to cast into hell the demon that came into my room in Eus to steal my soul away from this life. It was God who gave me the opportunity to hear the voice of my soul within my supernatural body begging to go beyond the door of earthly life into the unknown heavenly life. It was God's angel who ushered my premature, divinely transfigured or transcended body back to unite itself with my human body.

It was God the Father who told me inside His Son's old church building in Eus that if it were not for His Son's generous sacrificial love, all life on earth would have ceased and my soul would not exist. It was God's voice that warned me not to receive His Son's precious body and blood without first reconciling myself to His Son, manifested in the person of Christ the priest, in the Sacrament of Reconciliation and Penance. It was God's Son through the priest who called me up to the altar, the table of His risen Body, the church, to give my starving and thirsting soul some divine food and drink. And when I took that precious food and drink, Jesus, the Son of God, whispered in my ear, "Welcome home, my son."

This *"something inside me"* is a key and essential phrase that deserves to be understood. If you are someone who desires to know who God is, you need to know how to become conscious of His voice. For a person who lacks consciousness, that is, self-knowledge and awareness of "some good [divine] thing" inside his or her self, that person must give full and complete attention to learn from it. Otherwise, the person will fail to know God. To hear it means to focus on prayer. To pray correctly and effectively takes discipline. To pray well is easier said than done, to say the least.

Jesus did not give long and lengthy lessons to His disciples on how to pray. As a matter of fact, when He was asked how to pray, He taught them the Our Father, and that was about it. The rest of His lessons on praying or communicating with God the Father were done by bodily removing Himself from them and the crowds to go out into the desert to be alone, quiet, and still. These lessons in prayer take physical alertness, mental stamina, and spiritual control. These last-mentioned lessons are not easier done than said, but they are a must if one wants to see God and to hear God. In order to achieve these lessons, one must be disciplined in prayer.

Way before I traveled to South America, I disciplined myself to learn to be alone, to be silent, to be still, and to watch and wait on God. This is why I loved going to the desert in Nevada and various other wilderness areas in my travels. The desert, by virtue of its sheer solitude, helped me to avoid so many worldly distractions. Its natural silent and serene stillness calmed my mind and offered the perfect stage for my soul to move within me. In this ambience, I was able to catch glimpses of God and to discern His salient and sure voice from all the other unimportant, chaotic voices and thoughts in my head. Evil voices and silly thoughts can be silenced by a disciplined mind, especially if the mind has been trained to rely on God's tranquilizing presence. When I became aware of some (God) thing in me that could quiet my turbulent mind, I discovered a peace that afforded me more rest and the ability to create new ideas. When my mind was aware of the presence of God, it both rested and worked on new ideas that did not tire my brain or my body. Now the treasure and the pearl are never far from my heart's inner chest—the soul, "the innermost aspect of man."[24]

The Eternal Word Took on Flesh

It is also important to point out that long before I departed on my journey to look for God and experience His will for me, I had already read the entire Bible, especially the New Testament. People who try to discover God who are ignorant of the Old and New Testaments are spiritually handicapped. It is very difficult to understand the advanced teachings of Jesus on how to get into heaven without first having understood the basic fundamental spiritual messages one learns from the Old Testament stories.

---

[24] CCC, "The spiritual principle in man", Libreria Editrice Vaticana, 363

Isaiah and other prophets predicted that there would be a mysterious union of God with mankind, "Emmanuel, God with us" (Isa 7:14). God would one day come to the world to take on human flesh. The fundamental message of the Word was that God promised to send a Savior to free humanity from evil and that He would be a King of a new heaven and earth. For many people, it takes years of slow growth for the soul to grasp and comprehend the fundamental realities of God's Word and His plan of salvation from sin and eternal death. This is why a person who has no faith and knowledge in the ancient Hebrew Scriptures and does not desire to know God through His Son Jesus has little chance to fathom the depth of spiritual realities like the kingdom of heaven Jesus talked about.

Take the Sadducees, for example; they were religious authorities who denied the resurrection of the dead. In Luke's gospel they tried to nullify the resurrection by asking Jesus a trick question about which of seven husbands would possess the same wife in heaven. It is obvious to see that these men did not desire God above all things. They were absorbed in worldly matters and had not nourished their souls with God's grace by meditating on the Scriptures of old in deep prayer.

When they finished putting the question to Jesus, Jesus came back with an answer that disclosed their empty faith and lack of divine knowledge: "The children of this age marry and remarry; but those who are deemed worthy to attain to the coming age and to the resurrection of the dead neither marry nor are given in marriage. They can no longer die, for they are like angels; and they are the children of God because they are the ones who will rise" (Lk 20:34-36). This is an amazing revelation because Jesus is offering a concrete example of what the kingdom of heaven is like.

These so-called religious authorities raised one of the lamest-brained questions yet to Jesus. If any one of them had truly meditated on Moses' encounter with God at the burning bush, they would not have asked him that question. When God told Moses, "I am the God of Abraham, the God of Isaac, the God of Jacob" (Ex 3:6), He was talking to Moses in the *present tense*. God did not say, "I *was* the God of Abraham, Isaac, and Jacob." Nor did He say, "I *will be* the God of Abraham, Isaac, and Jacob."

What Jesus was pointing out to these foolish men is that you must change your perception of who God is. God is alive and ever present within those who have discovered some good divine thing. People like Abraham, Isaac, Jacob, and Moses know that God is all that anyone needs. There is no need to marry or be re-joined with some other person after death. A marriage is a commitment made between a man and a woman to help each other in life and procreate new life. The love shared between spouses while on earth has its ultimate goal in knowing and being with the Author of love—God. Therefore, spouses who once were bonded together for a worldly purpose are no longer indebted to each other in the next life because their love for each other will be turned toward the one who brought them together in the first place.

No human soul can fill another's soul like God can. Abraham, Isaac, Jacob, and Moses were one with God. They had learned to become one with God. Look at Elijah and Elisha. These two prophets were known to have worked wonders because of the Spirit of God working through them. They avoided temptation and sin. They were single, and they were united with God.

The Pharisees, scribes, and Sadducees should have understood what God said to Moses about the "I am." But because of their sinful lifestyles, they were spiritually ignorant of divine realities. Therefore, they were dangerously stupid leaders because instead of helping to open the way to God, they in turn blocked the people entrusted to them by God from learning who God is. They stifled the people from discovering two great mysteries: understanding the reign of evil entities and the kingdom of heaven within themselves. These poor leaders were too busy following their scrupulous laws to be bothered with Jesus, the man who saved people from evil powers, and Jesus, the man with the keys to true freedom.

If we read the Bible from a parent's perspective, from beginning to the end, God the Father takes painstakingly careful steps to raise and instruct His beloved child, humanity, through time on earth to eventually become one like Himself in heaven—an eternal communion. Through these parental lenses, we observe the child humanity slowly developing and spiritually maturing into an adult humanity. We can then appreciate an understanding of God's tremendous calling into existence a side of humanity that possesses true freedom, endless power, and a hunger to love beyond all telling without nullifying the limitations inherent in being a created human. In short, God is offering each and every one of us an opportunity to coexist and form with Him a communion of life full of boundless joy.

The Soul's Journey through the Bible

I am convinced that the Bible is like a blueprint or construction manual designed to help a willing person build his or her eternal soul. Every soul born on earth has the God-given capacity to inherit the reward of eternal life. Such a reward depends on how much the soul really wants to know its Creator. The Creator wants the creature with Him forever, but how much does the creature want the Creator? Only time and choice will tell. For those of us who choose to be with the Creator, let us explore our visible selves in connection with our hidden selves. A good place to start this interior journey of the human soul on its way to eternal life is by taking a walk through God's soul-building, self-revealing words—the Bible.

When, in his own image
God created man,
He included freedom
In creation's plan.
For he loved us even
From before our birth;
By his grace he made us
Freemen of this earth.

God to man entrusted
Life as gift and aim.
Sin became our prison,
Turning hope to shame.
Man against his brother
Lifted hand and sword,
And the Father's pleading
Went unseen, unheard.

Then in time, our maker
Chose to intervene,
Set his love in person
In the human scene.
Jesus broke the circle
Of repeated sin,
So that man's devotion
Newly might begin.

Choose we now in freedom
Where we should belong.
Let us turn to Jesus,
Let our choice be strong.
May the great obedience
Which in Christ we see
Perfect all our service
Then we shall be free.
—Fred Kaan[25]

Preamble

Since my youth, I have enjoyed contemplating on the words found in the Bible. When I was nineteen years old, I read the Bible from cover to cover for the first time. It took me approximately one year to finish it. My first impression of the book was feeling as if I discovered the diary written by my own father. My father's life was full of mystery and awe. As a child, I always looked up to him with reverence and awe. I did not fear his anger and punishment as much as I feared his not being present at home, missing his smile, or not hearing his words of encouragement and good advice. But more than all the above, I feared him not taking me into his arms and no longer hugging me because of my faults and unworthy behavior. This ongoing expression of God loving me like my father comes wrapped in one book called the Holy Bible, which I will always return to over the years. The stories of a chosen people within this book fits a pattern similar to the living experience of many faithful people, including myself as we age in our earthly existence.

Several years before my ordination as a priest, it slowly dawned on me that perhaps the Bible might be a reflection in words of the aging and maturing process of the human soul. Upon stepping back to look at the big picture, I saw how each Bible story is part of a whole. It was then that I began to realize that perhaps the book is telling the story of how an immature, ungodly disoriented, earthly soul develops into a mature, God-oriented, heavenly soul. The spiritual maturation process of the soul takes place in time from the beginning of creation in the book of Genesis to its end in the

---

25   Liturgy of the Hours, *Divine Office*, Vol. III Ordinary Time, Catholic Book Pub: N.Y. (1975) 801.

final chapters of the book of Revelation. I have no intention in this writing to suggest a rigid, no exceptions interpretation of God's inspired Word. This is an observation; it is a perspective taken from someone stepping back and looking at the whole picture of the Bible and relating it to the whole life experience of an individual human being's journey on earth. This is my personal observation of the inspired books of the Bible that could represent an important lesson God wants us to learn from it.

We are all familiar with the growth process of our physical bodies, but are we familiar with the growth process of our spiritual bodies—the soul? Thanks to science, we are able to survey and monitor the aging process of physical bodies. Scientists have access to books, data charts, and all kinds of information based on anatomical observation and experimentation that maps out and chronicles the gradual aging processes of the human anatomy.

What about the human soul? How much reliable information do we have available to accurately map out and predict the aging process of the human soul? Physical science cannot help much because there is no way to obtain solid, material evidence to support the existence of the human soul. Whatever information we have available on the existence of the soul comes largely from extraordinary experiences articulated by a variety of subjects throughout human history known as the mystical sciences of theology.

Out of all the written documents I have read, the Bible provides the best source of information that provides an accurate spiritual map toward a genuine and unique way to become familiar with the aging process of the human soul. The Bible acts as a theological guide that shows the way to good, spiritual direction. The Bible also acts as a chronological device that measures the different levels or stages of spiritual growth the soul passes through and experiences as it ages and matures during its lifetime within the human person. Let us take a journey with what I will call the soul of mankind or the biblical soul. Let us watch as God the Father slowly transforms His human being into a holy, heavenly being.

"In the Beginning," a Soul Illuminated Our Human Wilderness

The Author and Creator of life did not want to keep this mystery all to Himself. Instead, He decided to reveal His secrets of life to creatures He had stamped with His image and likeness, a freedom to know and to love. In order to do this, He needed time and material to do the job, so "God created the heavens and the earth" (Ge 1:1). There it was, a little, insignificant mass of stuff, floating in the midst of an immense universe. "The earth was a formless wasteland, a darkness covered the abyss" (Ge 1:2). The earth had no idea what was to become of it. It was just a disordered mass of elements suspended in dark space until "a mighty wind," a spirit of God said, "Let there be light, and there was light" (1:3).

I don't know about you, but for me this wind and light coming on to the primordial scene of a lifeless planet makes for a good comparison to the consent and conception of new human life. God wanted to create life just like spouses want to make a baby. With great joy, the Spirit of God blows in to impregnate the earth's elements. This Spirit enlightens and affords its elements with an idea, a code that enables its confused mass to order itself and conform to a certain shape. The same thing happens when the human egg is fertilized in the womb. With great joy, a spirit of love causes the impregnation of a formless mass of elements. A soul blows in and is received with an idea of how to order its elements to form and shape a new creature. A new human life begins, complete with body and soul. Human beings would be empty wastelands without souls.

The Dawning of Human Consciousness

I wish I could remember what it was like back in the womb. It had to be heavenly. There I was, free from all work and worry, tube fed, and just hanging out in the garden of my mother's womb, knowing nothing bad, only the goodness of being alive. The problem with all the above is that I was and remain totally oblivious to my prenatal experience. As a matter of fact, I can't even describe any recollection of my body's journey through the birth canal or even the first few years of my life outside the womb with any real cohesion.

I believe it is fair to say that children do not become conscious of themselves as having possession of an eternal soul until several years after birth. The same thing can be said of the infant beginnings of human life on earth. The dawning of a person's soul consciousness is a slow and often repetitive ordeal throughout most of the Bible's Old Testament. Modern science and literary studies have proven that without ways to articulate experiences in printed language, much of what early souls discovered about their relationship with their Creator was soon forgotten. They had to be reminded over and over of their mistakes much like parents have to punish their little ones over and over for repeating the same errors.

The Bible alludes to this discovery of the eternal soul by tracing the steps of certain characters who believed in God. The early stories in the book of Genesis describe a slow, childlike awakening of its key characters to the limits of their soul's freedom and selfishness. The story of Adam and Eve is the first stage of moral consciousness. The primeval souls were darkened by an evil angel's trick to make a choice that went against God's will. Unfortunately, they fell for it and made the fatal choice. It may seem like a tragic loss to their soul's spiritual advancement, but for those who loved God, some higher good came out of that original event. The infant biblical soul's childlike innocence was lost, but the biblical soul's willful perfection was just beginning.

In what follows, I do not wish to imply that God causes or creates evil to bring good out of it; rather, God can and does use evil to bring about good. In our fallen nature, without learning from the consequences of evil, we fail to make moral progress. Personal experience taught me that God used even my greatest mistakes to make me a better person.

St. Augustine taught that grace builds on nature, and grace perfects fallen human nature. My fallen human nature gradually understood that the existence of evil is allowed to intermingle within God's mysterious plan for the development of the human conscience. In the beginning, my young heart failed to recognize this malaise, and thus it failed to appreciate my free will's capacity to choose responsibly against evil. Therefore, I failed to see the perfection of love as my ultimate God-given purpose in life.

The presence of evil in the world motivates human beings to make a freewill offering in accordance with God's will. God wants us to freely choose Him and His love for life over Satan and his hatred of the living. The soul's eternal destiny depends on a person's free will to choose between good and evil, God and the Devil.

When I began to comprehend that my choices have eternal consequences, I was able to grasp the nature of the words, "You reap what you sow" (Gal 6:7). Ever since then, I try to think and do eternally. I choose to sow good seeds (thoughts and actions) in this life so I can reap (enjoy) good consequences in the next life eternally.

The Ups and Downs of the Developing Soul

Ever since Adam and Eve chose to know good and evil, sin entered the world and continues to destroy souls. Why? Because the Devil was condemned to a lower level than human creatures to slither on its belly forever (Ge 3:14). Conversely, men and women still have a chance to rise, stand, and walk in God's plan of redemption. Men and women are given a chance to gain eternal life by virtue of the holiness of their souls. By referring to souls, instead of the full human nature of body and soul, I do not mean to discount the importance of the body in God's purpose for human nature. My reference to the soul is meant to focus on the development of a human person's interior spiritual life.

The early biblical stories illustrate the horrible jealousy fallen angels harbor toward the souls of men for the promise of being redeemed and able to stand and remain with God again (Ge 3:15). Evil spirits, therefore, do everything they can to prevent living souls from listening to and knowing God's will. Abel started listening to God's will, which posed a threat to the Devil's hatred. Cain did not listen to God, so he was used by the Devil to murder his brother. God punished Cain by making him wander the earth away from home.

Evil continued to entice Cain's descendants, so like bad children who refuse to listen to their parents telling them time and time again to behave, their souls turned evil. Like an infectious disease, Satan and his evil spirits spread their poison throughout the whole infant humanity. They seemed to succeed in poisoning all prehistoric souls to sin and death. No people seemed to care about God, their Creator and Father, so God's heart broke when He saw His baby humanity in the throes of death. Baby humanity was about to perish forever, "But Noah found favor with God" (Ge 6:8). A non-rotting soul acknowledged God, for he was "a good man and blameless in his age" (Ge 6:9). So God whipped up a strong antidote to free baby mankind of poisoned souls to preserve the growth of a few healthy souls before it was too late. Evil could not destroy Noah, "for he walked with God" (Ge 6:9-10).

God Baptizes His Baby Mankind

In the story of Noah's ark and the great flood, the little soul of mankind went under a serious attack of the Devil. God, the loving Father that He is, had to take desperate measures to save the infant life of the human soul from a life-threatening spiritual infection. By submersion in water, He cleansed the onslaught of wicked spirits attacking the little body and soul of mankind on earth (Ge 7). Like concerned parents do to their babies in the first years of life outside the womb, they protect and care for the child until it can resist disease, strengthen, and grow bigger and healthier. After cleansing His infant mankind from both physical and spiritual disease, God nurtured and restored baby mankind back to health.

"Come, Let Us Build Ourselves a City and a Tower" (Ge 11:4)

Human beings increased in number and began to spread out over the land. The soul of mankind also grew into a child that learned to take its first steps. Then it began to wander away from its parental view to test its limitations. The first signs of unbridled freedom and lack of self-control can be seen in the little soul's united but foolish effort to build a tower to heaven. God had to discourage the wild imagination of mankind's toddling soul from playing such mindless and sometimes dangerous, occult games. Children often get lost in fantasy and can innocently open themselves up to evil enticements due to their vulnerable age. They have a tendency to do nothing better with their time until someone wisely instructs them how to put it to good use. God decided to help broaden His little mankind's foolish, self-oriented mind by introducing to the mind of His little soul all kinds of different words and sounds. Little mankind had to learn how to control, arrange, and coordinate diverse thoughts. This enabled the little soul to take on more meaningful challenges and to spread different ideas throughout the earth. When a child is given a challenge, its mind becomes more ordered and occupied with things that make more sense.

Abraham's Call to Covenant: a Bond of Mutual Love between Father and Son

The Creator of the universe made a pact of love with His little child on earth. "Will you love me?" asked God the Father to the son. "Yes I will," responded the child to the Father. The will of the Father was established in the heart of Abraham. Abraham's childlike will to love God brought about a promise of everlasting fidelity to mankind's soul on earth. "The covenant with Abraham is the covenant with us if we are the spiritual children of Abraham, for then we share in his faith and hope and love."[26]

Everyone knows how impressionable little children are. It does not take much to gain a child's attention when someone for the first time praises and makes promising remarks to a little child. Its little heart swells with elation. As a matter of fact, a child will either open its arms to you or run from you after the first initial contact.

When God called to Abram for the first time, it was love at first contact. "That is why Abraham obeyed when God told him to leave his hometown and everything he knew and loved."[27] When a little child learns someone loves him or her, he or she grabs on to that big person and follows him or her wherever he or she goes. There are no laws, only the law of attraction, only the law of love. The child gives all he or she has, his or her heart, mind, and soul, to such a person. But boy, if you scare a child or hurt him or her at that first encounter, you can pretty much kiss off any further communications with that kid. The child's entire being will react immediately with fear and rejection in your presence.

This is why for all time Satan has not made many points with souls who are introduced by their parents to the loving God of the Eucharist. It's an impression that lasts for a lifetime if nurtured and loved. For the first time in salvation history, God, like a loving Father, made a big impression on His little child's soul in human nature. Humanity's child soul latched onto God like a puppy and has followed Him ever since, never totally abandoning God. Even though this puppy will run away several times throughout biblical history, humanity's child-soul always seems to find its way back to the nesting grounds of Yahweh's house.

Freedom Comes from Choosing to Do the Will of God

Around the advent of Moses, the soul of humanity was arriving at an age that begs for reasons to be good. Through the stories of Abraham, Isaac, Jacob, and Joseph's descendants, we learn that the human child-soul has expressed basic cooperation and filial companionship with the will of the God and Father of the child's universe. The collected thoughts of little humanity

---

26   Kreeft, Peter. *The God Who Loves You*. Ignatius Press: San Francisco (1990) 122.

27   Ibid, 122-23.

begin to question God's authority. The child-soul wants to understand who this God is and why was it chosen to follow Him through such a deserted place for so long. The child heretofore has gone along with whatever the Father has said, but when a child suffers discomfort and doesn't like what his parents set before him all the time, the "whys?" and "why nots?" start popping out of his mouth. The age of reason has dawned on the human horizon.

There has to be a reason for obeying God. Ever since Adam and Eve ate from the tree of the knowledge of good and evil, God knew that the fruits of evil would seek to poison the souls of mankind. Therefore, the time was ripe for God to give, in writing, a rule of love to His beloved little son on earth. Before this moment in time, child mankind simply obeyed God's loving commands. "The law in Eden was love. The law in Eden is threefold. First, mankind is to be 'fruitful and multiply.' Second, the man and woman are to care for the garden. And third, they are not to eat the forbidden fruit, 'the knowledge of good and evil'. Each command comes from love."[28]

God saw that to protect His little son from falling into temptation and choosing to do evil, He needed to give him space to form a good, reasonable conscience. His little son was growing, and God knew it. Boy mankind's mind was growing too, and he was going to experience his own free will, a desire to separate himself from his father's wishes to someday choose to be his own man. He was going to have to learn how to make up his own mind. To safeguard this boy's soul from the twisted mind of Satan, God introduced his boy soul on earth to a set of rules, written in stone, to help him make good and healthy decisions throughout his human journey on earth.

These rules would serve as a steadfast anchor to the safe harbor of God's shoreline—a shoreline between the land of human nature and the deep sea of spiritual reality. Such a reality contains the promise of both heaven and hell. Depending on how the soul freely wills or chooses, only one reality will become its destiny, and it will exist in it for eternity. Will the soul reap fruit from the garden of love, or will it reap thorns from the desert of hatred? By these laws, God means to help steady the direction of His child-soul's boat as it begins to venture out, off shore on his own to float freely in the vast waters inhabited by irrational spiritual monsters under Satan's spell in search of its spiritual destiny.

---

[28]   Kreeft, *The God Who Loves You*, 118.

The Child Soul Grows Strong and Wise as
He Keeps His Father's Commands

From the time of Moses on up to the time of Samuel, the child soul of humanity basically followed the established laws of the Father's will. Typical of any growing child feeling its oats, it will test its parent's limits, break the rules, and get into trouble. Like one time, the boy soul misbehaved and ignored God by making a calf out of gold and acted like a Satan worshiper. The Father had to give His son a good beating (Ex 32). The kid soul, after licking his wounds of chastisement, wised up and basically obeyed the Father's will and conformed to God's commandments. The boy learned to accept the rules given to him by his Father, and there was order in the soul of God's boy on earth.

At the end of the book of Deuteronomy, the great Moses died, and Joshua took over to lead the chosen people into the Promised Land. The pagans had made a mess of God's house—the earth, that is. These godless souls had turned evil, and therefore, God gave the orders to His leading biblical son, Joshua, to clean house (Jos 1:1-9). The boy-soul obeyed and swept the land free from immoral debris as far as the eye could see. Every nook and cranny was thoroughly rubbed out.

Good children are obedient to their parents and do their chores without complaining. So it was for Joshua. He did as his Father asked, and the boy-soul advanced in wisdom and strength. The soul of humanity grew as well and soon entered into the age of early adolescence within biblical history. We can see the boy-soul gradually feeling a sense of power as he aged. He began to want to do things for himself and to be recognized by his Father as someone who could do bigger things by himself.

The voice of the adolescent soul of the son cried out to the Father, "Appoint a king over us" (1 Sa 8:6-8). In other words, "Crown me, so that I can have more control and power to do what I want to do with my life, Dad!" God was saddened that his little boy didn't want to totally depend on Him anymore but understood that He had to respect his son's free will. The Father reluctantly decided to give His son some slack and autonomy over himself. The Father said okay, but not without warning His spunky youth about the responsibility that goes with authority. Everyone knows that during the teenage years, a person feels invincible and thinks he knows what's better for him. This is the age of fearless chance taking. Parents dread these years of their child's life, but they know that forcing their youth to follow Mom and Dad's way all the time is not going to work. Therefore, they reluctantly give the kid some space, knowing that with authority comes responsibility.

Freedom "from" God versus Freedom "with" God

The books of Samuel and Kings truly reveal the agony and the ecstasy of freedom. God had entrusted the teenage soul with the privilege to take on more power to decide for himself what was best for his own destiny. The youthful soul in the person of the first king named Saul got off to a rough start. A son of man was put in charge to rule the whole of Israel. The first king of God's chosen ones was also put at the helm of leading mankind spiritually.

His early adolescent quest to rule and take charge of himself in the world showed signs of incompetence. In his incapacity to make the right judgment call against those (the Moabites, Amalekites, Philistines) who wanted to do harm to his kingdom, God the real King did not take back the crown of leadership from His little prince on earth. Instead, He left him alone and made suggestions only. The Father spoke to His son from the sidelines by sending in coaches with a play-by-play strategy. If His son listened, things would go well. If His son refused to listen, things went wrong. The teenage soul of the Bible did quite well through the persons of David and Solomon, but after their reign, things fell apart between the Father and His young biblical son on earth.

The young man-soul named Israel grew strong and glorious. Israel's teen soul on earth grew to be a strong young man. Never was there known in biblical times a more glorious collective soul in human history. The young man-soul regularly visited his Father in the temple and listened to his Father's advice coming from God's messenger prophets. Thus, the youthful soul of Israel advanced in strength, wisdom, and fame throughout the world.

Meanwhile, Satan planned his strategy as well, and by subtle seduction, he succeeded in slowly poisoning the young, healthy, princely soul. The Devil lured the son away from the temple by the use of such tools as pride, lust, and sloth. Saul's pride, David's lust, and Solomon's sloth eroded the young man's ability to remain faithful and attendant to God and His laws. The strong chain that anchored the son's boat to the safe shores between heaven and earth slowly corroded.

As a child matures both physically and mentally into adolescence, he wants to explore and dive into his own lifestyle. There is no other time more exhilarating in a person's life than the years of one's youth. As a teenager changes from a child to an adult, many wild and crazy things happen to both the body and the mind. New ideas, new growth, new looks, and new sounds are begging expression. All these new things are good, but how a person controls them depends on the very core, moral foundation a person has been formed and raised on.

Every adult has stories about his or her youth. The transition from child to adult is a zone full of excitement and fun. It is also full of challenge that dares the youth to go beyond familiar ground. Living in a culture that allows liberal arts and ideas to flourish is different from a culture that adheres to conservative traditions and values (i.e., a young person steeped in Christian morals experiences its transition into adulthood very different from one whose conscience was formed by liberal socialism). Whatever culture or religious formation a child has, it still will undergo change and what goes along with change. He will experience intense moments of knowledge and confusion, sureness and insecurity, bravery and fear; there will be times of emotional highs and lows, failure and success, peace and war, loyalty and betrayal (especially between friends), elation and depression. Whatever the experience, a good parent knows that he or she must not butt in and try to overrule his or her teen's decisions. As hard as it is to endure, parents know that their youths need to learn how to fend for themselves if they want to take control of their own existence in the world.

The strong and brilliant young soul in the person of the early kings was firmly convinced that in order to make the right choices during their reigns, it had to rely on God's laws and listen to His voice through the prophets. For the most part, all three kings started out their royal lives doing just this. Thus, because all three kings freely chose to be with God at the outset of their anointments, they each made significant accomplishments to humanity's soul on earth. David and Solomon were among Israel's most outstanding leaders. Through them, Israel's soul lived to experience its most glorious years in biblical history. No other nation could beat Israel because God was with him.

The same applies when comparing youth today who have been afforded a God-fearing, good moral and ethical foundation in their childhood. When parents and the culture supply their children with God's rules and the means to communicate *with* God (prayer), their children have the means to avoid distancing themselves from God. God has the opportunity to keep them *from* getting messed up and enables them to gracefully grow up safe and strong. As a result, these well-formed souls are more able to contribute to their community's as well as society's needs.

Young Israel Experiences the Agony and Ecstasy of Power and Glory

The reign of Saul represents a perfect image of a soul full of the vigor of youth that possesses the wild and often uncontrollable power of a young person who wants to make a big impression on the world around him. The *New Catholic Encyclopedia* describes Saul as someone "brave, active, and generous, but had an emotional instability that was his undoing. He was capable of frenzied excitement (1 Sm 10:9-13; 11:6-7)."[29] This sounds an awful lot like a typical young person today living in an affluent society.

Many youth put on airs that they have everything under control: no fear, no worries, all knowing, very mobile, and sharing among their peers, especially when their parents or someone else is footing the bills. The young soul of the first king of Israel wanted the people to see that he had everything under control when it came to defeating the enemy. He liked recognition and being the object of their cheers. This haughty pride was the cause of his jealousy and foolish behavior toward a young, little man who stole the show by killing a giant warrior named Goliath and routing the Philistine army.

When entering the cities of Israel, David became the preferred object of delight and was cheered by the crowd (1 Sam 18:6-7). Just watch what happens when a proud, promising, big, athletic, and heroic young man loses his claim to fame to a more agile, quick, smart, and cute little underdog player in front of his admirers, especially the girls. You will see a "very angry and resentful" (18:8), unimpressive display of expression coming from someone whose ego has been crushed. "An evil spirit" will come over him, and he will "rage in his house" (18:10). In other words, he will allow the dragon to enter into his heart and throw him into a tantrum.

The young man-soul of Israel enjoyed the taste of victory over its adversaries. Pride swelled over into the ranks and hearts of Saul, the king's valiant men, and all the people of Israel as well. God saw what was happening

---

[29]   New Catholic Encyclopedia, McGraw-Hill Book Co.: New York, Vol. XII (1967) 1100-01.

to His anointed son on earth and regretted having made him king because Saul "turned" from God and disobeyed His "command" (1 Sam 15:11). These early signs of disobedience to God's plans illustrate an offense to a parent's honor as stewards of God's creation.

A child no longer wants to honor his parent's wishes when he decides to act on his own. Even though the father, through life's experience knows better what the outcome could be, the son chooses not to heed his father's wise counsel and puts himself in harm's way. The young rebel says to himself, "What does he know about me? I'll show him who knows best in this situation!" God takes this kind of offense very seriously because the consequences are deadly. It is a sin that goes back to Adam and Eve. It is "rebellion, and presumption is the crime of idolatry" (1 Sam 15:23). I don't need God's advice because I think He'll agree that my way is a better way than His way.

God revoked and suspended his young rebel's privileges to rule, so Saul was beaten down and put to death by his own pride (1 Sam 31:4). Satan was allowed to enter within the courtyards of the young man-soul of Israel. From now on, the Devil will play havoc with the ever-increasing independence-addicted young man's heart, mind, and soul. The Devil will seduce the young man's intelligence in ways that will cause him to pull anchor and lure him out and away from the secure port of God's advice. With the exception of Kings David and Solomon's reign, the young man-soul of mankind will fall many times through his early adulthood. Each time he falls, however, he will get up, rub his wounds, and get a little spiritually stronger and wiser to the Devil's tricks.

King David is the shining example of a young person's roller-coaster struggle through the spiritually formative years of one's life in a relationship with God. Every God-conscientious young person will ride the roller coaster of discovering the truth over the lie. David discovered very early on in his boyhood that a heart focused on God eventually leads to a well-informed conscience. David communed with God in the hills as he watched over the sheep. When young David told Saul that he could beat Goliath, he was convincing. David was confident in his speech because he was familiar with God's voice and therefore conscious of God's will. God gave the young David the power to overcome fear and make such a brave decision to execute and accomplish victory over a large, visible enemy (1 Sam 17:32-37).

When a young person is not firmly anchored to solid moral ground and does not have recourse to a source of grace while involved in a serious decision-making position that only relies on an untrained, morally weak reason and uninformed conscience, he or she is headed for disaster. For example, I saw a recent documentary that depicts the sorry condition of several teenage girls who chose to have an abortion. Their stories describe how each one of them made a serious, life-and-death decision based on an ignorant or misguided conscience. Their decisions to abort their babies were due to things like threats from their boyfriends, culturally accepted rights, relativistic thinking, and emotional insecurity.

Now these young women are emotionally destroyed, mentally confused, and morally and spiritually broken. All of them showed low self-esteem and psychological distress. All of them expressed a lack of healthy spiritual direction. They all wished they had talked to their parents instead of hiding it from them for fear of shame. They all spoke into the camera to warn other girls to wise up to the fact that girls their age are being duped by a misguided culture—a culture full of lies that promises nothing else but to abandon their lives to a state of hellish decline. Hell for these brokenhearted young women is that they know what they did and they cannot go back and undo their choice. It's too late, and their consciences probably torture them for taking the Devil's advice over God's. They live day by day with this reality branded on their hearts, minds, and souls. Only God can come to their rescue and repair such damage. See the movie *Sophie's Choice* for another powerful example of what happens to the mislead and untrained conscience of a person who chooses to live a life lacking faith in God and poorly formed morals.

King David is the antithesis of the sick and sin-ridden King Saul. David and Saul are like two opposite personalities. Perhaps the author had intended by divine providence to link the two together, a kind of dramatic display that reveals the behind-the-scenes duel between the good side and the bad side of the human conscience. The two individuals make up one person in God's portrayal of the soul's battle for survival. Ever since original sin, every person struggles with the spiritual, real presence of good and evil spirits.

Saul represents the side of a person who is weak in faith, prayer, and trust in God. David represents the side of a person who believes, prays, and trusts in God's commands. On one hand, Saul had a tendency to rely more on his own godforsaken independence, which left him alone with his own diabolically driven thoughts. He proved this rebellion by meddling into spiritually unsafe waters, seeking spiritual guidance through the dangerous practice of fortune telling (1 Sam 28:8-11). Because of this disobedient behavior, God revoked Saul's power to rule and suspended His grace.

David, on the other hand, was almost totally dependent on the Lord's words alone. All throughout his life, David communed with God in prayer, fasting, psalm, mourning, lamentation, dance, and public worship. Whenever he was in trouble or under pressure of any sort, he consulted the God of Israel either directly or indirectly through reliable priests and prophets. When David sinned, he admitted to his guilt, took the blame, and did reparation for his sin (2 Sam 12:13). Because of this obedient behavior, God blessed David's rule and promised him an everlasting kingdom (2 Sam 7:16). God graced David with a long rule and a long life.

Pride, Wine, Lust, and Pagan Worship Are the Ingredients to a Soul's Disaster

The biblical soul entered into another stage of human history—a stage of history comparable to the fall of Rome. Israel's soul had begun to stagger around on top of the royal mountain. The Devil went to push the lightweight kings of the hill off the top because Israel's youthful soul had grown fat, dumb, and lazy. Power play and pleasure crept into the young man's heart because he had gone off to worship his wife's gods. God the Father sent messengers to call back His wayward son's soul, but rebellion brewed in the son's mind and heart.

At this stage, the great warrior kings had died, and a new peaceful king took rule in the person of Solomon. The young man-soul had conquered his enemies and established for himself a "stronghold of Zion . . . that was called the city of David" (2 Sam 5:7-9). King Solomon represented the well-formed and wise conscience of a man who had matured through adhesion and obedience to the moral law. This young man-soul of Israel had arrived at an age where past battles and lessons learned had paid off, because for the most part, he stayed close to God and His commandments. Because of this, he grew physically stronger and mentally wiser.

The young man-soul of Israel during Solomon's early reign experienced peaks of peace, wisdom, and glory. The young man-soul also experienced low valleys in between the peaks because Satan, up to his old tricks, wormed his way into the heart of the strong and wise young man-soul to dumb it down, to form bad habits, and to commit stupid moves for love of pleasure, leisure, and appeasement. Eventually, this would break the young man-soul's heart and that of God's too (1 Ki 1-10). Disordered pleasures would cause increased slothfulness and rebellion to grow within the young man-soul. The Devil would create a division between God and the young man-soul's kingdom, between God's will and man's will (1 Ki 12:28-30).

There comes a time in a young person's life when a youth yearns to fly the coop and can no longer be contained within the boundaries of his or her parents' house rules. The young person thinks he or she has learned life's lessons, having suffered a plethora of corrections and chastisements through childhood and adolescence. The youth is chomping at the bit, like a young racehorse ready to cut loose and head down the unknown tracks of life. Feeling strong enough to jump the fence and move on its own, he wants to detach himself from the stagnant security of his familiar surroundings.

The youth thinks and feels sure of himself and is ready to take on the world, come what may. He knows what he believes in is the source of his strength. Many young people, raised by good parents, have had instilled in their hearts a well-formed conscience that provides for them the opportunity to make a good start on their own path in the world. Once they are out on their own and surrounded by irreligious souls who could not care less about morals, God, and the church, it doesn't matter how much wisdom they learned. For many of them, it will leak out of their persons at party time.

When a person loses a reverence for God, all hell breaks loose. Psalm 111:10 says, "The fear of the Lord is the beginning of wisdom; prudent are all those who live by it." Fear of the Lord is the key to wisdom. In his book, *The God Who Loves You*, Peter Kreeft points out that most religious educators will "agree on the one thing that most stands in the way of religious maturity"[30]—the misunderstanding of the term *fear of the Lord*. When mature, religious people say fear the Lord, they mean something far greater than a change of attitude. Many young people detest authority, so when they hear some religious leader like a priest telling them they must fear the Lord, youth stigmatized by such a term automatically reject the message and walk away from the church screaming, "I don't want to believe in a scary God. I want to believe in a God who is love!" At their loss, the youth misunderstand and walk away with a wrong impression. They are deprived of a potentially powerful virtue.

So what does it mean that *to fear the Lord is the beginning of wisdom?* "It is not servile fear, fear that my enemy will harm me or fear that my cruel

---

[30]   Kreeft, Peter, *The God Who Loves You*, 187.

master will take advantage of me. It is awe, worship, and adoration of God as my friend but not as my chum. It includes the understanding that God can be terrible even though He is good—'terrible' meaning not 'bad' but 'great and high and holy.'"[31] Youth desperately need to identify themselves with an awesome God, not a misunderstood, mean, and scary God. This loss of *awe of God* means the loss of wisdom, the loss of praising, and the loss of adoring the most incredible designer of who we really are and what we were made for. All of us were created for an intimate and eternal purpose within God's plan for the entire universe. This intimate and eternal purpose has been mistakenly stigmatized by the fear of a harsh, loveless God. When a young person looks up to someone in admiration, he or she will gain whatever wisdom comes from the one he or she *truly* admires. When people admire God as a *true* friend, they identify their person with *true wisdom*.

Speaking of identity, one of the greatest tragedies taking place in the lives of our young men and women today is the loss of their true identity. They don't identify themselves with a religious way of life. The home, the family, and marriage have been so downplayed and attacked by every public institution in the modern world. Public schools, political systems, mass media, and public entertainment mislead young people into thinking that religion is old stuff and insignificant. To identify themselves as a Catholic is embarrassing to themselves and their peers. They live in two or more worlds today. They are one person at home and church and another person away from home, at school, or on a job. Their knowledge of themselves is interiorly divided. Many youth in jails or juvenile halls are there because they are clueless as to who they are, what they should be doing, and why they even exist. Their inner, spiritual kingdom is divided. They are like leaves blowing around in the wind. Troubled youth find it very difficult to identify with anything or anyone holy and healthy in this world.

With such a divided and broken identity, young people fall into the Devil's traps. In order to fill in the gaps of who they are, they begin to indulge in various harmful substances and activities. To cover up the pain of confusion, frustration, fear, anger, boredom, and the empty meaninglessness that fills their hearts, minds, and souls, youth today resort to all kinds of distractions. Drugs, alcohol, and sex are just a few of the more common intoxicants the Devil uses to anesthetize his victims.

---

[31]   Ibid., 188.

Modern technology has also imposed so many other means of keeping young people preoccupied and from learning how to patiently find their true selves. Cell phones, iPods, and the Internet offer quick and easy access to unhealthy distractions. Many youth have never experienced a social gathering because all they have to do is enter a chat room online.

In many European countries, the only way young people identify themselves is within a group that lives a unique form of social activity that roams the streets all night while the adult culture sleeps. There is a belief that only the youth are free enough to rule in the night because the adults are stuck in the daytime trap of work and responsibility. Young people cannot identify with marriage because they flounder in the emptiness and insecurity of being a product of a single—or no-parent home. They find it difficult to establish a relationship with the opposite sex because they lacked father, mother, or both to identify with. The whole gay and lesbian culture is a growing sign of mal-gender nutrition. In other words, they have been raised without a healthy dose of male and female psychosomatic vitamins. The malnourished, sexually unbalanced young person cannot identify with the opposite sex, so he or she engages in relationships with the same sex because it is more comfortable and less challenging to a psychologically insecure person.

Israel's soul was never more united and at one with God's will than it was during King David's entire reign and most of King Solomon's reign. After King Solomon's reign, however, the young soul-Israel developed into a split kingdom, a split personality similar to King Saul's and King David's personalities. God was offended by His young man-soul's behavior and decided to withdraw more and more away from His rebellious son's attitude. God allowed His son to fend and fight for himself against his enemies.

After the death of King Solomon, most of the following kings "did evil in the sight of the Lord." The strong, wholesome young man-soul split away from God and began his flight into sin and decadence. The soul of Israel plummeted into a miserable state of affairs—a condition that transformed a once-united, powerful nation-soul into a divided, beaten, and scattered slave-soul to an evil, pagan empire. Without the Father's protection and help, the son fell into the hands of his enemies—the Babylonians. God the biblical Father was hurt, but He had to let His son learn a hard lesson in obedience.

Everyone experiences some form of rebellion against his or her parents and the authorities. It is natural for a young person in the early stage of adulthood to want control of him or herself. Young people want their own freedom and independence. There is nothing wrong with this desire, except we want to do it our way (Satan's way), not someone else's way (God's way). The problem is that we all have to learn how to live with each other on the same planet. That is why God gave us the Ten Commandments, the moral law. That is what makes it possible to live together without deliberately stepping on each other's toes. God wants us to "be fruitful and multiply, fill the earth and subdue it" (Ge 1:28). But we must learn to get along with each other by sharing in ways that will bring harmony, not independent selfishness to each individual soul on earth. Obeying God's rules ensures peace and harmony within a group of individuals and arms us with the tools to defend ourselves from Satan's selfish suggestions.

When young people in today's world try to live their lives without God's protection and spiritual direction, they will get suckered into some form of addictive lifestyle because they do not possess the shield of wisdom—the healthy fear of God that warns and shields them from evil seductions. The Devil will seduce such a young, defenseless soul in subtle ways to convince youth that they can be their own gods and therefore invincible. Like the kings after Solomon, they will wither into spiritually weak, lazy, gluttonous, lustful, and prideful fools. Eventually they will do dangerous and stupid things that will cause them to harm themselves and others. All of these misguided souls either end up in an early grave or spend time in the exile of a prison cell. Physical incarceration is one thing to lament about, but spiritual confinement is another thing that is far more tortuous to endure.

Woe Is Me, God! Get Me Out of Here! I Want to Go Home . . . but Not That Much!

The young man-soul of Israel went astray to do his own will and left God in the dust. God retreated into the background and left His son to do everything for himself. The son ran wild and free, getting drunk on power and passion. His godforsaken ways made him sloppy and easy prey to his enemies. As a result, Jerusalem was ruined, and Israel's soul was caught in spiritual captivity and depravity. The once-free and strong young man-soul had now been thrown into the jail of exile and fell into depression. Full of remorse, Israel's soul lamented and pondered its sorry condition. The broken man-soul of Israel would undergo a period of physical and mental anguish. He would reminisce, reflect on, and review his past. Like a convict sitting in his cell, he would relive his past. He would remember his childhood, his youth, his home, and his days full of wonder and communion with God. He would remember all the secrets God whispered in the ears of his heart. Most of all, he would ask himself, "What went wrong?"

The young man-soul would pass through a type of "dark night of the soul"[32] experience. Although, he desired to go back to the pure and innocent relationship he once had with his Father, his reason wouldn't let him go back. Lost is that innocent, childlike faith and sure trust in God's providence. His mind was full of doubt and was torn between wanting to go back home and listening to his Father or being on his own and calling his own shots. He indulged in loneliness, self-pity, bad habits, and unhealthy behavior. (See the book of Lamentations.) The young man-soul had lost the capacity to recognize God. He was unable to discern the voice of God over so much inner turmoil and confusion. The din of noise constantly bombarding his mind surrounded his heart with sorrow. The enemy plotted to rob him of whatever memory of God and goodness he had so it could crush the son's feelings in sorrow and get him to despair.

Many of us pass through a period in our lives where wisdom ceases and we seem to live in a vacuum. Learning and gaining new insights about life and personal spiritual growth goes under arrest. We get into sensual preoccupations, possessions, and vanity. The light of reason and mindless fantasies battle for first place within our thoughts. Emotions and passions dull the conscience, where good decisions fail to be made. Days, weeks, months, and even years can spin around in the air, never touching the ground, like wheels on a suspended axel, the axel being our own false personality.

We drift through wasted days and wasted nights living in a desert wasteland of not knowing who we are, what we are, and why we are. Prisons, jails, and juvenile halls are examples of desert wastelands full of tumbleweeds blowing in the wind. Correctional facilities are devoid of much spiritual food and water. The inmates are the dried-up, disintegrated souls tumbling and bumbling around wherever the hot wind pushes them. The hot wind is the spirit of evil.

Young souls have a tendency to commit themselves to a repetitious and sometimes vicious cycle. A cycle of engaging in and performing all kinds of

---

[32] St. John of the Cross. *The Dark Night of the Soul.* Image Books: New York (1990). The experience of melancholy, embarrassment, dissatisfaction, abandonment, shame, withdrawal, solitude, and inner ruin. 63-69.

bad habits, like chain smoking knowing that it destroys their lungs, drinking beer after beer knowing that it slowly cooks the liver and makes a body swell up and bloat, and listening to loud music hour after hour that causes permanent damage to the ear. Whatever the addiction, the Devil will do everything he can to drown out the voice of the Holy Spirit and try to bring down the walls of the soul's house. The body contains the soul, and if the body enters death with a darkened, alienated soul, the Devil has a better chance at snatching and pulling the weakened and disintegrated soul into hell. People who commit suicide are broken souls who have been tricked by the Devil to give up hope and believe the lie that throwing off this life is the answer to a better one.

The young man-soul of Israel would sink to the lowest depths of anguish and sorrow. During the great exile in Babylonia, the Jewish nation entered into a massive state of depression. There were several prophets and traditional figures that spoke of profound reflections of Israel's pain and suffering due to its broken relationship with God and the consequences of sin.

In the book of Job, the Hebrew man-soul was reduced to the most extreme misery after having been blessed in his earlier life for his faith in God. Yet Job went into a deep soul search brought on by such suffering and loss. He discovered that the conscience, which is not at ease with the self, manifests a more profound evil than physical suffering. He realized the only thing that would relieve him of his miserable condition was to complain to God. Job's soul accused God for his problems as a way of crying out to God with all the strength of his unsatisfied hope. He wanted an answer. In the end, God heard the cry of a soul that did not give up hope but faithfully hung in there through great trials. God rewarded Job for such faithfulness.

Anyone who has experienced tremendous trials in life, whether they were brought on by themselves or by accidents, knows that if a person does not give up hope, a certain light, a spark of wisdom, or a new idea can arise from within the depths of his or her miserable and darkened soul. The Israelites yearned for a return to God, greatness, and goodness (Isa 63).

Israel's Soul Is Guilty for "She Rebelled against Her God" (Hos 14:1)

The prophets Hosea and Amos paint a gloomy picture of Israel's declining days before the fall of Jerusalem and the Babylonian exile. Their visions also saw the chastisement of Israel for its many sins. The young-man soul of

Israel had become utterly unfaithful to God due to its idolatry and ruthless oppression of the poor. For generations, the young man Israel worshipped false gods; he followed priests leading the way into general apostasy. The priests introduced ritual prostitution into sanctuaries dedicated to the Lord. Young Israel ate and drank in excess, and debauchery was a common practice. He bought and sold the poor; he abandoned the widow and the orphan. Israel's young unrepentant soul had become so derogatory that only a severe punishment could turn it around again. Therefore, God abandoned his chosen man-soul to the powers of evil without protection.

After many years of eating, sleeping, drinking, partying, flirting, fornicating, lying and cheating, stealing and killing, committing abortions and infanticide, and abandoning the elderly and euthanizing them, young people begin to wonder if this is all there is to life. If they do not turn to God for answers to their questions about life, they turn to more exciting and perverted ways to spend their empty existence. They look for ways to fill the void because as one drifts further away from the knowledge of God, or who one is in relation to God and what one is supposed to be doing, one will never find out one purpose in life. One will not learn why one exists or discover one's vocation in life.

During this stage in the Bible, the young man-soul is comparable to a typical young person today who has abandoned his or her soul to every direction except a spiritual direction. It is a godforsaken soul that must pass through the long, dark corridors of aimlessness and insignificance. There are moments where the soul surfaces amidst the turbulence and gets an insightful glimpse of wisdom.

Many youth who have been locked up for a time experience moments of enlightenment during their incarceration. They know what they have done and wish to correct themselves because they remember the person they once were; they want to return to their innocence and goodness. Once in a while, they receive a special insight full of good ideas, especially after lamenting and suffering through great sorrow for the wrong they have done. "Seek good and not evil, that you may live" (Am 5:14).

One young man in particular, full of repentance and deep sorrow, told me everything he had done in his life. There was not a day or night that went by when his mind did not torture him with the most unbearable forms of mental anguish and soulful shame for the kind of person he had become. He told me that nothing was sacred to him until his world got locked up inside a jail cell. He swore that he never wanted to offend God or another person again. He was going to go back to school and church and be a good citizen. He was tired of crying himself to sleep at night. He wanted to stop all addictions and lies. He was at his wit's end, at the bottom of the barrel, and living among the dead. "Conversion means being painfully cut loose from passionate dependencies, from the fascination of the gods, and being set free for the truth and right relationship with God and the world."[33]

> Return, O Israel, to the Lord, your God; you have collapsed through your guilt. Take with you words, and return to the Lord; Say to him, "Forgive all iniquity, and receive what is good, that we may render as offerings the bullocks from our stalls . . . We shall say no more, "Our god," to the work of our hands." (Hos 14:2-4)

The young man-soul of Israel had been in the jail of exile for over forty years. Suddenly, a ray of hope shone within his ill and dimly lit eyes. His soul begged to repent and return to the only one who could bring him out of his dark misery.

> Come, let us return to the Lord, for it is he who has rent, but he will heal us; he has struck us, but he will bind our wounds. He will revive us after two days; on the third day he will raise us up, to live in his presence. Let us know, let us strive to know the Lord; as certain as the dawn is his coming, and his judgment shines forth like the light of day! He will come to us like the rain, like spring rain that waters the earth. (Hos 6:1-3)

A New Light Dawns on the Wounded Man-Soul in the Dark Rubble of Ruin

I will bring about the restoration of my people Israel; they shall rebuild and inhabit their ruined cities. (Am 9:14)

---

[33] Schonborn, Christoph, *Loving the Church*, Ignatius Press, San Francisco (1998) 28.

The young man-soul had visions of truth, restoration of the temple, redemption, a New Jerusalem, and deliverance through a message of new hope—the coming messiah.

> Lo, I am sending my messenger to prepare the way before me; And suddenly there will come to the temple the Lord whom you seek, And the messenger of the covenant whom you desire. Yes, he is coming, says the Lord of hosts. But who will endure the day of his coming? And who can stand when he appears? For he is like the refiner's fire, or like the fuller's lye. He will sit refining and purifying, and he will purify the sons of Levi, Refining them like gold or like silver that they may offer due sacrifice to the Lord. Then the sacrifice of Judah and Jerusalem will please the Lord, as in the days of old, as in years gone by. I will draw near to you for judgment, and I will be swift to bear witness against the sorcerers, adulterers, and perjurers, those who defraud the hired man of his wages, against those who defraud widows and orphans; those who turn aside the stranger, and those who do not fear me, says the Lord of hosts. (Mal 3:1-5)

For over five hundred years, the broken and disoriented soul of Israel wandered through the deserts of a lost land and religion. With great sadness and fear, Israel's soul longed to remember the eternal God. Israel felt sadness because its beloved city Jerusalem had been destroyed and the temple was empty of the joyful spirit of God. The nation felt fear because Israel had abandoned God to worship the Devil and do evil. Therefore, it had to suffer the consequences of its sins. But God heard the cry of His poor people who kept the covenant made with Him (Bar 4:5-29) and sent messengers of hope to tell of the one who would come to cure the wounded man-soul.

> Jerusalem, look towards the East, and see the joy which is coming to you from God. Here come your sons whom you once let go, gathered in from the east and from the west by the word of the Holy One, rejoicing in the glory of God. (Bar 4:36-37)

When a young person who is addicted to alcohol or drugs in the worst stage remembers healthy days of his or her happy childhood and cries out to God for mercy, a spark is struck. And like a shooting star caught in the corner of His eye, God notices this glimmer of light streaking among the backdrop of eternal darkness signaling SOS and rushes to His fading soul's aid. Trust me, God is quick to respond to a lost soul's desperate plea for help!

I am convinced that God is the only one who can save and restore a young person's scattered kingdom. God spoke through prophets of old that He would restore mankind to its original, integrated self through a Son. A Son would come into the world promised to His servant David, and His name would be Emmanuel, "God with us" (Isa 8:8-10; 9:5-6). This God would come back to restore our youth's true identity as members of His own body on earth. They would no longer be divided but one with God and all men. Emmanuel appeared in Bethlehem, and the light of Christ dawned over Israel's land. The nearly dead soul of Israel slowly arose from its deadly slumber. For three years, the voice of God spoke through His incarnated Son, Jesus. Jesus spoke words of hope, consolation, and promise. For thirty-three years, God walked among the sick, poor, and messed-up souls of Israel, cleaning it up, fixing it up, and putting it back up on its feet.

When a person turns to God and believes in Christ, the Spirit begins its restoration project on that person's whole heart, mind, and soul. It is a long, ongoing process, but if a person decides to stay close to and communicate with this Christ of God, he or she will eventually develop the tools to disarm the enemy of the soul, the Devil and his age-old tricks. The soul will experience freedom from sin and death.

The road to a soul's recovery will be costly; however, it is necessary if the soul wants to rise from its worldly grave. Once the light of Christ is invited into a person's life, the Holy Spirit will never abandon that person. Foolish ones abandon the Holy Spirit, but the Holy Spirit will follow the poor person, always calling out to its lost one.

The road to a soul's recovery means taking the blows. Instead of going out to get drunk or stoned, cuss and fight, or lay or get laid, the soul decides to do penance and pay back its debts to God and neighbor. These pay backs can come in various ways and forms. Repentant souls will stop drinking and go get help at Alcoholics Anonymous; these souls will get laughed at for becoming nice, humble guys instead of being the proud, old jerks they once were. They will go back to the owner of a stolen thing and admit they did it. These sorry souls will return kind words when someone else cusses them out in their face. They will not blame their next-door neighbor when they discover a dent in their car. They will eat humble pie when another (especially an enemy) proves them wrong. They will accept whatever physical pain, sickness, or disease causing suffering that comes their way with an uncomplaining smile.

These souls will tell their spouse of their cheating ways and risk losing spouse, children, and home. They will get caught in a lie and will not deny the truth when confronted, even at the risk of total embarrassment. They will kneel before a priest in confession the way God wills reconciliation to Himself through His sons, the ordained priests in the church, instead of proudly telling their sins to a mountain, a beach, or a tree in defiance and rebellion to the teachings of the church.

All of the above causes the grace of God to rain down on the dried-up soul that has lived in a barren desert. Such a soul will revive in time and begin to sprout new leaves of spiritual growth. If the wounded man-soul perseveres in this cleansing of his soul by removing all the poisons of sin, he will restore his soul to a condition of spiritual health and strength, ready to serve God and other souls on earth.

The Darkened Soul of Israel Morphs into an Enlightened Soul of Christ

Jesus Himself showed everybody the way to heaven. He revealed the truth of God's plan of salvation from brokenness, disintegration, and death to total restoration, integration, and eternal life. Jesus brought to earth all the ingredients to start the process of a metamorphosis. The ingredients of *agape* love (unconditional, God-like love, unselfishness, service, sacrifice, and forgiveness) transform a broken person from living a sensual lifestyle into becoming an integrated person living a divinely inspired lifestyle.

Israel's soul and the soul of humanity was a scattered mess at the time of the Messiah's arrival on the earthy scene. There was so much confusion that not even the religious authorities, including Israel's king, were aware of the Messiah's arrival in Judea. When Herod heard about three foreigners asking, "Where is the newborn king of the Jews? He was greatly troubled, and all Jerusalem with him" (Mt 2:2-4). The experts of the law had to research what the prophets had said about the whereabouts of the birth of the Messiah. However, three outsiders, three non-Jewish foreign astrologers, were among the first to find and see the long-awaited, promised Savior of the chosen, covenanted People!

When talking about Christianity, it does not take long to find out just how confused and uncertain the average person is on matters of faith and its application in today's world. How many modern Catholic or Christian people possess a thorough and knowledgeable understanding of Christ, the church's teachings on social issues, and their own personal vocation in life on earth? Without knowing Christ, a soul is going to grope around in the dark and never really change and amount to anything much. I am sorry if that sounds awfully exclusive, but it is the truth. Jesus told His apostles and the blind men of his time, "I am the light of the world" (Jn 8:12; 9:5). A soul needs the light of grace to grow in knowledge and wisdom. The source of this amazing grace is Jesus who is the head of the longest lasting institution in the history of the modern world: the Catholic Church.

The Catholic Church contains an abundant supply of soul food. The best source of grace and nourishment for the soul comes from the Catholic Church because it has carefully preserved magisterial teachings on the source of divine grace. The Magisterium (bishops united with the pope functioning as teachers) reminds the faithful of the need to inform their understanding and interpretation of Scripture and the meaning of the church's sacraments.[34] Unfortunately, most people on this planet do not seem to care much about their soul's health and nourishment. But if a person wants to grow into a fully developed being capable of being transformed into an immortal creature made in the image of his or her Creator, the person needs to care about the welfare of his or her soul.

At this stage in biblical history, the man-soul's mind has been awakened and informed. His mind has been illuminated to the long-awaited sign that will lead his soul back in the direction toward the garden of Eden. In other words, it is suffering and dying as Jesus did that will be the key to a return of the man-soul's totality and immortality. The man-soul must now make a decision to believe in the Christ of God born in Bethlehem or not. History shows that Israel's mind was divided between believers and nonbelievers in the man-God called Jesus. The old split personality developed since the time of kings Saul and David would get in the way and make it hard for the current illumined man-soul of Israel to come together as one person again.

The Jews were split in agreement whether Jesus was "the truth, the way, and the life" (Jn 14:6). "Whoever believes has eternal life" (Jn 6:47). The acts of the apostles and the works of the early saints prove that the man-soul of Israel has been changing and growing in time. Mass conversions of

---

[34]   Otto R. Piechowski. *Catholic Teachings*. The Center for Learning (2000) 19.

Jews and people from other nations and cults to follow Jesus' words spread throughout the world.

Every man and woman who decides to follow Jesus and His teachings handed down by the church knows that changes take place in their lives. It is not an easy road to follow because it is painful and full of sacrifice, yet experience in living out the true Christian doctrine as taught by the Catholic Church tells the man or woman that it is worth the hard journey. After a person experiences a true and profound conversion, a life-changing event, that person gets busy at spinning his or her spiritual cocoon. True followers of Christ thirst for spiritual truth and knowledge. They do not want to be satisfied in only existing or being blown around and scattered by the winds of false spiritualities. They want to know where they are going in life, and they want to know their destiny.

The more a person searches and walks the straight and narrow Christian road, the more a person discovers his or her true self and final destiny. The *false personalities* of the past give way to the realization of the presence of a one and only Christ-like self that begins to emerge from deep within a person's heart. There comes a time during a caterpillar's life when it senses something deep within itself that calls for an all-out effort to shut down its old crawling and eating habits to ready itself for a major change into a new, winged lifestyle, and final destiny. The caterpillar goes on a long journey in search of an isolated place where it can concentrate all its efforts into allowing a mysterious, inner power morph its old self into a strangely beautiful winged creature. There is hardly any comparison to what it looked like before its journey to the cocoon stage; however, in essence, it is the same creature.

Much of my earlier life before returning to the Catholic Church was ridden with dark thoughts and deeds, rebellion, groveling, and a slow, interrupted process of spiritual awakening. But when I came back to the church, my slumbering self was revived by a new Christ-enlightened soul welling up from beneath the surface of who I once thought I was. Thanks to the Catholic Church, my once *false*, self-constructed, worldly conformed, half-fantasized personality was torn down and a new Christlike, truth-based, sacramentally nurtured *personality* started to rise up out of the old, dead me buried under the debris of sin. Jesus is the only way out of the belly of the dark whale full of corrosive, soul-disintegrating acids. By imitating Jesus Christ, we learn to sacrifice, suffer, and die in a way that ensures we will be rescued from the bowels of evil to stand on the beach between hell and heaven—the descent into deep darkness and the climb into the hills, valleys and mountains of Christ's light, beauty, and joy.

Deep within the heart of every man and woman lays the call of God to nourish the soul. God wants us to focus on Him so we can grow to a certain point in our lives where we become familiar enough to understand His voice, which leads us to commit our whole selves to do His will. What is His will? Focus on Christ, shut off the sense appetites, make the sacrificial journey, attach the old self on a cross, and once wrapped in the cocoon of a holy burial, let the mysterious power of God change His human creature into a new and glorious creature transformed into His very image.

The New Man-Soul Is Called to Be a
Saint and to Serve Humanity

In the Acts and in the letters toward the end of the New Testament, the early saints describe undaunted service in the name of Jesus Christ. A three-year conversion and formation process transformed twelve men and hundreds of other Jewish followers of Jesus of Nazareth into stalwart conquerors of the world, the flesh, and the Devil. Israel's soul, through Christ's influence, began to turn into a new person—a Christian. The old worm Saul, for the sake of souls on earth, converted and changed into a new butterfly Paul, a man totally dedicated to his faith and the service of God both as a Jew and a Christian. From the time of his conversion, he spent the rest of his life evangelizing and preaching the good news of Jesus Christ. Paul is an excellent example of a soul's conversion and the missionary spirit that results from such a conversion. Paul was a totally devoted Jew, a Pharisee, and a well-educated businessman. Paul's Jewish soul fervently defended his Jewish roots and religious traditions until the day he met the resurrected Jesus on the road to Damascus. Paul's soul, however, was suddenly informed and lifted to a higher level of knowledge of divine reality. Christ Himself gave him a crash course on faith and a new vocation. This Christ-enlightened soul enabled the man to change into a new person almost immediately. Paul's new soul would cause his whole person to go out and become part of a process that would radically change not only the soul of Israel but also the soul of all humanity.

The more a person's soul follows this call to conversion, the more he or she serves God and others. The saints are excellent examples of souls morphed from old selves to new ones. The church has plenty of documented conversion stories in its archives on the lives of saints, martyrs, clergy, religious, and holy men and women ever since the coming of Jesus Christ in the world. The saints nourished their souls on prayer, the Scriptures, the gospels, the church's teachings, and its sacraments. When they discovered their vocations (God's call), they changed and committed their new selves as consecrated Christian people who spent the rest of their lives serving God and others. They sacrificed their old habits and false personalities to walk the narrow road of giving all for all. Once the saints crawled out of the shell of their old selves, they flew in the service of God and to the aid of others. All the saints realized that by loving God, they were able to answer the world's problems. "They will die for the truth, and they will spend themselves totally for love."[35] Truth and love are what motivate saints to give until it hurts and even lose their lives for it because *it*, being truth and love, are one, meaning God.

The modern civilized world owes its gratitude to the work and devotion of the saints. There are countless souls who have contributed spiritual and humanitarian advancement to mankind over the centuries. The soul illuminated by Christ grows in wisdom and understanding. Such a soul no longer desires selfish pleasures; instead, it delights in being a benefactor for the needy and unfortunate members of society. The illuminated soul no longer suffers from the foolish torments of addictions and other self-destructive mechanisms offered to it by a secular society. A soul at this stage sips gently on God's grace and steadily matures into a whole and healthy spiritual giant like a tall Redwood tree planted by a gentle stream. The modern saintly soul chooses to live a hidden, quiet life nourished by prayer, the Word of God, the Holy Mass, and the sacraments, especially the Eucharist. The Eucharist is the action of the Holy Spirit working within the church's priestly ministry that changes ordinary bread and wine into the real body and blood of Jesus Christ. The Eucharist is the source and summit of a Catholic Christian's life. When a believer truly participates wholeheartedly in receiving the body and blood of God, such a soul is transformed into an extraordinary person capable of going out into today's streets, homes, businesses, and churches to contribute whatever gift, talent, or skill he or she has been blessed with by God to others.

Dorothy Day, Mother Teresa, Pope John Paul II, Martin Luther King, Edith Stein, and Maximilian Kolbe are among a few postmodern examples

---

[35]   Kreeft, Peter, *The God Who Loves You*, 210.

of such souls who served up their lives for the benefit of increasing the growth of humanity's soul. Like Jesus Christ, holy men and women who served the multi-faceted needs of the poor and unfortunate ones of the modern world possessed a certain extraordinary knowledge. The more a person serves God in prayer, in the word, and in Holy Communion, the more a soul advances in wisdom and in the knowledge of the nature of heaven. Jesus told His apostles, "The kingdom of God is at hand" (Mt 4:17). In other words, "If you guys pay attention to My words and follow My actions, you will discover something that will emerge from within the depths of your being that will catch on fire and manifest itself through the good works of your hands." Peter Kreeft says, "Love cannot be taught but only caught."[36] We can be caught on fire by the holy and loving example of good people in our midst.

I have personally been in the presence of individuals who exude the kingdom of heaven simply by observing their behavior. A woman who suffered from a painful, deteriorating bone cancer for the last five years of her life spoke only kind and uplifting words to me when I would visit her at her home. She spoke little of herself; instead, she would always encourage me to seek spiritual growth in Christ as she served me food and drink from her kitchen. It seemed as if time stood still to me while in her presence. I know a husband and wife with eleven children of their own living in near poverty who value the church and the reception of the sacraments more than anything else the modern American culture and all its enticements has to offer them. When I am with that family, I get a taste of what the communion of saints could be like. The kingdom of heaven is not something that comes from above only after death; it can come about right now. "It's at hand" (Mt 4:17).

The Mature Man-Soul on the Road to Calvary and a Redemptive Death

As the soul matures through loving service to God and others in its journey through life on earth, it becomes more aware and more prepared for the end of its life in a contradictory world of its decaying and ailing earthly body and its final battle with evil spiritual opponents bent on tempting a soul to

---

[36] Ibid., 214.

fall into despair, lose hope in God, and believe in nothing more than death itself.

In the book of Revelation we come to the end of Israel's pilgrimage on earth. Israel's soul has come of age and must give up its ghost. The book of Revelation is perhaps the most disturbing of all biblical writings. What disturb most of its readers are the disastrous images of a doom—and gloom-filled scenario of utter destruction of life on earth. Horrible interpretations of this book have been handed down from generation after generation. Old, medieval European artists have depicted the end of the world showing souls falling into the mouths of gross-looking monsters; some souls caught by insidious, demon-like claws reaching up out of dark holes; and other souls halfway submerged in lakes of fire.

The above depictions and written interpretations put a limit on God's words. They even try to bring closure to His loving plan of salvation. Some artists and scholars have tried to go so far as to predict the end of the world. These interpretations of God's Word can be very misleading as they attempt, through the use of its rich symbolism and numbers, to correspond to some actual date in the future when our Lord will return again. The author, who most likely was John the apostle, having survived all the other original apostles by living a long life, saw something entirely different concerning the second coming of Jesus Christ. This author saw God's saving love in action.

The book of Revelation is full of fantastic visions and images of power, knowledge, divine judgment, and victory. Much of the book reveals cataclysmic upheaval until the final judgment found at the end of the twentieth chapter. The last two chapters describe amazing consolation, promise, a New Jerusalem, and a reunion of all who believed in "the Lamb" (Rev 21:27) with God. These would be the souls who remained steadfast in their faith in the risen Christ and endured all the evils described in this book. They will be the ones who triumphed over Satan and his forces, including those who repented perhaps as late as the last moment of their lives on earth.

Now let us go back to the subject of the elderly. They are probably the most neglected social group living within our modern society. Many old people, however, who have lived holy and purposeful lives possess a certain knowledge of things beyond worldly matters that deserves attention, especially from the youth. The matured soul of a wise, old person is loaded with spiritual insight and knowledge of both good and evil. Imagine what it would be like to be confined to a room, laying in a bed unable to move, and suffering constant pain, loneliness, and isolation day after day. What goes on inside these poor old bodies?

Unfortunately, many of these souls are unable to communicate due to their physical condition and mental disabilities. But I assure you, if a person could tap into their souls, he or she would be amazed at what these matured souls are experiencing on the spiritual level. The souls that have been prepared to suffer their last days, months, and years on earth for Christ are walking the road to Calvary. Day by day they carry their crosses to co-redeem lost souls on earth and in purgatory (disembodied souls looking for God). They know the purpose of their final moments on earth. Their minds are struggling with Satan's negative, evil influence and God's positive, assuring goodness. Their faith helps them choose who rules their daily battleground. If Christ rules in their hearts, they have heavenly visions. If Satan rules in their hearts, they have hellish hallucinations.

Read the book of Revelation. It is all visionary. The author, in his last stages of life, could see the final spiritual battles a soul will undergo before it departs from its earthly body. It reveals Satan's last ferocious attempt to shake loose souls away from God or frighten souls to distract them from turning to say yes to God for the first time. An elderly, disabled person confined to a bed cannot get up to go for a walk in a park, go to a movie, visit a friend, or even turn on a light. The person's mind has no way to distract its soul from the very real attacks of demonic spirits. If the person does not believe in the presence of God within, then he or she is left with the tortuous confusion of past sinful memories, fearful thoughts, and hellish voices and visions. These poor trapped souls are at the mercy of their own, uncontrollable minds that threaten to play tricks on them relentlessly.

Evil spirits will do everything in their power to distract and prevent these souls from discovering inner peace with God. I have witnessed the elderly in convalescent homes where many of the residents lie in wait for their deaths with untrained minds and hearts. Many of these poor people go berserk. Some are constantly agitated. Others burst out shrieking at the top of their lungs, and still others sit or lay around all day long with a stare that looks like they are in some state of perpetual shock and hopelessness. The residents who seem to accept their state and condition in life cling on to some form of divine purpose and express themselves in some reasonable or cognizant way. If they are in pain, they try not to complain; instead they struggle to communicate in some way to show their appreciation for your presence.

In the book of Revelation, we see the mature, old man-soul of Israel in his final days, the end of his time on earth. We see his final battle between the forces of good and evil raging within his mind. During the last stage of life in its earthly body, the elderly confined soul experiences visions and locutions of the wildest and weirdest temptations ever imagined. At the same time, it can also experience the most beautiful and sublime moments imaginable. It all depends on the condition of the soul. If an old person's heart, mind, and body are integrated with the will of God, the soul will have magnificent thoughts, ideas, and visions. If an old person's heart, mind, and body are disintegrated and scattered by thousands of evil thoughts and desires, the soul will be driven to absolutely insane thoughts, ideas, and terrible visions.

It is possible that the author of the book of Revelations understood the difference between heaven and hell because of his own elderly experiences. Some biblical scholars believe that if John wrote the book, he probably died when he was around 110 years old. This means he could have spent more than half of his life confined in exile on Greek islands. Most of these islands are like giant, quiet, and isolated boulders sticking up out of the sea. There are patches of tillable ground, but most of their inhabitants survive on fishing. What could John do all day long besides fish, pray, and contemplate? Imagine what went on inside his heart, mind, and soul as his body aged and decayed. But knowing the way John loved his beloved Savior, his loving contemplation was all he needed to carry him through what the world, the Devil, and the flesh inflicted on him to isolate and rip his soul away from union with such a wonderful and eternal Friend.

Ever since Satan fell from grace and rebelled against God, he can never remain in God's presence, so out of sheer envy, he attacks creation. Out of pure spite and hatred, the Devil tries to destroy anything and everything God made and loves. God loves His creatures because everything He made was good. "God saw all that he had made, and it was very good" (Ge 1:31). It is this love that Satan and all condemned souls are unable to experience for all eternity. Good things and goodness threaten the efforts of evil spirits to bring other souls into their own company. The only satisfaction evil spirits have is getting more miserable souls to join them in their misery. As the old saying reminds us, "Misery loves company," and miserable people enjoy, in some perverted way, miserable companions. Miserable failures feel better when they know they are not the only miserable failures in existence.

Being good and doing good acts as a shield that protects and blocks out the efforts of the Devil. This allows a person the opportunity to grow in health and integrity. The heart, mind, body, and soul of a good person stay intact because a holy, integrated person is more capable of willfully choosing not to commit him or herself to the disintegrating powers of Satan's will. Integrity is the key to wholeness, and wholeness in heart, mind, and body provides for the formation of a strong and healthy soul. Disintegration is the key to chaos, and chaos in heart, mind, and body destroys the formation of a strong and holy (spiritually healthy) soul. Peter Kreeft uses a metaphor that depicts souls in hell as unrecognizable because they are like ashes. "A damned soul is one who has made an ash of himself." [37] In other words, the soul is so obliterated that it no longer resembles anything of its original, created human form.

A Soul's Destiny: a Glorious or Shameful Ending of the Biblical Soul's Road

The journey of the biblical soul offers its readers a spiritual roadmap to help guide other souls home. Heaven is home where all good people are destined to arrive if they choose to do God's will. Scripture reveals the story of the Creator's cherished man-soul's journey from the beginning of natural creation to the end of natural creation. One of the first commands God gave to man and woman was to rule over all creation (Ge 1:28). As long as man and woman remained faithful and obedient to God's command, everything went well, but when they rebelled, their relationship with God fell apart. The first commandment given to Moses was to worship no other gods before the Lord (Ex 20:3; Dt 57). When Jesus was asked by a young man which of the commandments was the greatest, He replied, "You shall love the Lord, your God, with all your heart, with all your soul, and with all your mind," and then He added, "You shall love your neighbor as yourself" (Mt 22:37-39).

These commands keep us together, and when we are all together with God, we can provide for and benefit the lives of others. If we are not together in heart, mind, and soul with God, it is impossible to help put other broken individuals back together again. "So, [let us] be perfect, just as [our] heavenly

---

[37]   Ibid., 155.

Father is perfect" (Mt 5:48). A perfectly healthy soul is like a light that shines on a dark mountaintop. It cannot be hidden but must be seen by others. "No one who lights a lamp conceals it with a vessel or sets it under a bed; rather, he places it on a lamp stand so that those who enter may see the light" (Lk 8:16). A soul that understands the message of the Bible can become a source of light that guides other souls to find their way back to the safe port of their Creator.

The soul has a longing to return to the safe and peaceful port of its divine Creator. During its earthly journey, the soul is at the mercy of the human will. The soul's life depends on the human person's decisions between good and evil. In His human nature, Jesus chose to do nothing but good instead of any evil. Jesus fulfilled the Scriptures and the prophets (Lk 4:21), who alluded to someone who would restore humanity to its original, pristine image of God.

Like the Old Testament character of the developing young soul of Israel, we all have to pass through a long, slow spiritual awakening and maturing process. Once the young soul of Israel passed through the cleansing fires of divine punishment, it was ready for change. The young soul of Israel matured to a point where it had to make a major decision to step into spiritual adulthood—a new way to worship God through His perfect example of Himself: Jesus Christ. Since that extraordinary event in time, the coming of the Messiah in salvation history, the soul of Israel has been spiritually quickened to understand the mysteries of God's redemption. Ever since the incarnation of the Word of God, the tree of Israel's soul has flowered and produced eternal fruit. Through Christ, the mature biblical-soul re-enters into the state of grace it once had before original sin.

This maturing process took time to unfold. The young man-soul reflected back from his interior prison cell while in exile; he remembered and came to his spiritual senses that saw and understood why he was being punished. No sinful soul can come back to heaven on his own to live with God. He must learn to respond to God's grace, stop sinning, cast out evil from his life, cleanse his soul through sorrow and suffering, and then enter into heavenly service. Christ showed the way back to heaven. To be a disciple of Christ is the doorway to heaven. Once a soul is free from sin and evil, he or she fully understands the call to sainthood. In other words, the light of Christ illuminates the upcoming saint's path to Calvary and death on the cross. By the mystery of Christ within, disciples gladly accept whatever pain and suffering they must endure for the rest of their lives because they know that in serving Christ and His church, they are going home; they know their destination.

The final battle symbolized in the book of Revelation will be with Satan in the last stage of life. It will happen while enduring the agonizing suffering of the cross. The cross could be the deathbed, the convalescent hospital, the battlefield, the highway, in the desert, or on the ocean. It does not matter where we die; it matters how we die.

Satan and his angels will be in your presence at the hour of your death. Will your soul be ready for the final battle? If you are a disciple of Christ, you will be ready. If you are not a disciple of Christ, are you sure you are ready for the evil spirits who await you? If you want to live on in heaven after death, how will you get there? If Christ is not on your side, what will you do to reach heaven? A theology professor in the seminary once said, "You can tell a man's life story by the way he died."[38] Saints die loving Jesus Christ, caring for their souls, and serving others. Sinners die hating God, not caring for their souls, and harming others. Compare Saints Paul, Perpetua and Felicity, Thomas More, and Maria Goretti to the likes of Adolf Hitler, Joseph Stalin, Margaret Sanger, and Saddam Hussein.

The Bible reveals in stages the hidden mystery of God's eternal promise. The promise is that whoever believes in Him and does what He says is destined to grow into one like Him. Not only will one span the entire universe with God, but one's love also will expand with Him beyond the universe.

Before opening the pages to this marvelous book, my knowledge of the God of Noah, Abraham, and Moses was very basic and limited. My understanding of God's love for me was naïve, childish, and shrinking with every passing day. My heart was as turbulent as the proud kings of the Old Testament. It was not until the I remembered my childlike innocence, the love and security of my parents, my life with my brothers at home, my Catholic school days, the mystery and joy of Christ's birth and Easter resurrection, and how I felt when I received my first Holy Communion that I decided to turn to the Christ of God long buried in the recesses of my heart. It was not until I started walking through the pages of God's good old book that I realize I had been shackled inside a spiritual dungeon and enslaved

---

[38] Fr. Jack Brennan. Professor of Theology. St John's Seminary. Camarillo, California.

by an evil master, who was slowly but surely leading me down an ever-darkening passageway destined to enter into eternal misery and death.

Over time, God enlightens and transforms the biblical soul into temples of glory where "night will be no more, nor will they need light from lamp or sun, for the Lord God shall give them light, and they shall reign forever and ever" (Rev 22:5). The author of the book of Ecclesiastes would argue that if a soul is not afforded a chance to grow in the knowledge of its Creator, it is forced to remain in the dark of earthly vanity and to experience nothing new of a divine plan. Qoheleth would say that someone who does not value the wisdom of God will experience "nothing new under the sun" (Ecc 1:1-11) other than the daily cycle of day and night, light and darkness, waking and sleeping, etc. When a person takes the challenge to journey through the Bible, the person's soul learns in stages to crawl, walk, run with Christ, fight the good fight, and eventually ascend victoriously beyond this world into a heavenly destination. Who knows, perhaps it will be able to at least keep up with the earth's daily spin, allowing it to bask in perpetual sunlight. Now that would be something new!

PART IV

THE REFLECTION

Give Him Time and God Turns Old
Shadows into New Shadow Makers

It was shortly after reading the Bible that I decided to put the God of Israel and Jesus Christ to the test. The good changes that took place inside my person during the year it took for me to read through the whole Book were astounding. It inspired me to break free from my miserable habits and to throw myself completely into the hands of God. I literally trusted in God to tell me whatever He wanted me to do and I would do it. When I went to Nevada to pray and fast in the desert above my uncle's ranch, I asked for a sign from the Lord for what to do with my life. Like the prophet Isaiah said, "Ask for a sign from the Lord, your God; let it be deep as the nether world, or as high as the sky!" (Isa 7:11). So there I sat day after day, night after night, waiting on the Lord until I heard His interior voice tell me to go with Him beyond the borders of my home, family, friends, town, state, and country to an unfamiliar land completely unknown to me in so many ways.

As physically and culturally shocking as it was, it was spiritually invigorating to me to be completely alone and vulnerable. People took advantage of my cultural naïveté and language disabilities, but I really did not let it bother me. This allowed me to stay somewhat anonymous and detached from getting involved in social trivia and worldly matters. My ignorance in such affairs afforded me valuable time to get lost, wander, and be alone with God.

Now after thirty years since my initial burning bush incident in the desert canyons in Nevada, I can give a mystagogical regurgitation on the more important and significant events that occurred in my domestic life and journeys abroad. The word mystagogy means moving from the visible event into the invisible mystery surrounding the event that took place. When a tracker finds a new footprint, he tries to envision the mysterious animal that made the print. Just as the reception of the sacraments signifies a divine and mysterious action taking place that continues to invisibly transform natural beings into supernatural beings, the reception of these extraordinary dreams that took place in my life continue to invisibly reveal more and more their mysterious cause and effects on my soul. So by regurgitation, I mean reflecting back on what caused the mysterious dream or vision to occur and that invisible, transformative effect it has had and is still having inside of me since the original event.

The dreams where I suffered several experiences of death shook the youthful high and mighty false image of *me and myself* right out of the upper branches of a proud tree down to the lower branches barely above ground. Death had a way of letting me know just how fragile a human life is. The most important thing I learned about death is how it can humble a person to abdicate—that is, renounce—physical and worldly power in order to pay more attention to the necessities of the soul. The soul needs to depend on God's power to mature spiritually. What keeps a soul from maturing and growing strong enough to defend itself from spiritual danger and everlasting death is sin. These dying dreams woke me up to the reality of sin and its deadly cause and effects. If it were not for these generous and beneficial peeks into the realm of physical dying and the supernatural effects they had on my soul, this book would not be available.

The sins we commit have a rippling effect on the world's pond. The sins of my past life caused ripples and waves that crashed and broke into the hearts of many souls. There is no doubt in my mind after experiencing so many horrible dreams that death is the direct result of sin. What God did for me was show me the effects of sin through dreams. Every death I suffered in dreams was a blessing in spiritual disguise. They abruptly but surely brought me to my knees in awe of God's mercy. It was His way of allowing me to be punished in spirit instead of judging me to be punished with final physical death. For all the evil deeds I indulged in and did to others, I deserved to be put to death. God, however, took notice of my efforts to change my attitude and behavior in life, so He granted me an extension of my stay on earth and has allowed me to make amends for my sins. Each morning that my eyes can open to see the light of a new day, I offer it as an oblation for the forgiveness of my sins and the sins of the world. Saint Joseph, my patron father, helps me humbly accept whatever physical pain, mental anguish, and spiritual attack I suffer as an opportunity to offer them as gifts to God for the healing and redemptive effects they have on my soul and the souls of others.

Looking back at the various encounters with elusive evil spirits that invaded my room at night, causing immediate physical paralysis, chased away all the doubts I had about their existence. Until I actually experienced contact with these supernatural entities, I refused to believe evil spirits even existed. It took several extraordinary dreams or visions of these despicable things for me to realize the truth of their presence in the world we live in. My early encounters with evil entities in the night always allowed me the opportunity to become familiar with the amazing power of the soul.

My soul gradually and eventually learned to defend itself by depending on God's grace to transform it into something much more powerful than the intruding spirit foe. When a trained soul becomes aware of an evil spirit in the vicinity, it opens the eyes and ears of every cell in the human body, especially to the more powerful demons on the prowl.

Over time as I look back on these incidents, I can see how my soul developed in strength and courage to react with less fear during and after evil attacks. My soul was catching on to their sneaky patterns of attack and had grown wiser to their nature and weaknesses. It was divine love that encouraged my soul to hold firm and to take action against the attack of an evil power. It took years for me to understand that the hidden love of God that manifested itself in images of family, people, and even animals I admired in my youth and had stored in my heart filled my soul with great power in its desperate hours of need. The power of love is real and effective when unleashed against evil.

The extraordinary event that took place in Eus, France, in 1982 when God allowed me to defeat the demon and walk in my transfigured body was and still is the most precious gift God has given to me from His great treasure box. So far in my life, I consider this event the most important and the most revealing encounter with spiritual entities and realities to this day. This particular event continues to unfold the mystery of God and the nature of His divine kingdom of heaven. This event and the one in Medjugorje, Yugoslavia, in 1991 are still revealing, depending on my spiritual behavior, hidden secrets to the ongoing discovery of God, my eternal soul, my vocation in life, and the purpose of God's plan of salvation through Christ's church in the world we live in. Unlike all the other extraordinary dreams or visions before and after these two particular events, I have discovered several new things about them during contemplative reflection.

"Night will be no more, nor will they need light from lamp or sun, for the Lord God shall give them light, and they shall reign forever and ever" (Rev 22:5).

If you can recall, as soon as one of these extraordinary types of dreams or visions was over, I would immediately reach for a light of some kind: a match, a candle, or a lamp switch. On that night in Eus, after the demon exploded, I found myself wide-awake and seated straight up in my bed. This was the first time that I did not desperately reach for any kind of light. Why not? There were two reasons. First, at that moment, I had absolutely no more fear of that evil spirit because it was gone. Second, the room was already lit up, so why turn on a light?

The thing I did not notice during the time of the actual event was where *the source* of light came from in the room. The relief of routing the ever-elusive enemy and being in the state of supernatural experience overwhelmed my consciousness with such intense joy that I did not care about where the light was coming from. But after the angel led me back to my body, I found myself laying down in the dark again. That is when I sat up, looked around the room, and noticed that the lamp was off, the moon was nowhere in sight, and I had no flashlight or burnt matches nearby. Before the bright angel dropped down through the ceiling and came into my front room, where did the light come from? How was it that I was able to see so clearly everything inside my dark house in the middle of the night with nothing lit? That's when it hit me one day years later during one of my many reflections on this event: the source of light in the room came from my glowing body! It had to be my own illuminated soul and body giving off such a light. And perhaps it was this extraordinary illumination that attracted the attention of the celestial being and brought it into my room. God has eyes and ears all over on the lookout to guide and care for His creatures that love Him and are at spiritual risk.

Up until this point in my life, I considered my soul to be nothing more than a sinful shadow—a shadow that hides and takes refuge within its human flesh. It did not occur to me that my soul was capable of generating enough light from God to not only ward off demons but also illuminate a dark room where a person could move about with fearless ease. This divine light seemed to grow brighter as I moved forward through the room. Every object I passed by before stopping at the front door was illuminated by the light emanating from some little known origin: my soul.

In contemplation of this extraordinary experience, God revealed to me in time that I was more than a shadow on the ground. Instead, I learned that my own glorified body contained the source of something that makes shadows out of material objects. In other words, God's divine light filled and illuminated my body. The idea that it was me, with the help of the Holy Spirit, making shadows of things that night would not come clear until nearly thirty years later. Plus, it was not until I had reflected on both extraordinary events (Eus, France, and Megjugorje, Yugoslavia) simultaneously that I realized the two luminous events were connected and verified each other. This God-given contemplation confirmed and sealed the reason to name this book *Eternal Shadows or Shadow Makers*.

One last thing to point out about this amazing event that continues in time to unravel hidden mysteries of God concerns the dream or vision itself. This dream was not a dream that controlled me. We all know how we are at the mercy of our own dreams. When was the last time you controlled your dream? In this supervised dream, it seemed to be my divinized will making or supervising my own destiny. By using the phrase *divinized will*, I mean that my will was so united with God's will that I knew for certain that it was what God wanted me to do. It was as if we were in tandem, so with God's permission, I was the one calling the shots and creating the dream. I willed the divine light to come out of my eyes to destroy the enemy; I willed my soul to create the beautiful light that lit the room; I willed my soul to move across the room with such ease that I could not feel the floor beneath my feet. It was I who wanted to go outside and play in God's backyard. But God being the Father that He is sent one of His wiser, hierarchical angels to interrupt me and say, "No, child. You are not ready yet. You are still too wild. Be patient. Be good. Watch and wait."

What took place in Medjugorje, which used to be called Yugoslavia in 1991, nine years after the French event, also continues to shed light on what it means to become a divinized creature made in the image of God. The results of this extraordinary event had a direct effect on my present-day vocation in life. After years of further reflection and contemplation on the event that took place behind Mt. Krizevac, my intuition tells me that Mary, the mother of God, asked her Son Jesus to make a shadow out of me. In that mystical night, the sun did not cast my shadow before my eyes; some divine light did. This extraordinary light not only cast a shadow from my body, but it also seemed to make a shadow of the condition of my soul. A soul darkened by sin appeared before my lowered eyes and shameful heart.

It was as if the Blessed Virgin Mary was showing me that if I turned back to participate in her Son's will, I too would be capable of receiving, by the gratuitous grace and power of the Holy Spirit, enough light to someday overcome my sins and erase my shadows. And if I may be so bold as to say, perhaps I would become someone who would possess enough light of Christ to cast shadows from other people as well. The one thing I am sure of is that the source of that light came from a divine being, not the natural sun, and certainly not from the Prince of Darkness.

Now in 2011, going on twenty years since the actual event happened to me, God continues to shine more light on His human subject. The subject of this event was me and myself alone—a limited human body with a limitless soul. Thanks to the wonderful gift God gave me nine years prior in Eus, France, what happened in Medjugorje, Yugoslavia, made me realize that we human beings are much more than what we think we are; that we hold within ourselves the incredible capacity to hear God's call; and that we can allow Him to transform our minds and morph our beings into beautiful, shadow-less creatures free from the shadows of sin.

Human beings are the only creatures on earth God invested with a soul, created in His "divine image" (Ge 1:27). Once He created man and woman, he told them to "be fertile and multiply; fill the earth and subdue it" (Ge 1:28). Then after that, He gave us dominion over all living things. Let's look at the words "be fertile and multiply; fill the earth and subdue it" from God's divine perspective for a moment. There is something more to these words than what usually meets the interpreter's eye. The ordinary preacher or interpreter is going to say, "God wanted man and woman to physically procreate and populate the earth with plenty of humans. God also wills all mankind to use all other creatures to his benefit because man has more value than any other created living thing."

Now let's look at the same phrase "be fertile and multiply; fill the earth and subdue it" from an extraordinary preacher's or interpreter's eye. This preacher will say, "There is something in man and woman that contains more value than any other created living thing. This something that we call the soul possesses an image and likeness of its Creator. And if the soul is carefully nurtured (fertilized) by the grace of God, it will grow (multiply) and fill the human body (earth) and overcome it (subdue it) with divine light: God's light."

If we take good care to water and fertilize the little seed of the soul within our being with the graces that come from God, our souls will fulfill their capacity to reflect the divine image and light of God's Spirit. Grace will fill our whole earthly bodies with enough power to eventually take over and transform into a new, resurrected, and immortal body, a Christlike being whose light will forever illuminate and cast out darkness from within.

The radiant, luminous being who gently came up behind me in the middle of the night and made a shadow of me convinced me that we human beings are designed by God to radiate God's light. All we need is to be filled with His enabling grace to transform our sinful bodies into holy creatures that reflect God's light, hence become shadow makers. The heavenly light, which I believe was sent by God through the efforts of the Blessed Virgin Mary and her Son Jesus, personally showed me that such a light was capable of not only casting a shadow from my body like the sun but that it was also capable of lighting up the entire landscape and surrounding atmosphere as far as the eye can see. Plus, everything touched by this lovely light moved and danced with living color and delightful joy. Written words fail to describe what my eyes gazed upon during that extraordinary night visitation.

What happened in Eus, France, and Medjugorje, Yugoslavia, revealed to me that God's plan has, is, and always will be to encourage His greatest creation—man and woman—to become an eternal shadow maker in union with His Son, Jesus Christ. This election, however, depends on our freewill choice and participation to accept God on His own terms. When a human being chooses to follow the teachings of Christ, the human creature is accepting God on his terms and conforms his or her will to God's will. Such people will witness three things in their lifetimes: First, the desires of the flesh will become obedient to what is good for the soul. Second, the world will no longer dictate the way one should live. And third, the Devil will cease to manipulate a person's will, thoughts, and dreams. When such a person is full of this grace granted by Christ, he or she can co-create a new surroundings, a new world, and a new life that casts out all shadows caused by sin, fear, and suffering. Such people no longer fear the pain of the cross. The mystery of Christ suffering on Calvary makes sense to a person enlightened by Christ.

Sin is a commitment to psychological and physical offenses that create dark, inner prisons of shame and misery we find ourselves confined to. People who live in the shadows of wrongdoing are afraid of exposing themselves in the light of truth because the shame would be painfully unbearable. This fear of exposure keeps us sinners locked in the shadows of misery and self-insecurity until one calls upon God in repentance to free us from our sinful, shadowy existence. People who refuse God's mercy are perhaps souls that eventually evolve into eternal shadows. Eternal shadow makers are souls transformed by the light of Christ into new, eternal creatures possessed by the Holy Spirit. Eternal shadows will forever be cast further into deeper darkness by the light of eternal shadow makers. Eternal shadow makers will always chase away evil spirit shadows like the sunshine of day chases away the darkness of night.

Shadow makers like the reflective souls of the Blessed Virgin Mary and saints can reflect the light of God by virtue of their love of God. Such a shadow maker's love of God that originates within the resurrected creature is what creates an extraordinary light capable of illuminating both earthly and heavenly existence.

God's ideas are not like our human thoughts. Earthly human beings think their thoughts create what they are. However, God's ideas cause our will to conform to His; therefore, the earthly man or woman who turns his or her thoughts toward God and conforms his or her will to God's will co-creates something new. The old shadow-like creature turns into a new shadow-maker creature that prays to express God's infinite ideas, which always manifest themselves in true goodness, beauty, and joy. Eternal shadows flee from Satan and are always on their own. Eternal shadow makers always communicate with God and are never alone. A shadow is someone who lurks in the dark. A shadow maker is someone who celebrates in the light.

Ten years before the Medjugorje event, God showed me that my soul was able to advance in His divine light and that my soul had enough power to cast off the darkness of sin, destroy demons, and eventually destroy even death itself. You might be asking yourself, "How do I immerse myself in this divine light?" You don't; God does. God calls, and you respond. In order to immerse oneself in God's divine light, you have to get to work. The work involves a process of prayer, discipline, and surrendering oneself in a way that allows God to move in and make His home within you.

First, clean your house, then invite God in it, and then learn to listen for His lovely voice. This is easier said than done. This is a real and difficult challenge, but it is a worthy challenge because we are talking about eternal life. The acceptance of this challenge means the difference between eternal life and eternal death. If you do not care about your existence, then do not take the challenge. The fruits of such work make all the labor, pain, sorrow, and tears worth suffering for. For when a person realizes his or her spiritual potential, that person realizes that life with God is good. In love, that person may have to lay down with pain and sorrow his or her old life in death, but that same person will also rise in joy to a new life that generates co-eternal love. God's will is that we share in His divine love and life.

Speaking of God's will, have you ever asked yourself why God allowed His Son Jesus, such a good and holy man, to suffer through three years of thankless work among those who were a bunch of losers and haters and then let Himself get tortured and killed in such a horrible way? Jesus! What did You get in return for that sacrificial lifestyle and ugly death? He received nothing but everything everybody wanted and is still looking for: He received and still receives love!

Ever since Jesus died, He has been receiving love from every soul He saved and is still saving from eternal suffering and death. He is the only one who saved me from destroying myself. He is the only one who protected my soul from being stolen and drug into hell by the Devil under its power of eternal darkness. Nobody knows how much I think about Him, pray to Him, talk to Him, and walk with Him every day. I have spent more time with Him than any other person in my life so far. Now, so what did Jesus get? I don't know about you, but I do know what Jesus received from me, and I know it made it all worthwhile for Him and His redemptive life. He received my total loyalty and friendship forever. If that's not real love, what is? This is what Jesus gained for His life, passion, and death. He won eternal love from all who believe in Him and want to be with Him.

Since we are on the subject of love, I must throw this little tidbit in here. It is funny how God sent the little cicada bug as a herald for the coming extraordinary main event. He must have known that I have always loved those singing insects ever since I was a kid in eighth grade. God knew that the cicada would make me stop thinking or doing whatever else to get my undivided attention. It worked because it drew all of me to itself.

One of my best subjects of love, nevertheless, I saved for the last. The one to whom I owe my recollections of the Medjugorje event is Mary, the mother of Jesus. There is a connection between my Lady of the Desert and Our Lady Queen of Peace. My admiration and love for Mary grow as I imagine her traveling through the desert on her way to visit and stay with her cousin Elizabeth. Somehow, I can see the young Mary thoroughly enjoying the profound silence and serene beauty of the open desert. I can also imagine her heart filled with awe and wonder during the hours of dawn and dusk. The immensity of the desert has a way of filling a soul with reverence of divine mysteries. She had to have felt the presence of the Creator in the midst of exquisite virgin terrain and pondered it with love. After all, she carried the Son of the almighty God in her pure virgin womb with love.

Our Lady of Peace has made her serene presence known to me ever since her visitation in Medjugorje. Somehow, I sensed that it was her who came up behind me that wonderful pre-dawn night. She came upon me gently, non-threateningly, and sweetly. When she was finished with her visit, she left something behind to confirm her presence. After the light of dawn restored the landscape to its natural colors, I stood there filled with incredulous awe, wondering if it was just all some kind of dream. When I took my first steps to go back down the mountain, my nose distinctly remembers leaving that area filled with the sweetest, candy-like fragrance in contrast to the natural odors coming from the surrounding wild brush. There was something very feminine in that sweet and lovely fragrance.

Also, in my thoughts, it was so easy to picture her enjoying the climb up the path to the top of the mountain anticipating how she would gently surprise someone who loves to be alone in the silence of the wilderness contemplating her and her Son Jesus. Whenever and wherever I sought refuge in the deserts around the world, I always found a mother's comfort and warmth in their midst, and sometimes that sweet and lovely fragrance. The spirit of the desert and God's mother are so alike. They both possess a purity and beauty that captures my heart and soul. I love them both so much.

Thanks to Jesus, Death Does Not Have to Be Eternal

Through His death, Jesus made available to me and anyone else concerned about eternity the spiritual ammo that His "children share in blood and flesh" (Heb 2:14). It is through the sharing of the body and blood of the risen Christ that "he might destroy the one who has the power of death, that is, the Devil, and free those who through fear of death had been subject to slavery all their life" (2:14-15).

Death comes only once for those who wait upon the Lord, but those who live without respect or fear of the Lord could experience the horrors of eternal death. Pope John Paul II constantly spoke on the culture of death. His message called for a respect for life in all its stages on earth, but it bore eternal consequences as well. Many people have abandoned the Catholic Church and its teachings. For Pope John Paul II, this was a real tragedy. I am sure he envisioned a world slipping into an obsession over death. He saw how young people were infatuated with death. In his philosophical mind, he saw how modern youth live fast, meaningless lives full of sensual cravings that lacked in any real vocation and purpose. His spirit saw they needed something to believe in.

In modern societies, especially since the sixties, the Catholic Church's teachings were pushed aside as being not hip, not cool, old, and boring. Hip parents gave birth to flower children instead of baptized children. The flower children were filled with a worldly spirit instead of the Holy Spirit.

This other worldly spirit alerted the pope, which motivated him to reach out to the youth in a way no other pope has done in church history. His famous World Youth Days called the youth of the world to stop thinking about death but life and to live it in the fullness of Christ.

A mind is a precious thing, yes, but an impressionable thing as well. If all a person does with his mind on earth is fill it with things and images of death, what will become of him or her after his or her soul leaves the body? Will a person remember and experience all the horrible images and thoughts he or she harbored in his or her mind while on earth? Will the soul transform into an ongoing montage of dying in a myriad of ugly ways? I think of people who plot ways of murdering their victims and serial killers who systematically exterminate their victims.

There are still others who meditate on horrific tales and write, print, and publish stories full of macabre details that cause fear, pain, suffering, and death. What happens to these authors whose minds are full of dark thoughts and images of deadly things? Where do the writers of tales such as *Frankenstein, Dracula, It, Quarantined,* and the more recent science fiction stories of *Aliens* that lurk around and devour humans in space end up? These images conjure up stuff so frightful that no one would want to experience them in real life. And yet, will they become a reality in the eternal spiritual realm? If you are what you think you are, will you become what you thought of? Saint Paul urged the early Christians to bury the old self and put away dead thoughts and bad habits to renew their minds and put on the mind of Christ.[39]

What do you suppose Jesus meant when He told a disciple to follow Him and "let the dead bury their dead"?[40] Jesus was not talking about physically burying dead bodies. Perhaps Jesus was saying, "Your parents are already spiritually dead. Leave them alone, and follow Me into heaven. They no longer look to God for newness of life. They have lost their faith, and they are no longer growing spiritually. If you want to be My disciple, let go of dead rituals, dead beliefs, and attachments to a meaningless way of life."

In other words, a life that lacks in the knowledge of God and His illustrious Son's spirit of new life and love is losing its eternal life. To follow Jesus means to shed the old, dead skin of the world and to put on a new, immortal, ever-growing mantle of God-like radiant life. Christ exhibited

---

[39]   Romans 12:2; Ephesians 4:22-23.

[40]   Mathew 8:22; Luke 9:60.

this new form of life to everyone He met, especially to those who believed in His words and actions.

Walk and Work with God until You Are Seen No More!

To walk with God is peaceful, to talk with God is insightful, but to work with God is wonderful. I have often thought of Enoch and God working together to build the only surviving one of the seven wonders of the world, the Great Pyramid on the Giza Plateau in Egypt. If Enoch was there, he must have been totally into it and so happy to make something with God. I remember the times as a child when my dad let me build something with him. Those were the most intense and enjoyable moments in my life. I'm sure Enoch felt the same way.

When I think back on my journey through life both in America and in so many foreign countries, it was just God and me walking and working together. Yes, family, teachers, and other people inspired me to learn and try new things, but ultimately it was God who patiently trained and coordinated my eyes and hands from start to finish on unknown challenges, projects, skills, and jobs. As a boy, God worked with me delivering newspapers to dozens of houses alone and in the dark during predawn mornings before school. God worked with me digging trenches and postholes in the Nevadan high desert. God worked with me on car motors torn apart in the backyard under a tree in Aptos, California. He showed me how to make them run again. God worked with me while making baskets alone in a room struggling to adjust to life in a small Chilean village in South America. God worked with me on learning to read and speak foreign languages.

God worked with me while I was farming in the fields, valleys, and hills of Nevada and Chile. God worked with me to show me how to find my bearings in some of the most remote and isolated areas in the world. God worked with me while repairing diesel power plants in the Andes Mountains and Brazilian islands. God worked with me while I was hanging off snow-covered rooftops above Swedish streets in Stockholm breaking off looming icicles. God worked with me while I was cutting stone in a riverbed so that a mason could fit them in a wall. God worked with me to place cut stones in buildings to shelter people in Southern France.

God worked with me while cleaning pools and hanging drywall in Southern California. God worked with me to build and repair houses in Northern California. God worked with me teaching children about His Son

Jesus in the Catholic Church in Santa Cruz, California. God worked with me to console and spiritually council teenagers in county correctional facilities (juvenile halls). God worked with me to open my heart to two little cousins in need of a man who cares about them in their lives. God restored my half-burnt brain and worked with me to maintain and comprehend truckloads of philosophical and theological material for eight years in the seminary.

The above are only some of the more outstanding things the Lord worked on with me to expand my knowledge and appreciation of Him and myself. Today, God is working with me in spreading His Son's message of love to people in Catholic parishes throughout California. God is working with me to form talks and retreats for groups of youth at the Marello Youth Retreat Center in Loomis, California. God is working with me to change ordinary bread and wine into the extraordinary body and blood of His immortal and eternal Son, Jesus. God is working with me to transform me into a saint. I sure hope He keeps working with me no matter how dumb I am at times and how many stupid errors I continue to make against His best wishes for me and His Church. It is wonderful working with Someone so in love with me, even with all my shortcomings and faults.

To this day, God continues to show me that if I keep walking with Him and His Son, Jesus, I too will possess enough of their Holy Spirit to work wonders—wonders that will set captives free, heal the sick, and cure the lame, the blind, and the deaf. These are real things to look forward to. Who knows, maybe I'll raise someone back to life. That would be cool! It won't bother me if I do not reach the miracle worker stage in this life. I'll do it from the next life like the saints do.

Indestructible Spiritual Beings II

Evil spirits hate the fact that we humans still have a chance to discover God and be with Him even while still on earth. They are so intensely jealous that humans can learn to go to heaven and they cannot because they had their chance and blew it. They are in an eternal state of misery and darkness. They are also in a state of eternal change. They get uglier and less mobile with every soul who exposes them to the power of Christ. They do not want human souls to increase in the knowledge of God because the more a human soul discovers its God-given powers, the more dangerous the soul becomes to evil spirits. Evil spirits hate being exposed. Evil spirits would rather be totally destroyed than experience being cast into the darkness of hell for eternity. What makes hell so awful is that they know spirits are indestructible; therefore, they are doomed to be enslaved and tortured by Satan forever. The event that took place in Eus, France, has become one of the best lessons God has allowed me to experience because it keeps teaching me more and more about spiritual realities ever since.

Every soul, whether it wants to or not, is going to experience an encounter with evil spirits. We cannot avoid it, just like we cannot avoid death. It's going to happen, so let us face up to evil influences now, not later. Once we are dead and outside of our bodies, we are at the mercy of either evil spirits or holy ones. If we have not taken the time to learn from God how to be prepared for these things, we will be in for a hell of a shock. Ignorant souls will be stunned by the realization of an unpleasant truth. But if we have taken the time to persevere in prayer and meditation, read holy Scripture, participate in the sacraments that Jesus Himself gives us, and do unselfish charitable acts, then the angels, saints, Mary, Jesus, and even holy people who died may be there to help us in that very intense, transcendent moment between the material world and the spiritual realm: death. All of Jesus' teachings are focused on preparing us for that moment, our rebirthing into a world beyond this one, heaven or hell that will continue to build or destroy us.

Demonic attacks do not mean that you are not protected by God. You are. He just allows them to happen for our further spiritual maturation. Before they became great saints, men and women of faith were attacked by Satan but not left unprotected. Ever since that night in France, I made plans to return to the United States and go back to my spiritual roots—the Catholic Church. I eventually crawled back into confession and began to receive the holy Eucharist with love and gratitude. Since then, on their approach, scary and ugly spirits cannot get near me anymore. Oh, they are around, and every once in a while they make an appearance, but I know them and can sense them way before they get close to me. I owe all this protection to my spiritual mother, the church. And I hope and pray I never abandon her again.

Every time I look back and reflect on that extraordinary event, I see something and learn something new that I did not see before. It is as if God keeps teaching me things as I graduate from one level of spiritual understanding to the next. What the demons or devils are doing is working overtime to prevent us humans from feeding our souls. They know that the most powerful food on earth comes from the altar. Every Catholic Church is a target for demonic warfare. They hate it with a passion because they know that every soul that feeds on Christ's body and blood is growing stronger day by day. Evil spirits know that the more a person goes to that source of spiritual power, the less tempting power the evil spirits have in tricking other souls to join them in their hellish condition. They do not like it that human beings have a chance to be with God while they remain in their miserable state of existence.

A spiritually developed person starts to see and understand things that make good spiritual sense. It is no wonder the Catholic Church has always suffered rejection, persecution, mockery, hatred, scandals, and a whole slew of attacks down through the ages. No other institution or religion threatens the demons and satanic powers over humans more than the Catholic Church, where Jesus comes alive and present within its believers. The evil spirits have no power over Christ, and they know it. So they go after the sleepy, lazy believers with a vengeance.

There were many moments while writing this book when my mind would be interrupted with thoughts like, *You're wasting your time. Go have a beer. People will think you're crazy.* Thanks to the Word of God and His Holy Spirit, I can see clearly what Jesus did during His temptations in the desert. The Devil probably told Jesus that He was wasting His time too. But Jesus kept fasting and praying to call out the enemy and to test his power. Finally, the Devil appeared. With the Spirit of God, Jesus blew the Devil away and went on His way to establish a new reign on earth: the kingdom of heaven. The kingdom of heaven is indestructible joy. The kingdom of hell is indestructible torment. Somehow, I know this book will help free at least one soul trapped in the Devil's snare and encourage it to trust in the Christ of God to blow sin and evil away.

God Designed Us to Walk on Water and Fly over Land with Him

Before Jesus was seen walking on the water, the gospel tells the reader that He had dismissed the crowd and went up a mountain to be alone in prayer. Keep this in mind when meditating on the next scene. The encounter in the middle of the night with Jesus walking toward a boat filled with the apostles is extremely revealing. According to Scripture scholars, the fourth watch would make it around 3:00 a.m. What do most ordinary people do at three o'clock in the morning? They sleep. Jesus, however, wanted to give them an extraordinary lesson in divine power.

Peter's spontaneous spirit fits right into Jesus' lesson on revealing our capacity to enter into the eternal realm. While Jesus was grabbing Peter's arm as he began to sink into the lake, He told Peter, "Oh you of little faith, why did you doubt" (Mt 14:31). Jesus was addressing Peter's spiritual self, not his human self. Any contemplative person would know that Peter's human self was back in (the past) the boat either in deep prayer or fast asleep (the present). Peter's spiritual self went beyond ordinary limits into eternity (the present). Peter was transcended into the divine presence of God (Jesus), but fear of the unknown (the future) caused Peter to descend out of immortal eternity back into a mortal and dying humanity. When Peter doubted his transcendent self's capacity to function beyond human limitations and power, he fell from the grace of God's omnipotent, ever-sustaining power back into man's limited, human power. Human power is slowly leaking out of us in a limited time destined for an earthly end—death of the body. Death is something to be confronted.

Peter's sudden fright and confusion caused by the wind and the waves over the deep waters also provides a lesson of warning. It warns us that outside the secure grasp of God and His loving presence, there is something insecure, frightening, and devoid of compassion below the surface. In other words, the surface represents death, a dividing line between two spiritual realities. One reality is being above the earth in God's light and surrounded by loving creatures possessing control of one's self, while the other reality is being below the earth in Satan's darkness and out of control of one's self, immersed in the confusion and panic of being surrounded by unseen powers and hostile enemies. When we leave this body to return to dust, our faithful soul is purified to revel in ecstasy forever, or our unfaithful soul pines in agony for eternity.

Other examples of ordinary men empowered by God to do extraordinary things can be found in the book of Acts. The apostle Phillip was moving cross-country in an extraordinary way. I would go so far as to say that he was in his transfigured or divinized body as Jesus was while walking on water. Notice how the angel of the Lord told Phillip to get up and head south to Gaza. What was Phillip doing at the time the angel came to him? Was he sleeping? Was he praying? How did Phillip happen upon a man traveling from afar just as he was reading Isaiah the prophet? Was it pure coincidence or just good timing? And then, how do you explain Phillip's disappearing act after the moment the eunuch was baptized? Phillip, I dare say, had to have been in the eternal presence. He had to have been in his supernatural/

divinized body. His physical body was somewhere else back where the angel first told him to "Get up and go south to Gaza" (8:26-39).

Legend has it that St. Paul was seen in two places at once during his travels throughout Israel, Greece, and Italy. He certainly covered a lot of land and sea for his time. He also seemed to have possession of extraordinary power to bring "a young man named Eutychus" back from the dead (20:9-12).

Eternal Sign of Liberation and Condemnation

The sign of the cross both condemns the Devil and liberates the soul forever. The sign of the cross is a daily reminder of our hour of death. The sign of the cross constantly warns us that we only have a limited time to know our purpose and choose our destination. The sign constantly begs us to use our time wisely by getting to know the Christ of God. Knowing and becoming familiar with Christ is our earthly purpose. Jesus' crucifixion was and is our spiritual model until the hour of our death. For the souls who served the Lord by giving their lives for His sake, the sign of the cross branded on a person's forehead will cast into hell the evil ones threatening it at the hour of death. When a soul is in heaven, there will be no need for reminders, for we will be free and in His constant presence beyond the grave. In heaven there is no more suffering, no sin, and no need to remember the dangers of evil.

For the wicked, however, the sign of the cross will continue to wield power of condemnation to evil spirits after death. For many souls who rejected the Lord by selfishly living a life for their own self gain, the sign of the cross will catch such souls off guard at death. The absence of the sign of the cross marked on the soul at death will be proof for Jesus to say, "I do not know where [you] are from. Depart from me, all you evildoers" (Lk 13:27).

Demons will try to influence human beings out of sheer envy for human souls that have a chance to go to heaven. Evil spirits dread going to hell, so they try to inhabit and hide in living creatures. The sign of the cross of Christ causes great difficultly for evil spirits to remain inside a person, especially if the person is faithful to the church and the reception of its sacraments. The sign of the cross will always remind the living to depend on the power of the Holy Spirit. The sign of the cross will always remind evil spirits that they are slaves to a hostile master. Even if evil spirits were to forget their names, they remember the sign of the cross. Each time an evil spirit sees the mark of the cross on the foreheads, the minds, hearts, and souls of every person they tempt, it will go on torturing the demon forever. It will be a constant reminder of something they can never have—love of God and being in His presence.

Babies and children who die before they have a chance to discover the meaning of the cross carry the cross. Their purpose is atoning for humanity's sins. If the divine Jesus can rescue a grown man like Peter from the depths of hell, He can catch His little ones on their crosses of abortion, domestic violence, accidents, and disease before they sink into hell. God loves His little innocent ones, and He will not abandon them in the hour of their deaths.

One might ask how Jesus can rescue so many little ones dying all over the world at once. The answer can be found in tabernacles all over the world. The tabernacle is the place where the true presence of Jesus' body and blood are reserved in every Catholic Church on earth. God, therefore, can be in all places at once, just like He is in every church building that houses His precious body and blood on earth. If He can rescue sinful adult souls and then gift them with the potential to do wonderful things for all eternity to enjoy, I do not see Jesus the Savior having a problem rescuing little innocent souls everywhere at the same time. He has had a lot of practice walking on water, clouds, fire, etc. I am sure He can handle anything, any amount, and any death in time because divine love has no limits. Such a love can stop time while Jesus' arms sweep across the face of the earth, gathering His little souls from their crosses to Himself.

PART V

THE DISCOVERY

We Exist Because God Does

There is a reason for our existence. We are not here in this life to eat, drink, be merry, die, and blow away. We are here to know God. If all we do in this life is eat, drink, and be merry, our lives on earth will end up in utter boredom and emptiness. Throughout the ages and all over the earth, ancient drawings and art forms tell us that men have not been satisfied with a mundane lifestyle or existence. Some curious thinkers depicted a life after death. The hieroglyphs of the ancient Egyptians truly paint a life expectancy beyond the tomb. The pyramids along the Nile and the Avenue of the Dead in Mexico tell us that there is some sort of transformation that takes place at the death of the human body.

Egyptian Pharaohs actually believed that they were immortal and that when they died, they would be transformed into a godlike being capable of transporting itself beyond the grave to live forever. In other words, human beings have long expressed, in symbols and words, the existence of an afterlife. Life here is like a seed in the ground. It anxiously awaits and prays to crack open its shell in order to pop up into the beginning of a new world—a new life full of extraordinary light, color, and sound that it only vaguely sensed within its old, dark shell of existence.

Some scientists tell us that the essence of life came from nothing but a stellar, black hole explosion. All of existence can be explained by science. There is no God in their minds. Okay, but how do you explain away the existence of love, compassion, mercy, and the I am? There is no scientific explanation for the existence of evil as in, "I hate you, therefore, I kill you." God is the only person behind the I am, just as God, who is love, is the only antidote to hatred.

The big bang theory has a beginning and an end. God has no beginning and no end. If the universe, on the one hand, had its moment of explosion somewhere back in time, it will end its expansion somewhere ahead in time. God, on the other hand, is eternally present, without a beginning or an ending. I would say God is the only true being in existence that simply is. When God told Moses, "I am the God of Abraham, Isaac, and Jacob," He is speaking in the present tense. God did not say, "I was the God of Abraham, Isaac, and Jacob." Nor did He say, "I will be the God of Abraham, Isaac, and Jacob." God is forever in the eternal now. We exist because God is, and therefore, we are because God loved us into eternal existence. No other natural thing or explosion formed or created me because it is incapable of loving. Love is the only thing that can design a life. Love is the reason for my existence. I discovered that I am because God is and that, I am because God loved me into existence forever.

Adoring Christ and Loving Others Has Eternal Consequences

In the beginning, God eventually created life in His image (Adam and Eve). God created them to lead immortal lives with Him, but Adam and Eve chose to destroy their lives by choosing death over life. Remember, God told them, "You can eat from all the trees in the garden except from the tree of the knowledge of good and evil because if you eat from it you are doomed to die" (Ge 2:16-17). Adam and Eve chose to be like God, so out of selfish desire, they disobeyed His one command. Selfish love broke the heart of True Love—God.

Mankind has been paying for this choice of false love—self-aggrandizement—ever since. Today, egoism and pride have created thousands and maybe millions of little false gods all over the face of the earth. Just take a look at how many recent world leaders have placed themselves up on a pedestal in their national plazas, like Hitler, Mussolini, Lenin, Stalin, Mao Tse Tung, Pol Pot, Moammar Qaddafi, Idi Amin, Saddam Hussein, and Kim Jong Il, to name a few. All of these poor souls had a misconceived understanding of what it means to love. History tells us that these deceased men were much more in love with themselves and their ideas than they were with God and others. It seems like they had no fear of eternal death.

A true way to eternal life and love goes something like this: A child comes up to you and is lost and crying. He keeps poking you with his finger. You don't know this kid, and he annoys you. Finally, you grab him by the hand and ask, "What's the matter? What do you want?" With tears running down his cheeks, he stands there and stares you in the eyes. You can't help but reach out to touch him. He grabs on to you and buries his face into your side. You stoop down and ask in a milder tone, "Tell me what's wrong." The child proceeds to describe how he can't sleep at night because he has scary dreams and sees dark things moving in his room. "Why don't you go to your parents' room?" you ask. "My mom sleeps with a man who doesn't like me." Suddenly, you realize the child is neglected and not cared for. You take him gently by the hand and begin to walk with him. You tell him not to be afraid and that everything is going to be better because he has found a friend who will teach him how to pray before he goes to bed and how to pray when he wakes up after having another bad dream until he is able to fall back to sleep.

You may have spent an hour or more of your day trying to help this kid get to the bottom of his problem; you didn't get a dime from him or his parents for counseling. You missed work and didn't even get his name or address. It was a total loss by all our worldly standards of self-interest and compensation. However, that child will remember you for all eternity. What you did for that confused little heart in his hour of need was plant a seed in its immortal soul that will never forget you. That soul will identify itself to you where time no longer exists and where only love occupies space.

Another way to eternal life is when someone prays and offers his or her sufferings, sorrows, and pains for someone who offended him or her while alive on earth. These people are aiding in the eternal salvation of their offenders. The perpetrator will forever be grateful for such a generous soul. People who understand that human beings are indestructible spiritual beings destined to enter heaven or hell realize that the least they can do while still alive on earth is pray for the souls that tortured or continue to torture them. Why do they pray for evildoers? Because by living a Christian lifestyle, they discovered the key to wisdom that opens the doorway to eternal realities. They know where they are at, whereas their offenders do not.

Jesus was tortured, ridiculed, and made to suffer a brutal death by ruthless men. Why didn't He fight back or at least curse them? After all the good he had done for them, did he deserve such treatment? Is this the thanks He got—spit, rocks, a whipping, a cross to carry, and nails through His hands and feet? Why didn't Jesus send fire down from the heavens and fry them all?

The answers stem from His eternal adoration of the Father and the Father's love for His creatures: us. Jesus mercifully and compassionately understood the eternal consequences of such odious actions. Jesus knows the reality of an abyss that separates souls in heaven from souls in hell. The last thing our Lord wanted was for His torturers to be cursed and condemned to hell. His love and mercy are so great that He took all that hatred to Himself to give slaves of the world, flesh, and the Devil a chance to break free from their grip and learn to turn around and reconcile themselves to God through His example and by His grace. Jesus is the ultimate role model who helps us begin to climb the ascending passageway in this life toward our glorious life that never ends.

If we do not spend time getting to discover God in our midst, we will never be free. It takes time and effort to become knowledgeable of God's interior design. The more effort we put into shutting off the world, the sensual desires, and the temptations, the more we allow the Spirit of God to move within our being. God can then slowly transform us—our real selves—into His very image. It is only through adoring Christ that we can truly be free from the material, sensual, and make-believe existence.

Contemplative people can see an empty heart, a certain miniscule presence of a person's soul when they look into the eyes of others they meet. These poor souls have not ventured to explore the vast terrain within themselves. They are like fish swimming aimlessly in a huge ocean, not knowing who and why they are. Either no one has passed any real information about God and His plans on to them or they do not care to learn about God. How can they get to know their souls if no one has led them to them? The answer is discovering God in silent adoration of His Son, Jesus. Fr. Ignacio Larranaga wrote in his book, *Sensing Your Hidden Presence*,

> In contemplation, there is no reference point in the self: the things that refer to the self are not important to the contemplative. The only things that have an impact are the things that refer to the Other. They are not elated by successes nor thrown by failures. Because of this, the great contemplatives are full of maturity and grandeur, with an unchanging joy, with the characteristic serenity of those who are in an orbit of peace above the ups and downs, storms, and troubles of daily living.[41]

The Other refers to God within the person. "In Him, we live and move and have our being" (Ac 17:28).

If eternal life is our goal, we need to submerge ourselves in silence, in adoration of the one true God who gave Himself up on a cross and whose body and blood remain in every tabernacle throughout the world, waiting to enter into a warm and pulsing communication with those who love and adore Him. The consequences of such adoration not only lift people to embrace their true selves and others on earth, but they also carry us through all the trials and tribulations of earthly life to embrace celestial beings with

---

[41] Larranaga, Ignacio. *Sensing Your Hidden Presence: Toward Intimacy with God.* Doubleday: New York (1987) 193.

a love yet untold. Adoration of Christ means we are willing to embrace the cost of pain and sorrow and even death for the one who comes alive to us through faith and trust in His divine presence. Such a faith and trust in an unseen God will not leave someone disappointed. God does not fail. God is ever faithful to those who truly love Him.

Souls Who Seek Eternal Relationships Adore the Christ

Adoring Christ in the Eucharist is the opportunity to develop not only our immortal relationship with Jesus; it is an opportunity to get personal advice from our Lord Himself how to develop our immortal relationships with others as well.

As Christians, our mission in life is to establish a lifelong relationship with Jesus Christ. This relationship spills over into eternity. I discovered that no matter how many broken relationships we go through in this life, they are not lost forever; they are in remission. People who think eternally know they will see the other person again, whether it will be tomorrow, ten years from now, or in eternity. It is important to keep this in mind because nothing is lost forever. We continue to grow or digress in our relationships right where we left off from our last encounter.

Our souls have an extraordinary capacity to recollect memories of each and every person we come in contact with. The degree of familiarity increases with every encounter. We either continue building a relationship in love with the other, or we continue tearing down in hatred the relationship with the other person. Innately, we want to be loving, but evil spirits try to break up loving relationships. They cause a hidden jealousy that only a person aware of divine things can understand. A person familiar with his or her eternal heart and soul knows how to respond against worldly suggestions and evil influences bent on dividing that person from God and others.

There are moments in the gospels where Jesus exposes His divine self. The transfiguration is by far one of the most revealing incidents in the New Testament. The apostles Peter, James, and John were alone with Jesus on a mountain in prayer. These three ordinary, humanly thinking men witnessed a man go from an ordinary human appearance to an extraordinary appearance. From this moment on, these three men learned something about Jesus that they could never stop adoring.

They were in all three dimensions at once. They remembered the Jesus who called them to follow Him; they were with Him in the present; and yet they saw a Jesus that will always be. They saw a person who could descend, ascend, and transcend into any dimension because earth and heaven are not separate from each other. The only thing that divides us human beings from experiencing each other's immortal innermost is sin. Sin blocks the entrance of divinizing grace to ourselves and from recognizing the immortal person stored within another person.

This is why the mission of Jesus the man-God on earth was so revealing and urgent. We human creatures do not have all the time in the world to play with. We must not waste our limited earthly existence, void of contemplative prayer, to discover our immortal selves. Eucharistic adoration means quietly sitting still, waiting on the divine Lord to help transfigure us into someone like Him. If we fail to use wisely this time on earth to free our natural selves from our sinful humanity, we may never be able to learn to discover what we really are capable of doing. We have the capacity to construct loving, ever-growing supernatural relationships with other immortal beings. If we do not learn how to perfect ourselves in the presence of God and others for all eternity, in whose presence will we find our unperfected souls forever?

Humbly Build Your House on God's Eternal Foundation

> No one can lay a foundation other than the one that has been laid, namely Jesus Christ. If different ones build on this foundation with gold, silver, precious stones, wood, hay or straw, the work of each will be made clear. The Day will disclose it. That day will make its appearance with fire, and fire will test the quality of each man's work. If the building a man has raised on this foundation still stands, he will receive his recompense; if a man's building burns, he will suffer loss. He himself will be saved, but only as one fleeing through fire. (1 Cor 3:11-15)

We need to be more concerned about developing our eternal character, not developing a worldly character. Those who know and understand that they will be around for all eternity will want to be remembered as good people. Since everything we built on earth is going to be exposed in the light of eternity, people will do everything in their power to do good things for God's sake and for the sake of others.

If all we do is cuss and slap people up the head all our lives, what can we expect from God, who rejects cursing and violence? What can we expect from the souls we mistreated? Maybe they will forgive us, but will they be able to love us if our hearts are still hard and empty? A humbled and contrite heart that builds on the stable foundation of the Christian spirit will experience the destruction and loss of a faulty character building, but he or she will build a new and everlasting house occupied by a Christ-like heart full of divine light, life, and love.

Ever since I jumped off a snow-covered cliff to fall hundreds of feet above the bottom of an Andean Mountain range, my thoughts and efforts to understand who I am and the purpose of my life have never ceased. I thought at that moment that I was a goner, but the eternal life force I thought God was heard a desperate call for help. This incident proved to me that God is not just some cosmic force but more like the biblical watchful parent who expresses immense mercy on his forlorn child.

Before this frightful incident, I thought that life's circumstances were created by the way we freely execute our own random ideas. At this particular moment in life, my reason for existing was in a state of flux. Instead of being a humble and obedient Christian serving God the Father by following the will of His Son, Jesus, I was looking for a spirit god, an impersonal power that would transform me into some non-paternal, cosmic being.

My body and its necessities were not that important. The past and future were considered useless things. The only thing that mattered was turning into an immortal spirit now. What I did not take into consideration was my humanity, especially the call that all human beings have by design: the call to learn to love and serve others. I discovered that all human beings go through a process of learning how to reach both human and Christ-like perfection. This was illustrated by the immature biblical soul's slow process of developing into the mature Christlike soul. God took this foolish and reckless moment in my life to brand into my soul, by virtue of His infinite pity and mercy, a personal love so excelling that His lost, misguided, and stubborn human child would never forget it again.

What did I forget? I forgot that all risen life originates through the Christ of God. I had forgotten that I was a baptized, Catholic Christian, an adopted son of God, who died and rose to new life! I forgot that before Jesus Christ came to earth, everything was created for Him. John wrote in his gospel, "In the beginning was the Word, and the Word was with God ... All things came to be through him, and without him nothing came to be. What came to be through him was life, and this life was the light of the human race; the light shines in the darkness, and the darkness has not overcome it" (Jn 1:1-5). I forgot that this "Word" was Jesus Christ "the first born of all creatures" (Col 1:15). St. Paul recognized this amazing truth when the light of Christ came to him on his way to Damascus (Ac 9:3). That is why he got baptized shortly after that event in Damascus (9:18). I forgot that the main reason I was on that journey to foreign lands was to walk with God and discover the truth. And that truth was, is, and always will be to serve God through His Son, Jesus Christ, and to serve others as Christ did.

Before that amazing plunge into the abyss, I was bent on building my own tower into heaven without paying much attention to the Christ of God or caring about the needs of others. Up until then, my proud and obstinate young heart refused to follow the safest route to eternal life. My proud and stubborn heart thought it could find another doorway into the immortal realm of heaven without the church.

As an innocent child, I once knew the way; it was so clear to see. It was plain and simple; it was black and white; it was through loving Jesus and the sacraments. As I fell to certain death, my proud and complicated heart was humbled to a level of sorrow never before felt in my life. It is funny how death forces the truth out of a person just like it forces the soul out of a body. Whether it was a thought or a feeling, all I remember was experiencing the deepest sorrow and shame for all my sins against God, the church, myself, and other people in my life. The truth was so overwhelming that I completely resigned and surrendered my life over to death. I had no one to blame for such evil deeds except myself.

All the souls that appeared to me in that mid-air, suspended animation of both time and space came to witness to the shameful personal offenses I had committed against them. I deserved to die. That was why I was sure I was dead when everything came to a sudden, booming stop. All I could see was a white light while lying in a frozen position six feet under powdered snow. This event put into action the wrecking ball on my proud tower. The demolition of my own personal designs and mistaken path to heaven was put in process.

The old, wild, wind-beaten sagebrush of a man started longing for the truth about Christ again. All the Native Indian and other crazy spiritual pursuits for some kind of cosmic bliss faded away. Slowly but surely, little Christian buds started forming on the old sin-withered branches of my soul. That was when I started recovering some Old Catholic prayers and phrases from the Bible. Being locked in the Argentinean military fort really helped me dig up my childhood prayers. The islands off the coast of Rio de Janeiro provided a good atmosphere for remembering and meditating on the life of Christ, especially how He cast out demons from people. It was His Holy Spirit that kept me safe from all the harmful demonic activity practiced on both the island and the Brazilian mainland. Even though I did not fully understand the witchcraft the people were involved with, I knew evil spirits were everywhere.

Another blast to my tower to heaven came in a dream where my body fell out of a plane and splattered itself in the middle of a busy city intersection. Why was I not able to turn on a light to see my reflection in the bathroom mirror? The job I had done thus far on my soul was deplorable. God could not let me see the condition of my soul. He probably spared me from falling into irreparable depression and self-hatred. The state of my soul was probably so hideous to look at it that it would have frightened even the most hardened criminals. Sin twists and perverts a soul to such a degree that it becomes unrecognizable.

I was unable to focus on the beautiful angelic creature who dropped in from above the ceiling on that amazing night in Eus France. My whole body was not allowed to turn and gaze on the radiant, sun-like image of the Blessed Virgin Mary standing behind me in Medjugorje, Yugoslavia. Deep within my heart, I knew my sins prevented me from engaging myself in further communion with these immaculate creatures.

These extraordinary events helped me to understand that my plans to avoid building on the rock-solid teachings of the Catholic Church so I could build my own way to heaven were plain stupid. There I was. Instead of building on the firm foundation of my baptismal faith, I had poured another foundation on the sand of self-pride and ego. But thanks to God's infinite mercy, He allowed divinely empowered beings to shock and awe His proud young baptized fool out of his selfish mission.

It took years of extraordinary spiritual interventions to shake my proud personality loose from its unsafe pursuit. It took deadly nightmares, demonic attacks, and free falls to death for me to humble myself and go back to building on the safe and secure foundations of the Catholic Church. An exorcist wrote in his book, *Unbound*: "Sometimes we think the Devil is after us and we need to take authority over him. But what is really happening is that God is after us and we need to repent and clothe ourselves with humility. Then we are better prepared to take authority over the Devil."[42] First, I humbly rediscovered God.

My foolish pursuit was not a total waste because in turning back to Christ and His teachings, I uncovered and exposed the hidden thief of a Christian's house. The robber does not want a person to clean house and resume building up his eternal soul on the foundation and designs of Jesus Christ and His church. The sacraments are powerful supports against the winds of evil attacks. When an evil spirit attacks a baptized Christian, it quickly discovers a threat. As soon as it recognizes that the body of the person it is attacking has the Holy Spirit inside of it, the Devil retreats. It knows that it is no match for the Holy Spirit.

This is why Christians have a big advantage over non-baptized people. When people are not baptized, they are easily won over and occupied by evil spirits. Many non-baptized people are not even aware that they are carrying around evil spirits inside of them. The real targets for evil spirits are the baptized because if they can win over a baptized person to apostasy, they take more pleasure in duping and torturing a consecrated soul than winning over a non-baptized person.

The biblical soul had to learn that in order to advance in the knowledge of God, it had to humbly adhere to the divine covenant, the divine plan of God. In order to discover God's plan of saving souls from eternal damnation, a person must work unceasingly to know his or her mission in this life. The Devil does not want a person to understand his or her mission in life because that would enhance a person's chance to fulfill a divine calling to sainthood.

This is why the house wrecker is on the prowl day and night. It knows that the more a person builds his or her house according to God's plan, the more difficult it becomes for evil spirits to inhabit human beings, human dwellings. "For a demon, to leave a body and go back to hell—where he is almost always condemned—means to die forever and to lose any ability to molest people actively."[43]

---

[42] Lozano, Neal. *Unbound: A Practical Guide to Deliverance.* Chosen Books: Grand Rapids, 165.

[43] Amorth, Gabrielle. *An Exorcist Tells His Story.* Ignatius Press: San Francisco (1999) 97.

It takes steadfast prayer and untiring work to fight off evil attacks. The only way to survive evil influences is to take courage and strive for a holy lifestyle. Many baptized Christians grow weak in their faith in God. They leave the church and the reception of the sacraments. They stop praying and get caught up in so many worldly distractions. When this happens, they are easily intimidated by evil attacks (i.e., evil dreams, nightmares, visions, voices, and other manifestations). Unfortunately, these disturbed souls turn to wrong ways to find relief.

Many people who have come to see me about spiritual problems in their lives turned to alcohol and drug abuse to sedate their miseries. They are afraid to talk to anyone for fear of being labeled "crazy" or "psycho." These people do not want to see a priest because they don't want to be considered "possessed" like images they have seen in the movies. Many people turn into workaholics, noiseaholics, TV addicts, or some other form of addict to drown out their emptiness, tortuous loneliness, depression, and fear of silence and solitude. They are deathly afraid to be alone and quiet because they are scared of another evil attack. But it does not matter how much a person takes or does to avoid the Devil; the only solution is to soberly take evil spirits on. We must not fear. We must go to God and *get high* on His grace necessary to defeat these evil intruders, because they will not stop until we are either victorious or dead.

In his book, *Sober Intoxication of the Spirit*, Fr. Raniero Cantalamessa describes the theme of "sober intoxication" as getting high, meaning "filled with the fullness of God." He discovered that from early on, the church fathers connected the Holy Spirit to a "spiritual drink." For Origen and many other fathers of the church, this *spiritual drink* theme alluded to things as being "filled with the Spirit . . . , experiencing true spiritual ecstasy . . . , and an intoxication of grace." Cantalamessa says that a Christian can act in both "a human way and a divine way, a natural way and a supernatural way."[44]

We are far better off gathering knowledge and strength from God's graces while alive than dead. It will be very difficult to fight off the evil spirits at the hour of death without possessing God's defensive grace. Evil spirits will strike hard and fast against an unprepared soul in its last battle on earth. The hour of death is their last chance to break into and steal the

---

[44] Cantalamessa, Raniero. *Sober Intoxication of the Spirit*. Servant Books: Cincinnati (2005) 149-50.

owner of the body: the soul. A person high and under the influence of the Holy Spirit has little or next to no risk of losing his or her soul to evil spirits.

God can provide all we need to build a strong fort loaded with ammunition—the grace we need to take on a legion of devils. All we need to do while in the flesh is allow God to fill our person with His sacramental grace. This sacramental grace begins at baptism and continues to strengthen through faith, belief in God, and trusting in His Son, Jesus. Jesus can expel demons in an instant. Those who believe in Him and have experienced the power of Christ by mentioning His name during an evil attack already know what I am talking about here.

But talk is cheap. Learning how to expel demons is costly and sometimes very painful, but take courage, it can be done. It takes unshakeable faith and virtue. Faith and virtue are what evil spirits do not want you to possess. Grab on to Jesus Christ, and let Him shake the evil spirits out of you. A good place to shake the Devil out of your person is in the confessional. Stop and think about how many excuses you make not to go confess your sins to a priest. If you have any kind of mental resistance or physical anguish about going to confession, it is very possible you have evil spirits in you. The best antidote against temptation and evil spiritual attacks is confession to a Catholic priest. Go and do it with a contrite heart and discover God's grace.

Believe me, I have tried many other methods and ideologies to rid myself of hideous enemies of the soul. Nothing worked until I humbled myself to a Catholic priest against my proud will and confessed every sin I could remember. Evil spirits flee from the man who has been ordained by God to change ordinary bread and wine into the extraordinary body and blood of His Son, Jesus. Evil spirits know this, and they cannot stand up against a priest's absolution because it comes directly from Christ working within and through the priest.

If you are not Catholic, become one. Your eternal life depends on it! I rediscovered that the reception of the sacraments of reconciliation (confession and penance) and Holy Eucharist are the most powerful sources of grace a person can receive on earth. Also, consistent prayer, fasting, and charitable works will supply a person with the virtues needed to reach the stage where one gains the opportunity to chase away evil spirits. Have no fear, and do not be lazy. Get to prayer and corporeal works of mercy, and build a safe spiritual house that will last for all eternity.

EPILOGUE

I wrote this book as a witness to encouragement. "Be not afraid" were the words of Christ echoed constantly by the late Pope John Paul II. I am not afraid of what people will think of me. If people want to call me nuts or psycho, so be it. I know myself well enough, thanks be to God. Nobody, no special person, and no alien from outer space taught me what I know about heaven and hell, good spirits, and evil spirits. God is the only one who never abandoned me through my life. Even after I ran away for so many years from His church and my baptismal promises, He was the only one who came to my rescue when I most needed someone to protect me from both physical and spiritual danger. And now that I have met and heard so many other spiritually enlightened souls' agony and ecstasy stories, I decided to share my experiences with those who would benefit from this life's witness.

Evil spirits are at the core of much damage to a person's character and well-being. All the sinful ways that strapped my youth have been slowly purged, eradicated, and chased out of who I am, a soul destined to be with God. I do not know how many devils or demons came out of me over my lifespan so far, but I do know that my earlier years involved the use of bad language, ugly, uncontrollable thoughts, frightful dreams, stress, anxiety, and self-centered desires. All of these things have nearly disappeared thanks to the grace of God. Every now and then the Devil tries to tempt me in my service to God and His people, but the matured soul within me knows how foolish it would be to throw away all the pain and hard work it took to get where it is now in its purification process.

The Lord Jesus was stripped naked before being nailed to the cross for our salvation. He allowed Himself to become totally vulnerable to both men and demons to encourage me not to have fear against my enemies. It looked like the Devil had won, but since the third day after His death, Satan has been on the run from the light of the risen Christ ever since. Like Jesus, I want to be vulnerable so my divinely empowered light bulb will turn on and make a shadow out of the Devil too.

A quote from one of the documents *On the Church in the Modern World* sums up man's call to be Christian. When one puts his or her faith in Christ, the Church reassures the person that there is no reason to fear the mystery of death.

> While the mind is at a loss before the mystery of death, the Church, taught by divine Revelation, declares that God has created man in view of a blessed destiny that lies beyond the limits of his sad state on earth. Moreover, the Christian faith teaches that bodily death, from which man would have been immune had he not sinned, will be overcome when that wholeness which he lost through his own fault will be given once again to him by the almighty and merciful Savior. For God has called man, and still calls him, to cleave with all his being to him in sharing forever a life that is divine and free from all decay. Christ won this victory when he rose to life, for by his death he freed man from death. Faith, therefore, with its solidly based teaching, provides every thoughtful man with an answer to his anxious queries about his future lot. At the same time it makes him able to be united in Christ with his loved ones who have already died, and gives hope that they have found true life with God.[45]

The late Pope John Paul II consistently reminded young people the world over of Our Lord's words, "Be not afraid." His speeches encouraged his Youth Day audiences not to fall into the traps of the culture of death. To paraphrase his favorite message to the youth, he would say, "Do not obsess over death. Instead, live life to the fullest." When I think of Pope John Paul II, I think of Saint Joseph of Nazareth. The pope was like a humble, wise father and good husband who provided his house—the church—a place full of God's graces and life.

Saint Joseph was not afraid to take the pregnant Mary into his home because an angel appeared to him in a dream. Why did God send an angel to this hidden, obscure carpenter from Nazareth? The Bible tells us that Joseph was a just man, and that meant a lot by the religious standards of his day. To me, Joseph was a man full of deep reverence and love for God.

---

[45] Vatican Council II. *Pastoral Constitution on the Church in the Modern World.* Costello pub. Co. New York (1992) 918.

For this reason, he was full of grace and confidence. When the angel woke him in the middle of the night, he was not paralyzed and full of fear and doubt. On the contrary, he was ready to make important decisions and take immediate action.

I believe that at the hour of death, an angel will come to give us an order. We will either be confident to execute it without fear, or we will be paralyzed and hesitate to take its orders. Such a soul may fall into the clutches of the demon if it is not familiar with God and His angels.

Death is like a doorway into a dark room. Take courage and pass through it carrying the torch of Christ. Heavenly creatures will recognize the degree of love for God you carry by the intensity of light coming from your torch, and they will hasten to flood the vast room with their light for your protection and a safe arrival home.

APPENDIX I

Practice Makes Perfect

My dad was born in Chicago in 1929. His parents were immigrants from Sweden. When he was seven years old, they moved to San Francisco. My grandfather was a piano maker in Chicago. When he moved to San Francisco, he worked in construction as a house framer. My mom was born in San Francisco in 1932. Her parents were immigrants from England and Ireland. Her father was a merchant marine in the navy. Her mother raised four girls.

My mother and her three sisters were raised in the Catholic faith. My mom went all the way through high school in a parochial school. She met my dad after she graduated. My dad was drafted into the Korean War and wanted to marry her before he was sent to Korea. She was his support and gave him something to fight for and return to.

My father was baptized a Christian in the Lutheran Church. He did not practice his faith like my mother did. He worked hard to put a roof over our heads and food on the table. He supported my mom in educating my brothers and me in a Catholic parochial school. My mother was the only real Christian in our family because she received not only the Word of God but the holy sacraments as well. My brothers and I all received the sacraments of initiation into the Catholic Church. It is to this universal church, and to the nuns whose sacramental love was planted into me, that I owe my life. If it were not for my Catholic roots and the sacraments I received in my boyhood, I would have died long before my ordination as a priest in June 2004.

It is one thing to just read the Bible, but it is another thing to live it. When a person receives the sacraments, the person goes on to live and practice higher levels of spiritual growth. The sacraments transform human beings into holy, whole persons (our humanity with God's divinity). My experiences living outside of the Catholic church and not receiving the sacraments, especially the Eucharist, starved my soul nearly to death. When Jesus said, "Unless you eat the flesh of the Son of Man and drink his blood you do not have life within you" (Jn 6:53), He was not kidding.

The grace and spiritual nourishment our bodies and souls receive in the reception of the Eucharist is indescribable and insurmountable. After many years of partaking in the sacrament of the Holy Eucharist, my understanding of His teaching grows day by day. I cannot help wondering what happens to those who refuse to eat His body and drink His blood. Do their souls starve to death? Will they be deprived of eternal life? May God have mercy on their souls.

I often hear people tell me, "I'm not perfect, and nobody is perfect." I have news for you: that is what you are called to be, so be it. In His sermon on the mount, Jesus told the people, "So, be perfect, just as your heavenly Father is perfect" (Mt 5:48). A person can practice being perfect in this life starting right now. All you have to do is stop sinning—that is, stop pushing God away—turn toward Him, receive His Holy Spirit through the sacraments as frequently as you can, and then love as Jesus did and as the Catholic Church teaches, and you will be perfect. It is not easy to be perfect, but it is possible with grace. Go get the grace!

The most powerful form of grace is in the sacraments. It is in the Catholic Church. The more a person lives and practices being a Catholic Christian, the more perfectly aligned a soul becomes in union with the three persons in one God: Father, Son, and Holy Spirit. In such a holy communion, we can become co-shadow makers with God, casting out darkness throughout the universe for an eternity.

APPENDIX II

Complacency and Mediocrity:
Modern Social Threats to Eternal Life

There is a scene in an old movie classic called *High Noon* where the young sheriff goes to visit the house of the old, retired sheriff. The young sheriff asked the older sheriff if he would help him fight off a group of lawless gunfighters coming to kill him and rob the town. The old sheriff made nothing but excuses and ended up refusing to go fight with him. In this particular scene, the old sheriff's character did a great job of showing how stuck he was living in complacent mediocrity, and therefore, afraid to get out there and fight against evil to the death if need be.

One of the most difficult challenges for me as a Christian today is not so much being afraid of death but falling into the traps of complacency and mediocrity. Reliable sources indicate that there are a number of Christians who are unwilling to give their all to fight against the modern manifestations of evil in America today. Complacent and mediocre Christians in the United States of America know that abortion is evil, but how many of them take a stance to fight against lawmakers who have falsely justified its use? Complacent and mediocre Christians know that gay marriage is evil, but how many of them stand up in court to fight legislation that redefines the meaning of marriage between one man and one woman only?

Complacent and mediocre Christians have bought into the whole political correctness trap that a handful of anti-Christian, social liberals use to keep children from praying to a Christian God. Christian parents need to tell teachers, school authorities, and the public school boards that their children have constitutional rights to pray to Jesus if they want to. The United States of America was founded on Christian principles. Complacent and mediocre Christians need to take a stand against the growing problem of Muslim Sharia law being imposed on certain US citizens. Radical Muslim fathers do honor killings on their American-born daughters for dating Christian boys. Complacent and mediocre Christians tolerate the demand for more Islamic mosques to be built for sympathetic reasons but condemn the building of Christian churches for environmental protection reasons.

Look at how many complacent and mediocre Christians go along with the whole environmentalism business. Not only are environmental laws choking the life out of private businesses, but this movement is also at the root of the extermination of human life on the planet. For years now, I have seen so many people throwing their love to the dogs. The desire for a pet has taken over the desire for another human being. Love for animals has replaced love for spouses and children. Environmentalism has allowed Satan to put into the complacent and mediocre heads of people the idea that it's okay to kill the unborn because the planet cannot afford to have any more human babies. People have been brainwashed to think there are too many human beings on the planet and not enough plants and animals. It is all a lie, but that is because evil spirits are in people's hearts, not the Holy Spirit.

Look how many influential Christian men of the cloth like Louis Farrakhan, Jesse Jackson, Al Sharpton, and Jeremiah Wright use the race card to squeeze money out of gullible, fearful, tolerant, mediocre, and complacent Christians who refuse to sue these wolves in sheep's clothing for what they are: race baiters. These deceptive reverends use black victims to line their pockets by extracting money from celebrities or rich non-black people they blame for using non-politically correct language.

As disturbing as it may seem, but for the sake of eternal existence, I want to revisit and call into question some of my uncle's extreme biases. Why did my uncle call black people the n-word? Why did he use that word when referring to a certain race of people? At first I was shocked. In my old social, liberal mind-set, I thought he was some ignorant, white trash bigot who came from a prejudiced household. But the more I got to know his personal history, the more I understood his usage of that word.

What he meant to say was this: slavery has been dead for nearly 150 years, but some disingenuous black leaders keep digging up the old, racial dead bones of "N" out of the grave and make it walk so they have a make-believe victim to show off in the public eye. They put new flesh on this old, rotting corpse of a concept so as to display a poor, abused, make-believe victim before a dumb, pitiful, non-black public. This keeps gullible, complacent, and mediocre people throwing money at the foot of this dug-up, fake, "N" victim.

Why are other black leaders not standing up to call out these hypocritical reverends on their deceptive race baiting? These black reverends incite hatred and cause violence by accusing non-black people of being racists. Why do black Christians not rebuke these false slanderers? Could it be that their livelihoods depend on keeping non-black people feeling sorry for so-called oppressed blacks to keep the money flowing into their deep pockets?

These evils threaten and tear at the social fabric and soul of modern America. As a man of the cloth myself, I am appalled by Christian, hypocritical reverends who use our Lord's words to justify race baiting as a means to a lucrative end to take advantage of a gifted group of people. Good, wealthy Christian people of any race reject racial bias, and they are offended by leaders who profit from dredging up old, dead stereotypes and using them for their own personal gain.

Where is the preaching of Christian reconciliation by these false preachers of Christian doctrine? Instead of teaching their followers to forgive and forget, they are telling their flocks to go on remembering shameful evils of the past and to use them to seek revenge against non-blacks. I do not know of a single good practicing Christian who holds racial bias toward any particular minority group. God-fearing people have no desire to discriminate against others on the basis of their race or income. Throughout American history, good wealthy people have volunteered to contribute much of their resources to minorities out of the God-blessed generosity of their Christian hearts

Racism has divided Americans and is kept alive by race baiters. There are many hardworking multicultural American men and women, but there are too many minorities who have allowed themselves to become slaves to a handful of rich, multicultural, government bureaucrats who hand out an allotted amount of entitlement tax dollars, which, by the way, was stolen from the pockets of hardworking, private sector citizens by the IRS.

Guess who are the new slave drivers? I'll give you a hint: it starts with a *g* and ends with a *t*. People who depend on the government are slaves to the government. My uncle's work ethic was this: "You don't work, you don't eat." He detested complacent black sympathizers because in his younger days, no matter where he worked, he observed non-black, pitiful bosses paying lazy black workers the same amount of wages for doing half the amount of work he did. He grew to despise black people who refused to work hard at anything. After observing their work ethic in school, in the military, in the warehouses, in the factories, and on the ranches, he concluded that black people refused to work because they had an attitude that said, "We deserve to be pitied and paid back by the oppressive, rich, non-black folk." If my uncle were still alive today, he would tell hardworking Americans to wise up to the old dead "N" victim game.

My non-politically correct uncle is probably rolling over in his grave for the way our complacent and mediocre society is caving into the desires of the likes of people he called "queers." This term specifically tagged sexually active homosexual men and women. In his mind, this group thinks the heterosexual public owes them pity and money for all their pitiable, hurt feelings. He called tolerant heterosexuals "stupid and gullible mice" for going along and listening to homosexuals whining about their right to play with each other's same-sex organs and then giving into their lies about unfairness, bias, and intolerance.

What do complacent heterosexuals do? They allow homosexual legislators to pass laws to protect the gay agenda, only to get bitten by gay homo-snakes as they turn on the gullible, complacent heterosexual mice. Homosexuals now use the law to sue the gullible heterosexuals for their money. What's worse is that the tolerant, complacent heterosexuals keep paying for the liberal court fees and for sentences imposed on them by biased (probably gay) judges. Homosexuality is a direct offense to the oldest natural institution known to man: marriage. Mediocre and complacent heterosexuals may end up watching the extinction of the human race if these misguided, possibly demonically influenced people get their way.

You might be asking yourself, what does all this awful stuff have to do with eternal life? It has everything to do with eternal life. When particular people like my uncle and Jimmy the Scottish truck driver cannot reason things out in their minds, they get frustrated, bitter, and angry. They cannot enter into a peaceful relationship with God because they are interiorly disturbed by the world around them. They blame God for not taking care of the world's problems, and they blame God for not taking care of their own personal shortcomings.

This poisonous frame of mind infects their hearts, which leads them into deeper inner personal struggles, where they eventually feel powerless when dealing with social evils and problems. The cumulative power of evil grows inside of them, and people like my uncle and Jimmy become fearful of the shadows and dark manifestations within themselves. As these personal spiritual problems increase in time, they become even more fearful, and they begin to curse and hate God for allowing them to suffer such unmanageable attacks. These poor, frightened, and empty souls end up blocking the only source of light that can clarify and heal their own personal problems and social dilemmas.

If my uncle had taken the time to go with me into the desert to spend a day away from all the business of ranch life—to go into the desert to be alone with God—he would have felt a presence of something among the vastness and tranquility of the desert that would have touched and affected his vast and chaotic inner self in a good and spiritually healthy way. His own mind would have settled down, and his heart would have opened its soul to God. God would have touched him with that grace he so desperately needed to forgive the black people, the gays, and whoever else did him harm or some injustice in his past.

His soul lived within an empty desert. Within him was the stormy heart of a man who refused to let God calm the roaring whirlwinds and twisters raging through him. Interiorly gathering in strength and numbers, evil intruders were bent on destroying his soul. These hellish intruders sneak into people's souls through cracks and holes in the shell (innocence) caused by sin that protects the innermost sanctuary of our being. Every time we sin we punch holes in our virgin shells, in our purity, and in our holiness, which protects us from these evil spirits and dark powers. Without God's healing presence and protective power, these destructive powers sneak in and attack the very core of our being to make slaves out of our souls or our immortal selves to the power of Satan.

Several generations of Americans, especially non-black Americans, have contributed a great deal of time and energy to bury old racial evils and to help black Americans. As a man of the cloth, I am deeply disturbed that complacent and mediocre black Christian leaders are not calling out the wolves in sheep's clothing. By causing division and racial hatred among American Christians, these so-called Christian men of the cloth, pretending to be Christlike, are leading their Christian flocks into eternal death instead of eternal life.

Most Americans I know are not race baiters and slanderers. Most Americans are Christians who beg for pardon from the Lord and from those they have offended. Most Americans want to live in eternity with friends of any color. How could they be in the presence of someone they mistreated or offended because of their race for all eternity? Most Americans understand this cannot be and know how dumb and empty it is to be a racial bigot. Racists will not exist with non-racists in heaven, just as the Devil cannot coexist with God.

Instead of raising up in their minds and hearts new, healthy, and wonderful living things like Jesus Christ intended, influential people, perhaps under the influence of evil spirits, have a fatal problem of conjuring up old, sick, and even dead concepts. In our current culture of death, too many of us praise dark stuff instead of light stuff and dead stuff instead of living stuff. Watch out, you modern hypocritical manipulators of God's Word, or you'll be screaming horror instead of singing praises for all eternity.

My prayers and sufferings are often being offered for leaders who manifest evil in government, in politics, in society, and in religion. I do not see how elite manipulators will be able to get into heaven without stopping their race baiting, especially if they are educated Christian leaders. Homosexuals might get away with receiving a marriage license by man's law, but there is no way same-sex relationships will receive a license for such a union by God's eternal law. Muslim religious people justifying the killing of innocent people of another religion for differences of faith will have no excuse for making life-and-death decisions in place of God. Legislators who passed laws that condemn babies to death while still in their mother's wombs will someday see the faces of their victims as they stand in waiting for eternal judgment.

Complacent and mediocre people who will not even lift a finger or a prayer to combat any one of these social evils will have a hard time convincing God that they had no idea what side to take in life: the good or the bad; the right or the left; the living or the dead. In Matthew's gospel, the evangelist tells us that when Jesus comes to judge the world, He will divide the good sheep from the bad goats. The sheep, who are hot for Christ, will go with Him to eternal life. The goats, who are cold for Christ, will go off to eternal punishment (Mt 25:31-46). In Revelation, John saw that God will reject the lukewarm. "Because you are lukewarm, neither hot nor cold, I will spit you out of my mouth" (Rev 3:16). There will be no eternal middle ground. After purgatory, there is no place for the mediocre and complacent to abide.

BIBLIOGRAPHY

Amorth, Gabriele. *An Exorcist Tells His Story.* Ignatius Press: San Francisco, CA, 1999.

Cantalamessa, Raniero. *Sober Intoxication of the Spirit.* St Anthony Messenger Press: Cincinnati, OH, 2005.

Catechism of the Catholic Church. Libreria Editrice Vaticana. Liguori Pub., 1995.

Doze, Andrew. *Saint Joseph: Shadow of the Father.* Alba House: New York, 1992.

Evert, J & C; Butler, B. *Theology of the Body for Teens.* Ascension Press: Westchester, 2006.

Griffin, Michael. *St. Joseph and the Third Millenium.* Teresian Charism Press: Hubertus, 1999.

Kreeft, Peter. *Heaven: The Heart's Deepest Longing.* Ignatius Press: San Francisco, CA, 1989.

Kreeft, Peter. *The God Who Loves You.* Ignatius Press: San Francisco, CA, 2004.

Larranaga, Ignacio. *Sensing Your Hidden Presence.* Image Books Doubleday: New York, 1987.

Lozano, Neal. *unbound: a practical guide to deliverance.* Chosen Books: Grand Rapids, MI, 2008.

Liturgy of the Hours. *The Divine Office.* Catholic Book Pub. Co.: New York, Vol. III 1975.

MacGraw-Hill. *New Catholic Encyclopedia.* Book Company: New York, Vol XII, 1967.

One Bread, One Body. www.presentationministries.com Advent Dec. 19, 2010.

Piechowski, Otto R. *Catholic Teachings.* The Center for Learning, 2000.

Pope John Paul II. *Theology of the Body.* Wednesday Audiences, January 13, 1982.

Rolheiser, Ronald. *The Restless Heart*. Image Books Doubleday: New York, 2004.

St. Francis de Sales. *Introduction to the Devout Life*. Image Books Doubleday: New York, 1966.

St. John of the Cross. *The Dark Night of the Soul*. Image Books Doubleday: New York, 1990.

St. Louis de Montfort. *The Secret of the Rosary*. Montfort Publications: Bay Shore, 1954.

Schonborn, Christoph. *Loving the Church*. Ignatius Press: San Francisco, CA, 1998.

Tomkins, Peter. *Secrets of the Great Pyramid*. Harper & Row: New York, 1971.

Vatican Council II. Pastoral Constitution on the Church in the Modern World, *Guadium et Spes*, Dec. 7, 1965.

Printed in the United States
By Bookmasters